The Legacy of
George W. Bush's
Foreign Policy

THE LEGACY OF
GEORGE W. BUSH'S
FOREIGN POLICY

. . .

MOVING BEYOND NEOCONSERVATISM

Ilan Peleg

A MEMBER OF THE PERSEUS BOOKS GROUP

Westview Press books are available at special discounts for bulk purchases
in the United States by corporations, institutions, and other organizations.
For more information, please contact the Special Markets Department at
the Perseus Books Group, 2300 Chestnut Street, Suite 200, Philadelphia,
PA 19103, or call (800) 810-4145, x5000, or e-mail
special.markets@perseusbooks.com.

Designed by Timm Bryson

Library of Congress Cataloging-in-Publication Data
Peleg, Ilan
  The legacy of George W. Bush's foreign policy : moving beyond
neoconservatism / Ilan Peleg.
     p. cm.
  Includes bibliographical references and index.
  ISBN 978-0-8133-4446-1 (alk. paper)
  1. United States—Foreign relations—2001–2. Bush, George W. (George
Walker), 1946– I. Title.

JZ1480.P45 2009
327.73—dc22

                              2008045541

10 9 8 7 6 5 4 3 2 1

TO MY DAUGHTER TALIA,

an idealist and a believer in civil and human rights

&

TO THE MEMORY OF MY FRIEND HOWARD MARBLESTONE
(1942–2008)

a scholar, a humanitarian, a mensch

CONTENTS

PREFACE

The last pages of this volume are being written as the administration of George W. Bush is coming to an end and Barack Obama is preparing to take office as the forty-fourth president of the United States. The worldwide reaction to the election of Senator Obama on November 4, 2008, was more enthusiastic than the reaction to the election of any other president in American history. To a very large extent this enthusiasm could be explained as the response of the world to Bush's foreign policy and as reflecting the widespread expectations that Obama will chart a substantially new international course for America and, indeed, for the world. In watching Obama's ascendance to the most powerful position in the world, we have witnessed a seismological change, a Richter scale "event" of 9.5 (or more) with potentially enormous consequences.[1]

The foreign policy of George W. Bush, the forty-third president of the United States, was greatly impacted by the prolific writings on foreign policy by the group of American intellectuals that has become known as Neoconservatives. While the debate on exactly who is a Neoconservative and what precisely Neoconservatism stands for might continue for years to come, the general contours or tenets of the Neoconservative philosophy, persuasion, or movement are sufficiently clear to have it as a subject of analysis. The Neoconservatives have promoted for several decades a muscular, unilateralist, militaristic, and hegemonic American foreign policy. The foreign policy of the Bush administration followed, in many if not in all respects, this Neoconservative prescription.

If foreign policy prescription can be judged by its results, Neoconservatism, as the ideational basis for the foreign policy of George W. Bush, ought to be regarded as a huge failure, an unmitigated disaster of historic proportions (see chapter 1). Not only did Bush's foreign policy not relieve the dangers associated with international terrorism, it aggravated them, making them more acute. Not only did this foreign policy not result in strengthening America's standing in the world, it diminished it significantly. The country's prestige, status, and legitimacy have never been lower than at the end of the Bush administration.

If Bush's years in the White House are not to be construed as a complete waste, they should serve as a historical laboratory, a testing ground for ideas that might produce a better and brighter future for America and the world. Those eight years ought to be examined empirically, and from as many perspectives as possible; then we should draw lessons for the future by better understanding the Bush years. This book does both.

While this volume focuses on the Bush years, 2001 through 2008, it is intensely interested in one fundamental, future-oriented question—what international role ought the United States play in the *post-Bush era*? Although some observers might believe that America's days as a world leader are numbered, chapter 6 of this book reflects a different perspective. By the sheer size of its economic and military power, the creative inventiveness and ingenuity of its people, the diversity of its population, and the openness of its culture (however constrained by prominent social forces within it), the United States is destined to be among the top world leaders and, in all probability, the single most prominent global leader in decades to come. However, to maintain its leadership position, to transfer it from the twentieth to the twenty-first century, America must not only leave the Bush legacy behind but also reinvent itself. It ought to be, and project itself as being, a thoughtful, deliberative, well-informed, moderate force on the world stage, not a unilateralist, militaristic, and nationalistic bully. In brief, the attitudinal prism described in this volume as Neoconservatism—present in and out of the Bush administration—ought to be relegated to the ash heap of history if the United States is to recover its traditional role as consensus-developer, institution-builder, and rights-promoter.

To move beyond Neoconservatism, we need to understand the essence and the core values of that persuasion, particularly as it was implemented by the Bush administration (see chapter 3). In many ways Neoconservatism presented to the world the ultimate unattractive model of US foreign policy, a combination of an exceptionalist America, militaristic and unilateralist in its modus operandi, imposing its will while dangling its values and promoting its narrow national interests (as perceived by the Bush administration) while presuming to represent universal ideals of democracy and freedom. No wonder that the policy inspired by Neoconservative ideas was met with rejection, resentment, opposition, and eventually active resistance, and that the push back was stronger and more profound than ever. The foreign and security policy based on Neocon ideology simply lacked the wisdom and the balance of Realist nuance. While the toppling of Afghanistan's Taliban regime was considered a reasonable act of self-defense on the part of America, when the Bush administration and the Neocons turned to the liberation of Iraq and the democratization of the Middle East they lost almost all international support. The well-deserved worldwide sympathy toward America of the post-9/11 era withered away. The genuine goodwill of the world toward the United States was squandered.

This volume argues that Neoconservatism, despite its name, is one of the most revolutionary, nonconservative movements in the history of American foreign policy. While Neoconservatives have often appeared to the world as tough-minded "realists," in fact they have been prisoners of their own ideological, revolutionary illusions and delusions. Accepting uncritically Francis Fukuyama's triumphal idea (or at least the way it was interpreted by many) that Western democracy has won and that it is bound to spread all over the world, the Neocons and their allies in the Bush administration were resolutely intent on imposing their democratic dream abroad. The Iraq war was conceived as an exercise in spreading democracy, a litmus test for benevolent hegemony, a dress rehearsal for bigger and better things. It turned out to be a model of overoptimistic, shortsighted zealotry, accompanied by a set of rosy predictions on the flourishing of democracy in the authoritarian Middle East. America's dream of benevolent hegemony turned into America's nightmare of endless war accompanied by the loss of legitimacy in the eyes of most of the world's citizens.

This book is not merely about America and its foreign policy. Because of the centrality of the United States in the global society, this volume is about the world at large. It reflects the great concern of the author about the global future. Two realities inform that concern. First, we need to recognize that the world has become more and more dangerous and unstable with the spread of weapons of mass destruction and international terrorism, environmental decay, the emerging competition for energy resources, and the increasing gap between the haves and the have-nots; global society faces consequential challenges that are unprecedented in their complexity. Second, we need to recognize that the multidimensional global crisis is, for the most part, not inevitable; much of it is the result of American actions (such as the Iraq war) or lack of actions (such as inaction on global climate change) over the past eight years. The net result of those actions and inaction has led to the dramatic decline of American power and influence and, more specifically, American legitimacy.

French foreign policy analyst Dominique Moïsi has captured the decline in US legitimacy rather well. He wrote recently about a 2008 West Berlin production of Beethoven's *Fidelio* that dressed the prisoners in orange jumpsuits resembling those used for prisoners in Guantanamo Bay detention center.[2] This vignette is an indication of how low America's reputation sunk during the Bush years. It is a measure of the ultimate decline in soft power of Bush's America— from a model of constitutionally protected human and civil rights to the ultimate "rogue superpower."

The 2008 election has the potential to change the situation in a significant way. Like most American elections since the end of the Cold War (e.g., the elections of 1992, 1996, and 2000), the 2008 election seemed to have been fought over and decided upon economic issues. Yet, the 2008 election was conducted against the background of not merely the troubled American economy but also the country's dramatic decline in the international arena. That decline benefited the candidacy of Barack Obama.

While Obama's victory opens the possibility for fundamental change in American foreign policy, the tasks of the new president are enormous. The Bush administration has left for its successor the most difficult situation since at least 1968, the height of the Vietnam War. The United States is facing a complicated situation in Iraq (since 2003), Afghanistan (since 2001), and increasingly in Pakistan. The so-called War on Terror, hostage to the definition given to it by Bush and the Neoconservatives (see chapter 1), remains inconclusive. The United States is facing an uncontrolled Iran with nuclear ambitions, an increasingly unstable and nuclearized Pakistan, difficult and strained relations with a resurgent Russia, and an emergent and competitive China. The dramatic decline in US prestige, standing, and legitimacy in the world (including among its closest European allies) makes a successful resolution to any of these problems difficult. While the Bush administration is not responsible for all those problems, this volume argues that it has significantly contributed to their development.

Barack Obama brings with him to the White House a set of characteristics that are quite promising in terms of the ability of the United States to recover from the disastrous years of the Bush administration. Obama has a first-rate analytical mind rather than the blind belief in an "instinctive" response that characterized the forty-third president (see chapter 4); he has sensitivity to long-term social and political gaps that ought to be dealt with both inside the United States and in the world (his experience as a community organizer in Chicago could prove highly relevant in that respect); he is biracial and thus reflects in his person the diversity of the world population; his mental world was not formed by the Cold War and he will be, in fact, the first truly post–Cold War American president; he understands that as president he must improve the global image and the international standing of the United States and that America's moral position is of critical importance for that task; and his campaign for the presidency seemed to show that he has absorbed the lessons from Bush's critical mistakes (carefully analyzed in this book). Obama is a terrific communicator with great oratorical skills, especially in large settings, capabilities that should serve him well in the White House. His visit to Europe and the Middle East in the summer of 2008 demonstrated his global popularity.

Although the world is facing enormous challenges, the *timing* for change is not unpromising. The enormity of the challenges is, in fact, a positive factor from the perspective of the likelihood of introducing change. The interdependence of all the world's economies is self-evidenced, accentuated by the threat of a long-term economic recession and even potentially a deep depression. The necessity of a unified action in which the United States will have to assume a leading role is clear. As the Bush administration draws to an end, there is a broad, albeit not universal, recognition of the fundamental mistakes committed by the departing president over the past eight years and the need to change course. The political trauma of the Iraq war is fading from memory and the rawness of the resentment toward the United States is gone; most European governments have resumed their traditional pro-American stance (especially important in this regard are the changes in governments in France and Germany, and the continuity of the pro-US position of the British government). The diplomatic efforts of the Realists under Condoleezza Rice during the second Bush term and in regard to Iran, North Korea, and Israel/Palestine have created a more positive atmosphere than the poisonous feeling produced by the 2003 Iraq invasion.

The issues on the agenda are many, and a sense of priority, as well as pragmatism, on the part of the new president will be essential. Here is a tentative list of possible priorities, over and above the stabilization of the American and the world economy: (1) initiate the early departure of American forces from Iraq, while focusing more on the challenges of terrorism in Afghanistan and particularly in Pakistan; (2) close Guantanamo Bay detention center as a symbolic act and declare an end to torture; (3) convene an international conference for dealing with global climate change and energy needs as a worldwide issue of the utmost urgency; (4) refocus American diplomatic efforts on "intractable" regional conflicts such as the Israeli-Palestinian dispute, Darfur, Somalia, and Cyprus; (5) reduce significantly the nuclear stockpiles of the United States and Russia as a reaffirmation of the American and global commitment to a new and invigorated nonproliferation regime; (6) strengthen international institutions, including the UN, NATO, and the G-8, while opposing ideas for exclusivist organizations such as a new "League of Democracies" (John McCain) that will undermine the UN and usher in a new Cold War; (7) work toward a comprehensive understanding with Russia that will include a commitment not to expand NATO in return for Russian acceptance of the boundaries of all states, including all former Soviet republics, and public commitment to nonintervention in the internal affairs of those states (a similar deal to the one we have had with the People's Republic of China in regard to Taiwan).

Most important, in the wake of the Bush years, the United States under Barack Obama must quickly restore its legitimacy in the eyes of the world, regain the confidence of other countries in the quality of its leadership, and get back the respect of people and governments around the globe. It must desert what many have conceived as its bully attitude, reaffirm its commitment to the rule of law and to civil and human rights, and join the world in an effort to deal with fundamental socioeconomic problems, including climate change, the energy challenge, and structural poverty. Soft power ought to complement and as much as possible replace hard power, but soft power, it must be remembered, requires the respect of the rest of the world and the legitimacy of the user of such power.

This book is dedicated to two individuals who have played an important, although quite different, role in my life. First, Talia Peleg, an idealistic young woman and my daughter, who shares my most fundamental values as few other people do. She will understand the heart from which my words have sprung.

This book is also dedicated to the memory of my dear friend Dr. Howard Marblestone (1942–2008). Howard was the most decent and generous person I have ever met; we were close friends and academic colleagues for thirty-four years, from the moment we met at Lafayette College until his premature death in January 2008.

Other individuals ought to be mentioned with appreciation. I had long and fruitful discussions with my son, Gil Peleg, on the subject dealt with in this book, as well as with my wife, Sima. Thanks are also due to my loyal and efficient assistants, Richard Krebs (who worked with me in the early stages of this project) and Matthew Goldstein (who assisted me in the final stages). More collectively, I have learned a lot from my students in the senior seminar on US foreign policy, offered during the tense but hopeful fall semester of 2008.

Thanks are also extended to others with whom I discussed this project from time to time, including Bob Freedman, Holmes Miller, Jonathan Mendilow, Paul Scham, Dov Waxman, and Eric Ziolkowski.

Ilan Peleg
December 2008

CHAPTER 1

THE BUSH LEGACY

Controversial Policy and Uncertain Future

The purpose of this introductory chapter, written during the last months of the administration of George W. Bush, is dual. The first goal is to present a general thesis in regard to the foreign policy of the forty-third president of the United States, its consequences, and its implications for the future of America and the world; this thesis is explored in full detail throughout the volume. The second goal here is to briefly describe the structure of the volume as a whole and that of each of its six individual chapters to facilitate a relatively easy, painless reading for experts and laymen alike.

The past eight years of American foreign policy were among the most dramatic, rocky, and consequential in decades. It was a period that defied simple, univariate, reductionist explanations. A unique and complex combination of factors shaped American foreign policy. Among them, five are of particular importance: the personality of President George W. Bush, the foreign policy decision-making process established by his administration, the impact of the extremely traumatic events of September 11, 2001, the challenge to the United States' unipolar supremacy within an ever-changing international system, and the influence of a determined intellectual elite often referred to as Neoconservative.[1] Each is analyzed in detail in chapters 2 through 5 of this volume.

The thesis of the book is that the controversial foreign policy of the Bush administration, reflected in the sharp decline of America's legitimacy in the world and the increase in threats to its security, was a result of the manner in which President Bush, a small number of his advisers, and ideologues outside of his administration defined and responded to the events of September 11, 2001, and to the international challenges faced by the United States in general. The "power of definition"[2] enabled the president to shape reality and lead the United States toward a new, indeed revolutionary, foreign policy and to adopt, in effect, the overall ideational framework and many of the specific proposals offered by a group of Neoconservative intellectuals and policy advisers. While it cannot be denied that President Bush's policies often reflected American traditions, institutions, and ideologies,[3] he pushed many of those further than any president before him ever had.

Bush's definition of the situation after 9/11, the adoption of policies based on this definition, and the response to these policies on the part of others in the international political system produced a new and, in general, highly negative reality. Because the initial definition by the president and his Neoconservative supporters was erroneous and misleading, it has led to a significant deterioration in America's global standing, a process extensively described and analyzed in this volume.

Bush's misguided leadership can be better understood through the lens of a fundamental sociopsychological phenomenon first described over forty years ago by Columbia University sociologist Robert K. Merton. The concept offered by Merton was the "self-fulfilling prophecy." Wrote Merton,

> The self-fulfilling prophecy is, in the beginning, a false definition of the situation, evoking a new behavior which makes the original false conception come "true." The specious validity of the self-fulfilling prophecy *perpetuates a reign of error* [emphasis added].[4]

In the high-stakes area of international politics, the extreme behavior of a very powerful actor who adopts what Merton calls "a false definition of the situation" could potentially lead to catastrophic results. The more catastrophic the results, the more perpetual the "reign of error" and the deeper the belief of the perpetrator that his initial actions were, in fact, right. This belief does not allow the perpetrator and most of his supporters to liberate themselves from the initial action.

In a self-fulfilling situation in international politics, as in other fields, the very prediction (or prophecy) causes itself to become reality *via the behavior of the party making the prediction.* Put differently, the "prediction" is continuously validated by the perpetrator, regardless of how deceptive and misleading it may be in reality. The key in a self-fulfilling behavior is the three-stage relationship between the way a situation is initially defined by an actor, the behavior it causes this actor to adopt, and the new situation resulting from that behavior.

The systematic application of the notion of "self-fulfilling prophecy" to the foreign policy of the Bush administration is carried out in this book on several levels of analysis, starting with the international system. In chapter 2 ("The Challenge to America and the World"), international factors contributing to the development of the "false conception" are identified. The Bush administration arrived at the White House in a time of post–Cold War instability, with America challenged by the emergence of new or "rogue" nations (e.g., China, Iran, Iraq, and North Korea) and the continuous instability in several of the world's most volatile regions (e.g., the Middle East and the Balkans). From the beginning, the approach of the new administration was to act unilaterally and militaristically to tame and control the world. This attitude received great "validation" in the eyes of its supporters by the events of September 11, 2001. Thus, what began in the Bush administration as a hesitant, ill-defined prescription for a unilateralist and hegemonic foreign policy became a full-fledged elaborate interventionist ideology, with the actual implementation of several remarkable doctrinal innovations emphasizing preemption and prevention. On the international level, the self-fulfilling prophecy resulted from an overly pessimistic perspective, which transformed into an aggressive policy and led eventually to a much worse global situation.

A deeper and more comprehensive understanding of the specific self-fulfilling behavior associated with the foreign policy of the Bush administration must penetrate, beyond everything else, the ideological assumptions adopted by that administration. Chapter 3 attempts to offer such an understanding by focusing on what it calls the Neoconservative revolution. It examines the proposition that the Bush doctrine has been organically linked to Neoconservatism, the hypothesis being that the Neoconservatives produced the "prophecy" that gave the rationale for the foreign policy of the Bush administration.[5] Neoconservatism is a right-of-center nationalist ideology that emphasizes American exceptionalism and calls upon the United States to act, even militarily and unilaterally, in order to establish hegemonic control abroad. While not all so-called Neocons endorse all elements of this definition with equal vigor, those are some of the core ideas of Neoconservatism as promoted by members of the movement, particularly following the traumatic events of September 11, 2001.

Chapter 4 focuses on the personality of George W. Bush as the man at the very center of the foreign policy from 2001 to 2008. While many observers have perceived President Bush as merely a puppet of other policy makers, particularly Vice President Richard Cheney, that position is rejected in this volume as fundamentally unsubstantiated. Chapter 4 argues that, in fact, Bush seems to have guided his own foreign policy, although he was deeply influenced by others. In this volume, it is also maintained that the Bush personality showed an *inclination* to adopt self-fulfilling prophecies and potentially self-fulfilling disasters. By his own admission and by the testimony of many others, Bush's reactions to different situations tended to be nonanalytical, "gut" responses (that is, reactions that could have easily produced "false definitions of a situation"). More important, Bush had an openly Manichean worldview; he defined the world as a stage for the struggle between good and evil.[6] The president tended to be utterly inflexible in pursuing his foreign policy goals,[7] thus perpetuating what Merton has called "a reign of error."

Chapter 5 assesses the impact of the decision-making process in the Bush White House on the establishment and perpetuation of the self-fulfilling behavior. It examines the argument that the worst inclinations of the president and the ideological impact of the Neoconservatives were exacerbated by a decision-making process in which some of the most hawkish members of the administration, particularly Vice President Cheney and Secretary of Defense Donald Rumsfeld, were in full control or were at least disproportionately influential. The decision-making process lacked self-criticism and intellectual openness.[8]

Chapter 6 ("Lessons for Future Presidents: America and the World beyond Bush and Neoconservatism") reflects on how the United States might deal with its current and future challenges, some produced by the self-fulfilling mechanisms of the foreign policy of the past few years. Chapter 6 also offers and analyzes a new agenda for the next presidency. Among the ideas analyzed in this comprehensive chapter are demilitarizing American foreign policy, reinstituting "the diplomacy of consultation," refocusing the United States on serious regional conflicts, emphasizing multilateralism and globalism, avoiding overreaching via clearer priorization, and, above all, preventing self-fulfilling disasters by limiting ideological blindness.

THE LEGACY

While foreign policy is invariably the result of numerous factors—and the function of the analyst is to identify the factors that are most significant—it is the particular relationships between the factors (e.g., the extent to which they reinforce each other) that often determine the actual result of the foreign policy adopted by a particular administration. In the case of the Bush administration, the ultimate result of the multifactor constellation (which includes the president's personality, the Neoconservative ideology, the international challenges to America's supremacy, and the White House decision-making process) has been a genuine, far-reaching *revolution* in American foreign policy.[9] The dimensions of this revolution are comprehensively assessed in this study.

In promoting its revolutionary program, the Bush administration has adopted what could be described as an ideology-based rather than fact-driven foreign policy, an attitudinal prism somewhat detached from the reality of the international system. In historical terms, the new policy has amounted to a dramatic shift from the traditional principles of American foreign and security policy, particularly the strong American tendency toward pragmatism. Many observers have come to believe that this shift threatens not only the long-term interests of the United States but also, given the prominence of America in the global system, the well-being of the world community at large. It is argued in this volume that more important than any other factor, the United States *lost legitimacy* between 2001 and 2008.

While Bush's foreign policy was sometimes perceived as "hard-nosed," the fundamental problem in both its conception and implementation has been not its tough pursuit of realpolitik but precisely the opposite—its lack of realism. The policy had excessive utopian ideological commitment to unilateral American hegemony;[10] in the minds of its supporters it reflected both the interests of the United States and of those dominated by it. Notions such as *benevolent hegemony* (assuming that even those controlled by the United States could benefit from its hegemony or would even appreciate it) were introduced into the lexicon in order to justify the new policy. The problem has been the considerable gap between what the United States could actually do to pursue that hegemony and what President Bush and his advisers believed it could do. Chapter 3 of this book provides a detailed account of the rationale that led to the hegemonic policy prescription, the Neoconservative ideology adopted by the Bush administration. The Neoconservatives, the people who gave Bush's foreign policy its intellectual coherence and laid down its foundations, seem to be captives of their own ideological formulae. They began with the assumption that the United States could do all it wanted to do and that it could do it on its own. Therefore, they concluded, the United States *should* act alone.

When the terrorist assaults of September 11, 2001, occurred, the Neoconservatives, most members of the Bush administration, and many others came to believe (or acted as if they came to believe) that the world had dramatically changed overnight and that under the new circumstances US freedom of action had become limitless. This attitude is reflected in the words of Christian Brose in *The National Interest*: "What the September 11 attacks revealed about the nature of the unipolar world compelled the Bush administration to initiate an unprecedented reevaluation of international political thinking. Foreign states could come along willingly, reluctantly or not at all with the new US-wrought dispensation, but they certainly would not be allowed to 'live past' this monumental event. They would be compelled to realize not that God was dead, but that the old order was no more."[11]

Brose's words, and those of numerous other commentators, reveal the centrality that many observers have tended to assign to the terrorist attacks of September 11, 2001, an event that is fully assessed in chapter 2 of this volume. The argument promoted is that September 11 was, in a way, a *dual* tragedy. First, it brought about the death of thousands of innocent people. Second, it allowed the Bush administration to introduce and implement a series of new but misguided initiatives that revolutionized American foreign policy. The last chapter of this volume examines the possibilities of returning to the bipartisan, pragmatic, Realist Washington consensus of the pre-Bush years.

In assessing the United States' response to the events of September 11, 2001, it ought to be noted that despite the genuine psychological trauma of the terrorist attacks, the world has not changed in terms of the distribution of power. September 11 demonstrated that the United States could be hurt by nonstates and, more specifically, by terrorist organizations. Experts in the field have been aware of that reality and for years have warned policy makers about it. Whatever changes did occur as a result of September 11, 2001, they were surely not as fundamental as those that occurred in such overwhelmingly important years as 1918, 1945, or 1989. The United States remained the only genuine superpower after September 11, as it had been before. From the perspective of this volume, it is most important to note that the Bush administration and its ideological supporters inside and outside of government *chose* to react to September 11 as if it completely changed everything. This followed their particular "definition of the situation," revealed in a long series of presidential speeches and comments. Moreover, the Bush administration successfully pushed policies based on the assumption that "everything changed," thereby deepening and widening the crisis.

Secondary powers had begun to emerge as potential competitors with America even prior to September 11, although none of them genuinely threatened the overwhelming advantage of the United States.[12] Ironically, the Neoconservative recommendation that America ought to act unilaterally in the post-9/11 world, and the Bush administration's adoption of this ill-conceived policy, strengthened those emerging secondary powers. This new policy made the challenge to the United States more serious than it had been before.

The fundamental assumption of a "changed world" that presumably threatens America's global position, well-being, and even existence, and the unshaken resolve to revise US foreign policy on the basis of that assumption, meant that the Bush administration was willing to act after September 11 in an even more unilateral, hegemonic, and militaristic manner than before. Assertive, overly militaristic unilateralism became the preferred option and eventually led to the Iraq invasion. In adopting such policy, the Bush administration deviated from accepted norms in American foreign policy and from the well-established, bipartisan Washington consensus, a consensus that some analysts have called liberal internationalism. Although deviation from liberal internationalism might have started "well before Bush took office,"[13] the Bush administration completely abandoned it. In adopting its new policy, the administration accelerated and energized processes *unfavorable* to the United States and intensified worldwide anti-Americanism.[14]

Despite arguments to the contrary, it is important to realize that the Bush revolution in foreign policy has not been merely a change in terms of the *means* used to implement that policy.[15] Much more important, the Bush revolution must be understood in terms of its overall *strategic goals*. Thus, for example, Bush administration functionaries and ideologues have called for regime change in "rogue states" and in general endorsed a policy of preemption and even prevention against America's adversaries. In broader terms, the changes introduced by the Bush administration reflected the Neoconservative desire to establish a worldwide, American hegemonic control, a position announced to the world quite openly by several prominent Neoconservatives. Some of these proclamations were issued already in the 1990s during the Clinton administration (and even the administration of George H. W. Bush); they represented a concerted effort on the part of leading Neoconservatives to reshape American foreign policy despite the existence of relatively moderate administrations in Washington.[16]

An example of the growing assertiveness of the Neoconservatives and their allies is the Statement of Principles of the Project for the New American Century (PNAC), signed in 1997 by twenty-five prominent individuals. This important document asserted the need for the United States government to embrace a hegemonic position. "We need to accept responsibility for America's unique role in preserving and extending an international order friendly to our security, our prosperity, and our principles,"[17] the statement declared. Robert Kagan, a leading Neoconservative ideologue and cofounder of the PNAC, stated in an article published in *Foreign Affairs* in 1996, that America's goal should be to establish "benevolent global hegemony." Placing this goal in historical context, Kagan added: "Having defeated the 'evil empire,' the United States enjoys strategic and ideological predominance. The first objective of US foreign policy should be to preserve and enhance that predominance by strengthening America's security, supporting its friends, advancing its interests, and standing up for its principles around the world."[18]

While the Neoconservative obsession with a hegemonic United States was already present during the presidencies of Bush-41 and Bill Clinton, under Bush-43 that obsession became an operational program directly influencing the administration's policy. In an early, now famous essay published in 1990, Charles Krauthammer described the post–Cold War world as reflecting "a unipolar moment"; he demanded that the United States turn it into a unipolar era. He stated, without equivocation, that "the center of world power is the unchallenged superpower, the United States."[19] The presidency of George W. Bush tried to make those dreams of unlimited power a reality.

While it has been argued that US foreign policy has been, in effect, "hijacked" by the overzealous Neoconservative camp and several of its "assertive nationalist" allies within the administration (e.g., Vice President Cheney and Secretary of Defense Rumsfeld[20]), there is a substantial amount of evidence to suggest that President Bush himself has shared or at least adopted their policies out of conviction, weakness, or inexperience, or possibly a combination of all three factors. Evaluating this debate, chapter 4 asserts that Bush ought to be understood as *the master of his own revolution* rather than, as he has often been portrayed in the media, a puppet of others, a sort of caricature. While Bush's image was indeed that of "a deer caught in the headlights," there is little real evidence to show that he did not control the most important aspects of his foreign policy.

While chapter 4, drawing on many sources, assesses the impact of the personality and convictions of the president,[21] the overall thesis of the book is that in addition to those personal factors, Neoconservative philosophy, the attitudes of key administration officials, the unique decision-making process established in the Bush administration, and, above all, the world situation in the post-9/11 era ought to be taken into account in a major way in presenting a full explanation of the era from 2001 to 2008. Equally important in explaining US foreign policy for the past eight years is that the terrorist attacks stunned and paralyzed Congress and, to a large extent, even the American people. This reaction (or overreaction) allowed the president and his assistants to chart a new course for US foreign policy.

Analytically, the key to a thorough understanding of the new, post-2001 American foreign policy is in a multilayered, multidimensional approach to all actors involved in it—the president, the people around him in the White House, and the vast Washington bureaucracy, the Congress, the mass media, and ultimately the American people. Any partial, segmented approach to American foreign policy cannot even begin to capture the full story of the "Bush Revolution." This volume tries to explain US foreign policy between 2001 and 2008 in terms of global changes (chapter 2), ideological formulae (chapter 3), the personal characteristics of George W. Bush (chapter 4), and the decision-making process adopted by the president (chapter 5). Reductionist explanations that focus on one of these factors to the exclusion of others are rejected in favor of a multidimensional analysis.

DISASTROUS CONSEQUENCES?

While it might be too early to assess comprehensively the long-term consequences of Bush's foreign policy, a partial evaluation can already be made. In regard to Iraq, the president's major initiative, Bush adopted "a high-risk, high-reward strategy";[22] most observers seem to believe that it has not been successful, particularly in terms of its own ambitious goals (such as democratizing Iraq and the entire Middle East, or substantially reducing the terrorist threat). If we take an appropriately broad view, incorporating into the analysis the long-term consequences for America's standing in the world, the war in Iraq and the "war on terror" in general have been rather unsuccessful. The invasion of Iraq (and particularly the unilateral way in which it has been carried out) has been not merely unnecessary but, in fact, a self-fulfilling disaster, a result of the administration's overall approach to foreign policy.

An assessment of the past eight years also ought to include a look at the highly negative reaction of what might be called world public opinion to the foreign policy of the Bush administration. The level of criticism of American foreign policy in the world since 2001 is historically unprecedented. This increase in criticism reflects the decline in America's prestige during the presidency of George W. Bush. In general the vast majority of the countries in the world have intensely opposed the new US foreign policy: for example, in a February 2006 international public-opinion poll conducted by GlobeScan and the Program on International Policy Attitudes, 60 percent of the respondents said they believed that the Iraq war had increased the threat of global terrorism, while only 12 percent believed it decreased the probability of future terrorist attacks.[23] In addition to world public opinion as a whole, the public opinion of America's traditional transatlantic allies, Britain, France, and Germany, also showed dramatic decline in the months and years following the invasion of Iraq. In a poll released by the Pew Research Center in March 2004, US favorability ratings decreased in all three nations by 15 percent to 25 percent between the summer of 2002 and March 2004.[24] On the whole, those results were quite typical.

People in most countries have perceived Bush's foreign policy not merely as revolutionary in terms of America's traditional behavior, but also as blatantly ignoring their interests, preferences, and sense of what is right. The almost universal rebuke of the United States stood in sharp contrast with the almost universal identification with and sympathy for the United States following the tragic events of September 11, 2001. Although traditional opponents of US foreign policy might have been expected to offer criticism of the changes in America's positions, new opponents emerged as a direct result of the new initiatives. While France, as expected, failed to "comprehend" the new policy,[25] countries traditionally friendlier toward the United States, such as Germany, have become just as critical.

Ideologically speaking, the critics of the new American foreign policy included liberals as well as conservatives. Liberals have traditionally been suspicious of interventionist policy on the part of the United States. As could have been expected, the military campaign in Iraq, beginning March 20, 2003, failed to convince most of them of the necessity of the operation. The failure to locate weapons of mass destruction in Iraq or to substantiate the link between Saddam Hussein and Osama bin Laden strengthened the liberal position that the United States was involved in an imperialist war.

Somewhat more surprising was that many conservative commentators joined in critiquing the new foreign policy, attacking it from an analytical, realpolitik perspective, not from the perspective of liberal ideology. John Mearsheimer and Stephen Walt, prominent scholars of the Realist tradition, argued against invading Iraq on the grounds that it was an unnecessary operation. The two academics supported a more traditional containment policy toward Iraq and argued that such a policy would work simply because "the United States and its regional allies are far stronger than Iraq." They warned that an invasion would result in "high US casualties, significant civilian deaths, a heightened risk of terrorism, or increased hatred of the United States in the Arab and Islamic world."[26] Brent Scowcroft, national security adviser under Bush-41, stated in a *Wall Street Journal* op-ed piece that "there is little evidence to indicate that the United States itself is an object of [Saddam's] aggression"; he warned that an "attack on Iraq at this time would seriously jeopardize, if not destroy, the global counterterrorist campaign we have undertaken."[27] His powerful op-ed piece left a strong impression but was unable to stop the march toward war.

Pat Buchanan, representing a more isolationist position among conservative Americans, pointed out that "the Bush threat of war upon nations that have not attacked us was unprecedented." In offering a contrast between the Bush administration and previous presidencies, Buchanan reminded his readers that "Truman never threatened war to stop Stalin from building atomic bombs after Russia tested one in 1949. LBJ did not threaten war on China when it exploded a nuclear weapon in 1964. While it had been US policy to prevent the spread of nuclear weapons, Russia, Britain, France, China, Israel, India, and Pakistan had all acquired nuclear weapons without serious retribution from the United States."[28] While Buchanan's position on US foreign policy was unconventional for years, his emphasis on the deviant nature of Bush's foreign policy was telling: it reflected part of a broad antiwar spectrum in the United States.

The exceptionally activist policy adopted by the Bush administration, and specifically its insistence on the right to launch preemptive and even preventive operations,[29] generated unprecedented opposition all over the world. The assumption of unlimited and unrestrained American power, accompanied by the moralistic tone and occasional arrogance of the administration's spokespeople (particularly Secretary of Defense Rumsfeld), infuriated the United States' opponents and allies alike.

The radical nature of Bush's new policies stood at the center of the criticism. Gail Russell Chaddock of the *Christian Science Monitor* described the National Security Strategy as "the boldest restatement of US national security strategy in half a century."[30] It is important to note within such broad historical context that Bush's policies have indeed deviated from a bipartisan foreign policy that has dominated the country from the mid-1940s, despite certain splits (such as in regard to the policy toward Vietnam).

Some observers, mostly on the Left, have argued that Bush's foreign policy has been, in effect, a continuation of American imperialism rather than a revolution in US foreign policy. Carl Boggs, for example, maintained that the use of force by American presidents has been a by-product of imperialist intent and, as such, "cannot be understood in terms of specific administrations, leaders, and policies."[31] Seyom Brown saw the policies of Bush as a continuation of trends that have taken shape since the end of World War II; he explained recent foreign policy developments as "not just a temporary reaction to crisis but a reflection of a general trend in elite thinking and public attitudes."[32] Their arguments, it is maintained in this book, are not altogether very compelling. This book attempts to show that Bush's foreign policy was clearly revolutionary in the sense that it deviated from traditional American foreign policy in terms of both *declaratory policy* and *actual actions*, particularly in the military sphere. Thus, the ejection of Saddam Hussein from Kuwait under Bush-41, the humanitarian intervention in Somalia under Bush-41 and later Bill Clinton, and the bombing of Serbia (Kosovo) under Clinton were nonrevolutionary actions, and in many ways even conservative ones, trying to maintain the existing political order. They were designed to maintain the existing patterns of world politics, not to wreck them. The second Iraq war, starting in 2003, on the other hand, was a revolutionary act, and it was perceived as such by most political actors as well as by most observers.

As is explained in detail in chapter 4, it is extremely difficult to ascertain whether George W. Bush himself was truly a revolutionary at heart when he took office,[33] although his actions and policies prior to 9/11 and particularly after 9/11 suggest that he indeed saw himself as an agent of change in the world.[34] First, the forty-third president had little record in foreign policy prior to ascending to the highest office in the land. Moreover, during the presidential campaign of 2000, he quite specifically expressed preference for a modest and humble foreign policy.[35] Chapter 4 provides an assessment of the extent to which these aspects of Bush's personality and background have influenced his ideas and policies relating to American foreign policy. While it is easy to establish that after 9/11 Bush pursued what must be looked upon as a revolutionary policy, it is much more challenging to authoritatively establish that he arrived at the White House with an ambitious agenda in the field of foreign policy.

Although the interpretation and analysis of the foreign policy of the Bush administration must take into account the preferences of the president, the positions of his chief lieutenants, and the ideological pull of the Neoconservatives inside and outside the administration, it must be realized that President Bush and his supporters could not have pursued the new policies in a geostrategic vacuum. The general situation in the world at the end of the Cold War, as well as the particular "moment" in world history after 9/11, facilitated what has to be seen now as Bush's deviation from traditional American foreign policy.

Chapter 2 introduces the essential challenges American leaders faced in the post–Cold War world and then analyzes the more immediate challenges presented to America following the terrorist attacks on September 11, 2001. That combination holds the key for a comprehensive understanding of the foreign policy of the Bush administration.

September 11, 2001, gave the Bush administration a golden opportunity to introduce new policies, a topic more fully developed in chapter 2. Emphasis must be placed on the unprecedented, reevaluative, unilateral nature of the policy eventually adopted by Bush, and its departure from the "old order." The roots of the post-9/11, self-fulfilling behavior were evident before the terrorist assaults. In fact, a close examination of the period between January 20, 2001, the day Bush took office, and September 10, 2001, is useful in uncovering the signs of a new policy.[36] Although some observers have argued that unilateralism and military intervention were already present even under Bush-41 and Clinton, the intensity and consistency of these presidents' pursuit of such policies stand in stark contrast to the policy of Bush-43.

While the situation in the world has to be taken into account as a general facilitator of the Bush revolution, a fuller explanation of the way in which the dramatic change was introduced ought to focus on the decision-making process in the Bush White House. Thus, the roles of Vice President Cheney and other key figures in the Bush administration have to be thoroughly analyzed, as indeed they are in chapter 5. Cheney's influence on Bush, including the decision to invade Iraq, seems to have been highly significant, probably even crucial. In the mind of Cheney's critics, an invasion of Iraq fits the vice president's vision of "a hegemonic United States making the Middle East safe for democracy and oil and gas production."[37] Cheney's role in the administration's decision-making process was so great that some Washington officials, such as Secretary of State Colin Powell's assistant Lawrence Wilkerson, believed it was Cheney and not Bush who was truly in charge.[38]

But beyond the description and even the analysis of the decision-making process in the Bush administration is what that process implies for the future of American foreign policy. Chapter 6 addresses that particular question, offering an analysis of a variety of decision-making models used by American presidents (including George W. Bush) and draws conclusions about their potential effectiveness in dealing with America's current and future challenges.

UNCERTAIN FUTURE

Even a cursory review of the foreign policy of the Bush administration reveals its problematical nature, particularly in the context of the future of American foreign policy. The launch of the Iraq invasion in March 2003 was as controversial an initiative as any taken by the United States since the end of World War II. Even the controversial Vietnam War could have been, and has been, justified as a necessary action to contain the spread of communism. The Iraq invasion, in contrast, rested on two apparent falsehoods—one, that Saddam Hussein had weapons of mass destruction, which constituted an imminent threat to the United States, and two, that his regime was linked to the terrorist attacks of September 11, 2001. The failure to verify, prove, or convince the world of either of these claims caused America's unprecedented loss of credibility, reputation, and prestige. The future of American foreign policy rests on the ability of the United States to recover from this serious setback.

The invasion of Iraq ought to be seen—as it is in this volume—in a much broader context. Iraq was merely one decision, part of a larger behavioral pattern. This pattern, forming the foreign policy of the Bush administration between 2001 and 2008, revealed to many observers in the world a new face of US foreign policy—unilateral, militaristic, bullying, and even morally problematic. The invasion of Iraq was the type of initiative that could eventually lead the United States to a loss of its political standing in most parts of the world and even to its decline as the global leading power.

The departure of Bush from the White House in January 2009 left his successor a difficult, challenging legacy. Although this successor will confront many specific issues—Iran, North Korea, the Arab-Israeli conflict, nuclear proliferation, terrorism, relations with Russia and China, and more—the fundamental issues will be broader: restoring confidence lost, reviving alliances wrecked, rebuilding coalitions dismembered, and above all, presenting a credible international leadership to a chaotic world. Chapter 6 identifies the challenges that the next commander-in-chief will have to confront; it argues that only a multilateral and global approach to these unprecedented challenges of the twenty-first century can succeed.

This book offers a comprehensive, multidimensional, multifaceted analysis of Bush's foreign policy in an effort to develop a series of ideas for the foreign policy of Bush's successor. The thesis of chapter 6 is that the next president of the United States will need to fundamentally change US foreign policy in all or at least most respects in order to recover America's position in the world. The forty-fourth president will need to adopt a Realist foreign policy, combining the traditional American bipartisan Washington consensus of 1947 to 2001, with close attention to *new challenges*, particularly the emergence of a new and self-confident Europe, the rise of a much more vibrant and engaging China (and potentially India), the possible intensification and even diversification of global terrorism, the progressive environmental decay, the persistent poverty around the world, and so forth. What I call the "old-new policy" will need to be based on the rare use of force and the continuous reliance on international norms as these are reflected in post–World War II international institutions. New norms might have to develop as well, intensifying the cooperation among international actors.

It will be crucial for the next president and his administration first to identify clearly the goals of US foreign policy and then to adopt the strategy and tactics (that is, the overall ends and the specific means) to achieve these goals. Prioritization will then become the key for success in an ever-changing world. While the Iraqi quagmire might be a litmus test for this new approach, the agenda will be much broader.

The challenges for the United States, and particularly the new president, will be complex and full of contradictions. One of the toughest questions will be the following: how can the United States maintain relative stability in a fundamentally unstable world? While the United States will continue to be the dominant military power of the world in the foreseeable future, it is likely to be balanced and challenged economically by several new actors, primarily the European Union and China. What might be called the new political matrix—the overall political distribution of power and influence—will likely be polyarchic,[39] ethnoconflictual,[40] and surely balkanized.[41] The most difficult question for the United States will be how to prevent its potential opponents (People's Republic of China, Russia, and others) from uniting against it, as they should in accordance with the predictions of the Balance of Power theory. This problem is called the Bismarckian Dilemma.[42] The fundamental issue for the next generation of American foreign policy makers will be the following: how can the United States maintain a leading position in the international arena *despite its military dominance?*

The overall argument in chapter 6 is that the new, post-Bush American foreign policy must have a carefully calibrated, calculated, and balanced set of positions that avoids overreacting to manageable challenges. A detailed analysis of the policies since 2001 indicates that the Bush administration clearly overreacted to 9/11 and what many within it perceived and defined as a worldwide, generalized Islamic terrorism. The broad definition of the situation they chose led to an exaggerated reaction, including the Iraq invasion. Assessing the future against this background, the last chapter of the book maintains that what is needed is a dramatic readjustment of US policies, emphasizing the need to create something that approximates as much as possible a new and much broader worldwide ideological consensus. This consensus will amount to a coordinated global action designed not merely to fight international terrorism in a more multilateral fashion, but also to double the efforts to avoid a nuclear holocaust,[43] refocus attention on achieving the nonproliferation of nuclear weapons and technology, and organize a much more effective worldwide campaign against endemic, systemic, socioeconomic problems (the looming conflict over energy resources, AIDS, poverty, underdevelopment, environmental decay, etc.).

Although a call for a worldwide ideological consensus sounds highly ambitious and therefore might be regarded as unrealistic, it is important to note that there is already a partial and increasing consensus on many crucial issues. This consensus includes a commitment to democratization (despite different definitions of what democracy actually means), opposition to the proliferation of nuclear weapons (demonstrated in the coordinated actions toward North Korea and Iran), the existence of central and authoritative international institutions and especially the United Nations (despite differences of opinion on its effectiveness), and a coordinated action on many environmental, health, and poverty issues. In the context of working toward enhancing such global consensus, it is important to note that the Bush administration was never really committed to this concept as an ideal or to the principles that might flow from it—the strengthening of international organizations, the promotion of genuine democracy rather than forcing US rule on other countries (via leaders such as Pervez Musharraf in Pakistan and Nouri al-Maliki in Iraq), and the strengthening of the environmental commitment (which was evidently limited at best and became slightly more assertive toward the very end of the Bush administration). The new American president will have an opportunity to *reverse course* and do so *dramatically*. Specific proposals for how it might be done are explained in full and analyzed in the final chapter of the book. Yet, these ideas will emerge organically from an analysis of what went wrong with the Bush-Cheney, Neoconservative approach to foreign policy.

While the United States must desert Bush's unilateralist approach as inherently dangerous, ineffective, and counterproductive, it cannot simply resign as the natural, historical leader of the post–Cold War, post-9/11 world (as some isolationists on the Right or moralists on the Left would have it). The book endorses British prime minister Tony Blair's position as reflected in his speech to Congress several years ago, when he stated that history has placed the United States in a leadership position.[44] In fact, Blair boldly pronounced that "there never has been a time when the power of America was so necessary."[45] In a polyarchic world, it is argued, it is more important than ever for the United States to lead. John Ikenberry stated that in the absence of American leadership a much more oppressive hegemon could take root, one that might not be as "liberal . . . and expansive" as is America.[46]

The American leadership role in the world was relatively easy to define during the forty-year Cold War. It is a lot more complicated to define in the post–Cold War, post-9/11, and especially post-Bush-43 era, when the United States has lost prestige, reputation, and credibility. This book argues that to a large extent *the wounds of the Bush years were self-inflicted*. If this is indeed the case, *self-correction is possible*, however difficult.

The goal of this book is to systematically analyze Bush's foreign policy, learn in detail from its mistakes, and develop a comprehensive agenda for significant improvements that will serve the next president. The president, in particular, could lead America and the world in a significantly more successful manner than the Bush administration has done.

CHAPTER 2

THE CHALLENGE TO AMERICA AND THE WORLD

The policies of the Bush administration ought to be understood within the broader historical context of American foreign policy and its ideological foundations. This assessment cannot be done merely within the time span between 2001 and 2008, or even the ideological framework of Neoconservatism or the American Right in general. While the United States faced serious challenges in the world during the Bush presidency—ethnic instability in several regions, nuclear proliferation among so-called rogue states, an unprecedented act of terrorism, continuous ecological decay, and so forth—the reactions of the Bush administration did not fit the challenges and did not deal with them efficiently and responsibly. Rather, the reactions were largely incompatible with the challenges and, as a direct result, exacerbated the conditions that brought those challenges about. The initial, fundamental inclination of the administration was to react to international challenges unilaterally, even though only in a military sense could the United States act unilaterally due to its superior power.[1]

The increasingly diverse post–Cold War world, especially in terms of economic power, ideologies, and the polyarchic nature of the global society,[2] required a much more nuanced, balanced, and multilateral approach on the part of the United States than the one exhibited by the Bush administration. This kind of nuanced approach was lacking from the very beginning of the administration (that is, in its "formative," or pre-9/11, period), although on rare occasions a balanced approach did prevail within the Bush administration.[3] Such a nuanced approach was almost completely and even progressively deserted following the September 11 terrorist attacks.[4] During George W. Bush's second term in office, there were public attempts to recover the Realist approach or to present the Bush administration's foreign policy as Realist. For the most part, these attempts were not successful, despite genuine efforts by several prominent people within the administration. Although some of these apologists have tried to shed softer light on the record of the Bush administration—presenting it as less of an aberration than it actually was and was widely perceived to be—the truth remains that President Bush's overall policy deviated dramatically from that of other presidents, including, most important, those who have headed the American administration in the post–Cold War era.[5]

This chapter focuses on the systemic challenge presented to the United States by the world and the American reaction to that challenge. It begins with the fundamental challenges of the post–Cold War world, challenges inherited by the administration of George W. Bush in January 2001. The second section deals with the reaction of the administration to the specific challenge of September 11; the general argument in that section is that, for the Bush administration, September 11 did not define but merely *reaffirmed* the analysis and the policies to which the administration was committed from the very beginning. The final section is dedicated to the examination of Bush's doctrinal innovations. It would be suggested that the revisions introduced by the Bush administration have dramatically changed the character of American foreign policy.

The Post–Cold War Challenge:
Alternative Responses to Uncertainty

The sudden, unexpected end of the Cold War left the United States with a great, historically unique opportunity to reshape the world in a way that reflected its values and interests. With the collapse of the Soviet Union and its main military instrument, the Warsaw Pact, in the early 1990s, American leadership was the only one left available. Another potential rival, the People's Republic of China, was still far from being a superpower, even in purely economic terms. The unification of Europe was still a future dream. Thus, the United States found itself as the one and only remaining superpower. Yet, as Condoleezza Rice observed almost twenty years later, "We [the United States] knew better where we had been than where were we going."[6] Although President George H. W. Bush spoke at the time about the emergence of a "New World Order," this concept remained ill defined and too general.[7] The predictable certainty of the Cold War, with its stable, structured, nuclearized bipolarity, was forever gone. Some observers of the international scene thought from the very beginning that the future looked bleak.[8]

Indeed, in terms of the overall implementation of American foreign policy, the post–Cold War era has proven to be much more difficult to handle than the Cold War era due to the lack of clarity of US goals, the unpredictability of many international events, changes in the world's balance of power, the return of militarized conflict to the international scene (Iraq, Yugoslavia, and Rwanda are but a few examples), and other factors. Some analysts have argued even that in terms of relative power, the end of the Cold War did not enhance the relative power of the United States but rather reduced it.[9] Although it might be hard to prove this thesis in terms of real power, psychologically the post–Cold War era seems a lot more complicated than the Cold War era. The complexities and challenges of the "unipolar world" are unique.

While some analysts of American foreign policy in the post–Cold War era have been quite critical of the country's performance in its totality,[10] it would be argued here that, given the objective difficulties of this period, both presidents George H. W. Bush and Bill Clinton performed, in fact, quite well. Thus, neither of these presidents allowed the United States to get involved in a prolonged, costly, and large-scale war, despite the considerable "imperial temptations"[11] of using America's huge military advantage. When these two presidents ordered the military into action—Iraq in 1990 and 1991 and the former Yugoslavia in the 1990s are prime examples—they guaranteed the political support and military participation of a large number of additional countries, attempted to gain the endorsement of international organizations such as the UN Security Council and the North Atlantic Treaty Organization (NATO), and assured a reasonably quick military decision on the battlefield. Consequently, in both Iraq and in the former Yugoslavia, US leadership stature grew as a direct result of both diplomatic handling and military intervention. Politically, those interventions strengthened the United States as the undisputed leader of the world.

In the case of Bush-43, the situation was clearly different.[12] From the very beginning, the attitude adopted by his administration was significantly more confrontational, unilateralist, and militaristic than that of either of his two predecessors.[13] While in hindsight it could be argued that under Bush-41 the United States showed a lack of clarity in terms of specific, large-scale vision for the world,[14] in defense of the first post–Cold War president it ought to be noted that he faced an extremely complicated and entirely new situation, particularly in Europe and the Middle East. The collapse of the USSR, the reunification of Germany, and Iraq's invasion of Kuwait were earthshaking events and, more important from this book's perspective, new challenges for the United States. President George H. W. Bush dealt with those new situations cautiously, patiently, and thoughtfully, producing positive results for the United States and the world. Similarly, Clinton's position toward the international crises faced by his administration (mostly in the former Yugoslavia) was pragmatic, carefully calibrated, and quite cautious.

Several authors have noticed the increasing American tendency in the post–Cold War era to intervene militarily in various parts of the world.[15] This generalization might be true in a statistical manner: in terms of the numbers of American interventions, it ought to be noted that most interventions under Bush-41 and Clinton were relatively limited in size and duration. The exception, the Iraq war in 1990 and 1991, was not only recognized almost universally as a necessary and justified intervention; it was also brilliantly executed and politically highly successful, propelling the United States to an unprecedented, strong leadership position in the world.

Whatever the case may be, the American interventionist tendency intensified significantly with the arrival of George W. Bush in the White House. The new president appointed several known "superhawks" to key positions in his administration (including Dick Cheney, Donald Rumsfeld, and Paul Wolfowitz), and the results began to show even prior to the September 11 assaults.[16] Moreover, the *character* of the American military intervention has changed quite dramatically. This reality could be demonstrated systematically by comparing four large-scale American military interventions in the post–Cold War era—Iraq I (1990–1991), Kosovo/Bosnia, Afghanistan, and Iraq II.

The following table offers such a comparison between the four major US military interventions. It focuses on four major characteristics of those interventions: (1) the level of international support received by the United States in pursuing the military intervention; (2) the legal or moral support obtained by the United States for a military intervention; (3) the manner in which the military intervention was executed; and (4) the level of success achieved by the United States in pursuing the military operation.

Several comments ought to be made to highlight the essence of the table: (1) While Iraq I, Bosnia/Kosovo, and Afghanistan were strongly supported by public opinion in the West and beyond, Iraq II met with strong opposition from numerous governments and in world public opinion; (2) while the legal and moral basis for Iraq I, Bosnia/Kosovo, and Afghanistan was firm, it was highly questionable in regard to Iraq II, an intervention perceived by most observers as imperial; (3) the execution of the wars in Iraq I, Bosnia/Kosovo, and Afghanistan was impressively efficient, which is not so with Iraq II;[17] (4) finally, while the overall political success of Iraq I, Bosnia/Kosovo, and Afghanistan (at least in the first few years of US engagement there) was self-evident, strengthening the American position in the world, Iraq II has proven to be politically damaging in terms of America's legitimacy, reputation, and prestige.

	Iraq I (Bush-41), 1990–1991	Kosovo/ Bosnia (Clinton)	Afghanistan (Bush-43)	Iraq II (Bush-43), 2003–2008
International support	UN Security Council Resolution; Arab support	NATO involvement	Broad international support	Relatively little international support and fierce opposition in world public opinion
Legal and moral basis	Responding to Iraqi aggression toward Kuwait (politicide)	Responding to ethnic conflict (including ethnic cleansing) and a refugee problem	Responding to a direct attack on US soil in self-defense against the Taliban regime	Preventive war, justified in terms of the regime's alleged link to al-Qaeda, the existence of WMD, and the democratization of Iraq and Mid-East
Military execution	Many (750,000) US troops and non-US troops	Air bombardment	Using the Northern Alliance	Few troops (140,000)
Success	High, quick success	Relatively quick success	Initial success, but more problems with reduction in troops	Undetermined, but doesn't look good

The bottom line is that the decision to invade Iraq in March 2003 could and ought to be seen as a watershed in terms of US foreign policy in the post–Cold War era. It reflected the attitude of the president and his chief advisers, an attitude that existed before September 11, 2001, but in all likelihood was reaffirmed as a result of that eventful day.

In comparing Bush-43 to his two predecessors, it could be reasonably argued that, in general, the United States was ill prepared to lead the world when the Cold War came to an unexpected end in 1989. After leading the Western alliance against the Soviet-dominated bloc for over four decades, America found the post–Cold War environment complicated, unpredictable, and challenging. Against this background, it is important to recognize that both Bush-41 and Clinton brought to the White House a healthy dose of pragmatism and caution, as well as bipartisanship.[18] Each of them pursued a low-risk strategy in trying to adjust to the volatile new world. The past eight years, in sharp contrast, have witnessed a dramatically different approach. The key policy makers in the administration of George W. Bush saw the post–Cold War system as giving the United States a free hand in pursuing its interests unilaterally and militaristically. This position—unilateral, militaristic, and on many occasions publicly arrogant—was strengthened following the events of September 11, but it has characterized the attitude of the Bush administration toward the post–Cold War world in general. Thus, emphasizing the differences between the pre-9/11 world of the Bush administration and the post-9/11 world of that administration does not capture the genuine character of the Bush regime. A more useful comparison is between George W. Bush and his two immediate predecessors.

Nowhere else has the contrast between Bush-41 and Clinton, on the one hand, and Bush-43, on the other hand, been clearer than with regard to the relationships between America and Western Europe. During the long years of the Cold War, the Atlantic alliance rested on the mutuality of defense interests, as well as commitment to a similar value system, by the United States and its Western European allies. Despite some tensions and even public crises, as over the issue of deploying American missiles in Europe during the administration of Ronald Reagan, the overwhelming rationale for continued and close cooperation between America and Europe was sustained for more than forty years.

The unexpected fall of the Soviet empire, a momentous historical event, had to have significant impact on American-European relations, although not necessarily the impact produced by the administration of George W. Bush prior to and following September 11. Zbigniew Brzezinski, along with many others, has noted that after the fall of the Soviet Union, America found itself as the world's clear military superpower, with no rivals: "America has a monopoly on global military reach, an economy second to none, and peerless technological innovation, all of which give it unique worldwide political clout."[19] While this assessment is undoubtedly correct, it ought to be emphasized that despite a change in the situation, the desirability of close American-European relationships remained, although the fundamental rationale for it has changed. The complete disappearance of the Soviet threat made the original rationale (military deterrence) obsolete, but alternative reasons for maintaining the American-European alliance emerged.

Many observers have lamented that the American-European alliance declined.[20] Yet, it is crucial to emphasize that this was only to a limited extent the result of the end of the Cold War and the disappearance of the Soviet or Russian threat. Equally important were the attitudes and policies adopted by the administration of George W. Bush prior to and following the traumatic events of September 11. Even before September 11, the Bush-43 administration carried out a policy that most Europeans looked upon with profound disdain, both in terms of substance (Kyoto, International Criminal Court, Missile Defense, etc.) and in terms of style (unilateral and militaristic).

Seyom Brown has noted that there were "early post–Cold War visions of the United States exercising global hegemony in a 'unipolar' international system, largely through its economic power and its dominance in multilateral diplomacy."[21] Although such "visions" were indeed presented from time to time, there is little evidence that they were based on the actual policies of either George H. W. Bush or Clinton. On most if not all mutually important issues, Bush-41 and Clinton consulted heavily with other leaders, particularly Western European heads of government. Brown is right that those visions of American hegemony have proven to be "overly optimistic simplifications of the more complex realities."[22] This reality was recognized by Bush-41 and Clinton; the administration of Bush-43, on the other hand, chose to act as if those hegemonic visions were both realizable and desirable.

During the 2000 campaign, there were no real signs that if George W. Bush became president a dramatic deviation from the traditional US foreign policy would occur. His chief foreign policy adviser, Condoleezza Rice, came from a Realist background and strong links to the Realist-based administration of Bush-41, specifically Brent Scowcroft, national security adviser of Bush-41. In her article published in *Foreign Affairs* during the 2000 presidential campaign, Rice argued that the United States should act to further the already active trends toward democratization and liberalization.[23] The priorities she outlined were entirely within the overall Washington consensus: ensure military dominance (the reality of the post–Cold War era guaranteed that position), encourage free trade and economic growth (a position acted on by the outgoing president, Clinton), strengthen relationships with American allies "who share our values" (an area in which Bush-43 failed), focus on Russia and China, and act against rogue regimes and terrorists building weapons of mass destruction.[24] Of all these goals, the Bush administration will be remembered by the last one more than by any other. A hint that this was the administration's intention was included in Rice's article when she stated, "The next American president should be in a position to intervene when he believes, and can make the case, that the United States is duty-bound to do so."[25] Yet, few imagined the extent to which this position would be carried out.

Part of the 2000 campaign by George W. Bush was an attack on the Clinton administration's commitment to pursue "nation building." That attack was carried out in the name of "national interest," emphasizing particularly the traditional military mission of the armed forces. In emphasizing "national interest," the Bush people called, or so it was understood by most observers, for a return to the type of Realism that had characterized the policies of Bush-41. In this context, Rice stated that the American military was "most certainly not designed to build a civilian society" and was "best used to support clear political goals."[26] It is important to note that Bush-43 clearly did not follow this advice. On the contrary, Bush's policies were greatly impacted by the ideological input of Neoconservatives supportive of what might be called the democratization project.

The post–Cold War era has been characterized by a variety of perceptions as to the precise nature of the "new" world. The bipolar world of Soviet-American rivalry was replaced by what looked like a unipolar world, although it was unclear and probably unpredictable how long this unipolarity could and would be sustained. Bush-41, an experienced internationalist, and Clinton, less experienced in global politics and mostly committed to domestic economic development, tried to carefully navigate in a world not yet fully understood. These presidents sometimes gave the impression of being indecisive. The administration of George W. Bush acted more decisively but also less cautiously. Moreover, his administration, coming into power a decade after the end of the Cold War, seemed to assume from the start that the post–Cold War era would be, and should be, hegemonic.

Most important, from the theoretical viewpoint of this book, is that in acting hegemonically and unilaterally, in a blatant and even provocative manner, the Bush administration helped usher in a world that is closer to the *balance of power* system than the one it has inherited.[27] In effect, the Bush-Cheney vision of a unipolar world in which an all-powerful hegemon must exercise unilateral force to keep its competitors from destabilizing the world order became a classic *self-fulfilling prophecy*. Even prior to the ascendance of Bush-43 to power in 2001, there was "an increasing disposition on the part of US officials to threaten the use of force in order to keep the most dangerous aspects of the emerging polyarchy under control, particularly the growing hostility to US global hegemony and presence."[28] Although this disposition was kept under control by both Bush-41 and Clinton, it was significantly enhanced with the arrival of Bush-43 at the White House, and it completely took over after September 11, 2001. This new behavior, based on a new depiction of the situation, tipped the balance of the global opposition to the United States. It exacerbated the anti-Americanism that was already present. In other words, we had here a clear-cut case of self-fulfilling disaster.

In *The Sorrows of Empire*, Chalmers Johnson asserts that "the end of the Cold War represented both an opportunity and a crisis for US global rule—an opportunity because the Soviet sphere of influence was now open for imperial expansion, a crisis because the fall of the Soviet Union ended the justification for the global system of naval bases, airfields, army garrisons, espionage listening posts, and strategic enclaves."[29] There is some evidence that the administrations of Bush-41 and Clinton used the opportunity Johnson mentions for expanding American power. Thus, there was an expansionist policy on the part of the Clinton administration reflected in the initiative to add the Czech Republic, Hungary, and Poland to NATO. Yet by and large, this expansion was heavily supported by American and Western European public opinion.[30]

Although neither Bush-41 nor Clinton took positive action to dismantle the global strategic presence of the United States, there was little political pressure or demand for such a move. Moreover, to do that would be to deviate from the well-established, bipartisan Washington consensus. While the policy of Bush-41 and Clinton fully reflected the superior American power, neither of these presidents could be viewed as particularly aggressive in promoting this power.

In the case of George W. Bush, on the other hand, there was a clear-cut, unmistaken commitment to not merely maintain the strategic presence of the United States but to greatly expand it. While a variety of sometimes competing explanations for the 2003 invasion of Iraq have been offered, establishing a long-term American presence in that country and enhancing its overall military presence in the Middle East are surely among the leading explanations for the war. But the imperial expansion on the part of the Bush-43 administration could be easily documented by focusing not only on the policy toward the Middle East. The establishment of a missile defense system in several Eastern European countries (the Czech Republic and Poland, and possibly Lithuania) is another example of this military expansion. The increasing size of defense allocations is yet another indication of the militarization of US foreign policy under Bush-43.[31] In 2006 and 2007, for example, administration requests for defense allocations amounted to huge increases over previous years. There can be no question that 9/11 gave the Bush administration a truly unique opportunity to significantly expand US military domination.[32] An examination of the pre-9/11 policies of the Bush administration, as well as the ideological inclinations of key people within the administration, renders compelling evidence that the fundamental goal has always been to expand the military dominance of the United States.

An examination of the policies pursued by the administration after 2001, as well as an evaluation of the positions taken by several key officials and other people linked with the administration of George W. Bush, indicates that those policies were based on what some analysts have called the hegemonic stability theory.[33] The idea behind this theory is that a world with a hegemon is inherently more stable than a world without one, which has analytical as well as prescriptive and normative implications. Those who proclaimed the post–Cold War era as America's "unipolar moment"[34] fully accepted the hegemonic stability theory, viewing the United States as the stabilizing hegemon. Their position reflected the situation: by the end of the Cold War, "the United States found it-self without a military equal and in a position, from a narrow military stand-point, to act without a serious prospect of external restraint. . . . Since the post–Cold War world continued to hold many dangers, it was easy to make the case that the international order required a guardian."[35]

Yet none of the analysts endorsing the new hegemonic "moment" dwelt on the necessity of *restraining* the guardian's power via either domestic opposition to overly hegemonic policies or an international balancing action. By and large, little domestic or international restraint was needed under Bush-41 and Clinton because self-restraint seems to have been practiced during both presidencies. This kind of restraint, however, completely disappeared under Bush-43, partic-ularly after September 11, 2001. The era of unconstrained unilateralism arrived in full force in the wake of the terrorist attacks on American targets.

Looking at the post–Cold War world, Robert D. Kaplan has focused on the particular challenge of environmental degradation. He stresses that it would cause great crises across the globe: "We are entering a bifurcated world. Part of the globe is inhabited by Hegel's and Fukuyama's Last Man, healthy, well fed, and pampered by technology. The other, larger part is inhabited by Hobbes's First Man, condemned to a life that is 'poor, nasty, brutish, and short.' Although both parts will be threatened by environmental stress, the Last Man will be able to master it, the First Man will not."[36] There is little evidence that either Bush-41 or Clinton was ready to invest the necessary resources in closing the gap be-tween the haves and the have-nots. In the case of George W. Bush, his commit-ment of possibly trillions of dollars to the Iraq war practically guaranteed that funds for a worldwide Marshall plan would not be available.

Commenting on the post–Cold War era, and particularly on the position taken toward it by some observers, Kaplan states that he "began to suspect that the optimistic future many predicted for a democratizing sub-Saharan Africa in the wake of the Cold War was no less naive than the Wilsonianism of a previous era."[37] Kaplan's pessimistic point of view is quite valid but has to be expanded beyond sub-Saharan Africa, as well as beyond the democratization project. Some Neoconservative observers, most notably Francis Fukuyama, painted a bright but also triumphalist picture for the post–Cold War era. In the context of the analysis offered here, however, it is important to note that that triumphal-ism was significantly less evident in the Bush-41 and Clinton administrations than it was in Bush-43's administration, where it came to truly dominate American foreign policy.

Richard Haass, a foreign policy centrist associated with several administrations in Washington, captured very well the American mindset prior to September 11, 2001: "Most Americans perceived a seemingly inexorable positive trend in international developments. From the American perspective, therefore, foreign engagement appeared to be a matter of discretion—of choice, not necessity. With the demise of the Soviet Union, the oceans once again seemed to afford us privileged security. Even in the face of growing transnational threats from the proliferation of weapons of mass destruction, terrorism, infectious diseases, and environmental degradation, we continued to feel secure in our homeland. Preserving our way of life against external threat seemed a low cost, second order proposition."[38] Haass's moderate language seems to represent more accurately the administrations of Bush-41 and Clinton than the "fighting spirit" of the Bush-43 administration. In a previous book, Haass described the role of the United States in the post–Cold War era as that of "a reluctant sheriff."[39] However, this description did not apply to the administration of George W. Bush. His administration looked more like an enthusiastic enforcer.

THE CHALLENGE OF SEPTEMBER 11:
THE TEMPTATION OF AN ÜBERPOWER

The post–Cold War challenge for the United States became even more difficult as a result of the events of September 11, 2001. The traumatic experience compounded the uncertainty and became part of an already unstable foreign policy environment. In the eyes of the Bush administration, the global milieu of a world in transition, and the specific challenge posed by global terrorism, became a cardinal national challenge for the United States. The belief of the key people in the Bush administration and its most vocal Neoconservative supporters, that the world was a dangerous and menacing place that required American hegemony, was reinforced.

The new environment allowed the Bush administration and its ideological supporters to carry out a revolution that many within it had been contemplating for a long time. For people like Cheney, Rumsfeld, and Wolfowitz, the post-9/11 era presented a golden opportunity, a uniquely powerful temptation to revolutionize the matrix of world politics in a fundamental way. They were not about to pass on this opportunity.

The fundamental issue following the terrorist attacks was, and remains even today, how to precisely *define* September 11 so as to properly respond to it. The assault on America could have been defined in several different ways: the 9/11 events could have been viewed as an attempt by al-Qaeda to capture the imagination of hundreds of millions of Muslims by attacking the great superpower, thus making al-Qaeda's chief, Osama bin Laden, the leader of the Islamic world. On a tactical level, 9/11 could be seen as an act designed to tempt the United States to overreact, a bait of a sort that would eventually benefit the provocateur. Equally convincing is the hypothesis that the assault was an attempt to convince or coerce America to change certain policies, such as withdrawing its forces from Saudi Arabia. Be that as it may, all of these are straightforward, relatively narrow definitions of the assaults.

Whatever the original goals of al-Qaeda, President Bush and his ideological supporters decided to define September 11 in the *broadest* possible manner. For Bush, in his own words, 9/11 represented not merely an attack on America and its policies, but also an attack on such fundamental values as freedom, democracy, and human rights.[40] This definition led the administration to pursue the *most radical policies* compatible with this definition and resulted eventually in the *disastrous* situation that such self-fulfilling behavior can produce. The Neocons and eventually Bush himself chose to define 9/11 as a genuine existential challenge to America, comparing it to the Nazi-Japanese challenge of the 1940s and the communist challenge of the Cold War era.[41] Such a definition of the situation led the Bush administration to an attack not merely on al-Qaeda but on the Taliban regime in Afghanistan, which protected the organization. That definition implied that other states and possibly even large regions of the world— primarily the Middle East—ought to be targeted by the United States to be completely changed. The theory adopted by the Bush administration and its supporters was that the only way to deal with what they defined as the root causes of terrorism was to democratize the societies (and regions) that give birth to terrorism. The reaction to 9/11 thus reflected the convictions of some key members of the Bush administration and so-called Neoconservatives out of the administration, convictions that were held before 9/11 by many years. This definition of the situation led eventually to fundamental changes in US foreign policy doctrine; the invasion of Iraq was the behavioral expression of the new doctrine.

The problem of defining the situation was not merely limited to the broadness of the definition offered by the Bush administration; it was also in identifying the United States as the only or even the main target of the attacks. The terrorist assaults on America could have been defined in broad terms but very differently: the barbaric acts of September 11, 2001, could have been defined as a challenge to *humanity,* the *world* community, and the *world order* as a whole, not as a challenge limited to America and its national interests. Had the terrorist challenge been defined (and applied) in that fashion, it could and would have generated *a much more coordinated, internationalized, multilateral response,* combining the power of the United States, its traditional allies, and its most important potential foes (particularly China and Russia). While the Bush administration paid lip service to the international nature of al-Qaeda's challenge, there is no question that its approach was fundamentally unilateral and narrowly American. For Bush and his people, al-Qaeda was America's problem, and America alone had to find a solution. By expropriating the right to act alone, the administration lost a golden opportunity to reshape the international system.

So a critique of the Bush definition of the true meaning of September 11, 2001, could proceed from two perspectives. First, the administration could have defined the challenge of 9/11 in a narrow fashion, as an al-Qaeda attack requiring the elimination of that organization and possibly the Taliban regime. Most of the world would have endorsed such a definition and the action that followed as eminently reasonable. Alternatively, the administration could have defined 9/11 broadly, not as primarily a challenge to America but as a challenge to humanity and the international order. Both these alternatives were rejected in favor of viewing 9/11 as a challenge to the United States that required it to adopt a comprehensive but utterly unilateral action.

But the problem with the Bush reaction to 9/11 was not merely in its unilateral and comprehensive nature. It was also in the administration's insistence on discussing the challenge in *moralistic, religious, and even missionary terms* (rather than in political ones).[42] By insisting on describing the terrorist challenge as a biblical struggle of good versus evil, the Bush administration propelled itself into an irrational space. In the process, it managed to lose the support of the rest of the world, including some of its closest allies, despite the overwhelming sympathy of the world immediately following the attacks. The intervention in Iraq and the doctrinal revisions introduced by the Bush administration made it and the United States as a whole as unpopular and as resented as the terrorists responsible for 9/11.

The mistakes committed by the Bush administration in reacting to 9/11 reflected broader attitudinal problems that were evident from the very beginning of the administration. From its first day in office, the administration tended to act unilaterally, to introduce dramatic changes in the international system (as in withdrawing from the Anti-Ballistic Missile Treaty, in force since 1972), and to overreach in pursuit of its goals. Yet while the stakes at the beginning were relatively small, they became substantially larger after 9/11, and so did the potential for disastrous results.

The mistakes of the Bush administration are highlighted particularly by comparing what might be considered appropriate and inappropriate responses to the events of 9/11. Most observers thought that in deposing the Taliban regime in Afghanistan the United States acted quite appropriately, justly, and legally. This action was almost universally supported, and the United States acted within the confines of contemporary international law. Article 51 of the Charter of the United Nations permits self-defense; the United States was attacked on September 11, 2001, and the Taliban regime, as protector of al-Qaeda, bore at least some responsibility for the attack. By attacking Iraq, on the other hand, the United States crossed the line of an appropriate, just, and legal action, suffering in the process a huge loss of international support and long-term legitimacy. To most observers, the Iraq war was an interventionist, imperial war, not a war of self-defense. Wrongly defining the situation led the administration to its highly problematical behavior and produced the wrong and highly damaging results. Iraq was the clearest case of self-fulfilling disaster during the Bush era.

The complete Americanization of the response to 9/11 became a lost opportunity for creating a global response to the terrorist atrocities. Such a response could have been based on a revived and energized notion of collective security (a concept introduced to global politics by the United States at the end of World War I), mutual responsibility, and close cooperation of the nations of the world. The individualized, unilateral, and totally militarized action preferred by the Bush administration, reasserting the position of the United States not merely as the world's only superpower but as its unchallenged hyperpower, with unlimited interventionist rights, proved both ineffective and costly in all respects. An alternative response, one that reflected genuine international cooperation, could have been devised in one of humanity's most opportune moments. It could have rested on a value system emphasizing *both* global security and universal justice, a combination of hard and soft power, around which a powerful coalition of nations could have been unified. The Neoconservative alternative, which Bush embraced uncritically and with missionary zeal, led the United States in precisely the opposite direction.

Although some Neoconservatives and others have argued that whatever the United States did, it was destined to be criticized, the truth of the matter is that the international community was quite discerning in its reaction to America's response to 9/11. Thus, the Bush administration's decision to invade Afghanistan, and the claim of a right to do so, was mostly uncontroversial both domestically and internationally. It "commanded almost universal international support,"[43] reflecting strong emotive sympathy with the United States in the wake of the terrorist attacks. This was quite remarkable given that past American military interventions have rarely been popular in the world. Afghanistan was considered a legitimate operation. After September 11, 2001, no country defended al-Qaeda or its Taliban supporters, and nearly all accepted America's inherent right of self-defense in striking back against those who had attacked it. But most who supported the United States in the Afghan war and its aftermath believed that military action would end there.[44]

In chapters 3 and 4 of this book, the argument is developed that the Neoconservatives and their allies in the administration (e.g., Cheney, Rumsfeld, and Wolfowitz) saw 9/11 as a prime opportunity to persuade an inexperienced president to attack Iraq and possibly other countries, whereas the Realists (e.g., Colin Powell, Richard Armitage, and Haass) favored moving against al-Qaeda and overthrowing the Taliban in Afghanistan.[45] Thus, 9/11 can be seen as a genuine moment of truth, a watershed in the evolution of the Bush administration foreign policy. This momentous event was followed by the development of what became known as the Bush Doctrine (discussed later in this chapter), itself a reflection of the Neocons' ambitious strategic design preceding 9/11.[46] The Neocons and others on the political Right, although tellingly not everyone on the Right, promoted the idea that "that morning's [9/11] terror attacks were the symptom of a larger geopolitical condition: the 'unipolar' world, now stripped of its illusions of order and seen in the reality of its violent resentment and upheaval. Though it had been a long time coming, a US administration finally awoke to the collapse of the old order and began working through the attendant implications."[47]

Many Neoconservatives chose to connect the events of 9/11 to the possible decline of the West, and that of the United States in particular. They saw those tragic events as a golden opportunity to reverse a trend that they had feared. They tended to support a comprehensive, tough, unilateralist position as a way of achieving that goal. Interestingly, following 9/11 the United States could have used the event as an opportunity to reaffirm its unique leadership position and establish its world image via cooperation with other like-minded countries. The Iraq invasion harmed the United States by antagonizing the world.

The position that President Bush eventually adopted in response to 9/11 was entirely compatible with the position advanced by the Neoconservatives and in clear opposition to the position advanced by the Realists in his own administration and beyond. Rather than reacting to the attacks in a measured, pointed manner by focusing on deposing the Taliban regime in Afghanistan and pursuing al-Qaeda, the president chose to view the September 11 attacks in a much wider manner. For Bush and his advisers, 9/11 was a challenge to the very future of America. This position led eventually to the military attack on Iraq, carried out as a way to spread liberty and democracy;[48] the Bush administration thus placed the events of September 11, 2001, and the American response to them within a new and much broader ideological, religious, and even evangelical framework. For Bush, the reaction to 9/11 became about promoting American ideals. The vast majority of observers saw the US response, particularly the invasion of Iraq, as promoting America's narrow interests. In Bush's mind, September 11, 2001, was a demarcation line between the 1990s and the new century;[49] ironically, it was perceived as such by Bush's critics as well.

In effect, the decision of the president to define the lessons of 9/11 in the most general ideological terms, rather than in a specific political and military manner, determined all of his policies from that day forward. His definition of the situation was deterministically self-fulfilling. More moderate, Realist elements within the Bush administration chose to define the challenge to the United States in narrower terms. Thus, Richard Haass, director of policy planning at the Department of State under Colin Powell, wrote on the significance of 9/11: "The attacks on the World Trade Center and the Pentagon did not create the post–Cold War world. But they helped end the decade of complacency. They forced Americans to see clearly that foreign policy still matters. . . . They brought home the stark reality that if we do not engage with the world, the world will engage with us, and in ways we may not like."[50] Bush, however, did not engage with the world; he saw 9/11 as a license for a unilateral, military action.

BUSH'S DOCTRINAL INNOVATIONS: FAREWELL TO REALISM

The arrival of George W. Bush at the White House was a controversial event. The legitimacy of the Bush-Cheney administration was questioned by many from the very beginning in view of several facts: (1) Bush was awarded the presidency by an unprecedented decision by the US Supreme Court; (2) Bush won a minority of the popular vote in the 2000 presidential election; and (3) many believed that throughout the campaign Bush revealed an appalling lack of knowledge of foreign affairs and unfamiliarity with international issues.

Nevertheless, in terms of foreign policy, the prospects for a calm, successful era in the early twenty-first century looked excellent: (1) Bush rose to the presidency in a time of unprecedented economic prosperity in the United States and clear-cut, unchallengeable American superiority in the world; (2) some of the most challenging issues on the agenda—including the realignment of forces in Europe and the chaos in the former Yugoslavia—were well on the way toward resolution; (3) the foreign policy "Washington consensus," a fundamental bipartisan agreement on the American approach to the world, was as solid as ever.

Within a remarkably short period of time, all of this would change due to the attitude adopted by the president to both international politics in general and several specific world events, and particularly the interaction between those two. A genuine revolution was initiated and then implemented by a man probably less familiar with the world than any other president in the post–World War II era. This revolution came to be known as the Bush Doctrine, a set of principles enunciated and implemented by the president.[51]

The Bush Doctrine could be summed up by a combination of principles and policies adopted by the administration between 2001 and 2008. These fundamental ideas were codified in several documents (such as the National Security Strategy of the United States of September 20, 2002) and expressed in several of President Bush's speeches (including the "Axis of Evil" speech of January 29, 2002, the president's speech at West Point in June 2002, and his second inauguration speech, in January 2005).[52]

The Bush Doctrine can be summed up by seven ideas:

1. State terrorism: The United States should treat countries that harbor or give aid to terrorist groups as it treats the terrorists themselves. While including states, rather than only organizations, among those who are terrorists, this was the narrow definition adopted publicly by the administration.[53] This initial principle was used to justify the 2001 military operations in Afghanistan. It was later used in regard to Iraq in 2003 as well, but much less convincingly. The difference between Afghanistan and Iraq highlighted the difficulty inherent in the policy itself. Many observers felt that "terrorism" was used by the Bush administration indiscriminately in order to punish states opposing the United States. As indicated by the cases of Iran and North Korea, also identified as terrorist states, this broad definition was very difficult to actually apply.[54]

2. Preemption and prevention: The United States has a right to initiate a preventive war against regimes representing a threat to its security, especially when terrorism and weapons of mass destruction are involved. Since this threat does not have to be imminent, this policy supports not merely preemptive strikes but also preventive wars. The invasion of Iraq in March 2003 was justified by that rationale. After 9/11, preemption became "the centerpiece of US national security policy."[55] Based on the writings of several prominent Neoconservatives, observers thought that the United States committed itself to prevent any rival from ever challenging America's preeminence (see chapter 3).[56]

3. Spread of democracy: In an effort to prevent or undermine terrorism, the United States should be committed to what is called regime change in "rogue states." Put differently, in more positive terms, the United States should promote democracy in the Middle East and in other parts of the

world as an antiterrorism measure. This principle emphasizes the theme of "democracy versus authoritarianism" and the right of involvement of the United States in other countries' domestic politics (that is, interference in their internal affairs). To a large extent, this policy has been deserted and it has never been consistently pursued, although it was still the centerpiece in Bush's second inaugural address, in which the president declared that the United States' "ultimate goal" was "ending tyranny in our world."[57]

4. Unilateralism: The United States should pursue its interests unilaterally. This go-it-alone principle was already evident in 2001 when the Bush administration took over. It antagonized even some of America's closest allies (e.g., Germany) and led to unprecedented condemnation of the United States in world public opinion. Bush's position was clear and decisive: "America will act on its own, irrespective of the views of its allies."[58] One analyst observed that "the Bush strategy is one of the most aggressively unilateral US national strategies ever."[59]

5. Ad hoc coalitions: Within the Bush Doctrine, existing alliances, such as NATO, are significantly less important than so-called coalitions of the willing, ad hoc alliances designed to promote US interests in a particular situation. Some supporters of the Bush Doctrine have gone even further by classifying the nations of the world in terms of their usefulness for US operations—"Affinity Allies" (United Kingdom), "Strategic Allies" (Pakistan), etc.[60]

6. International organizations: These groups, particularly the United Nations, are not to be trusted. If they do not go along with US policy, they should be ignored. While Bush never states this idea as a "principle," he surely treated the UN, and specifically the Security Council, in that fashion during the Iraq crisis. Bush's Neoconservative supporters were persistent skeptics about international law and institutions.

7. Moralism: The Bush Doctrine asserts that the United States is on the side of goodness, while its rivals are evil. This position is an ultimate deviation from Realism. The War on Terror has been described by Bush as a war between good and evil.[61] Bush eventually expanded it to all tyrants. This moralistic tone has been based on exceptionalism as a characteristic of American culture.[62] It reflects a tendency toward black-and-white thinking.[63] Bush sup-

porters continue to promote this good-versus-evil analysis,[64] even if some of them have been highly critical of the management of the Iraq war.

By and large, the Bush Doctrine reflects quite closely the principles of Neoconservatism. A leading Neoconservative columnist stated authoritatively and quite correctly that "the Bush Doctrine is, essentially, a *synonym for neoconservative foreign policy* [emphasis added]."[65] While defenders of the Bush Doctrine often describe it in a more modest manner as reflecting "assertive Realism,"[66] their arguments do not withstand critical analysis.

In its totality, the Bush Doctrine has "alienated friends and emboldened enemies"; its critics judged it to pose "a greater danger to the United States than do the perils it supposedly guards against."[67] The doctrine constituted a major deviation from the bipartisan Washington consensus of the past several decades.

In analyzing the Bush Doctrine, it is useful to distinguish between its *substantive parts* (elements 1 through 3 above), the *methods* it adopts for implementing its goals (elements 4 through 6), and its overall *tone* (element 7).

Possibly the largest, most significant substantive deviation of the Bush Doctrine from traditionally successful US policy was in adopting preemption and prevention as guiding principles for inter-state relations in place of the two pillars of US strategy in the post–World War II era, deterrence and containment.[68] These two pillars have proven to be enormously effective in promoting US interests for fifty years, and with reasonable cost. These policy-controlling principles have proven very effective as long as the following conditions could be maintained: (1) the United States' clear superiority over (or at least parity with) the deterred and contained country; (2) the ability of the United States to sustain that superiority in the foreseeable future; (3) the public and private annunciation of a clear-cut deterrence posture; and (4) the dedication of sufficient resources to maintaining the policy in the long term.

Toward a country like Iraq, US deterrence and containment had an excellent chance of working successfully, given the United States' enormous power advantage, the opposition to Saddam Hussein's designs by many regional forces (including Iran and Saudi Arabia), and the severe sanctions imposed on the Iraqi regime by the international community since 1990. The Bush administration's desertion of containment and deterrence had to be interpreted as an imperial move designed to wreck the status quo in favor of American hegemony.

The policy of preemption and prevention had many negative consequences: (1) it pushed potential targets like Iran and North Korea toward intensifying and accelerating their nuclear programs; (2) it invited international chaos and the frequent use of force; and (3) it confirmed the worldwide suspicion that the United States was determined to act on its own in promoting its interests, thus wrecking the international order established after World War II.

In commenting on the characteristics of the Bush Doctrine, Fukuyama has argued that "neither preemption nor unilateralism was a new feature of American foreign policy" but has suggested that "what was revolutionary about the National Security Strategy [the main document summing up the Bush Doctrine] was its *expansion of the traditional notion of preemption to include what amounted to preventive war* [emphasis added]."[69] Several important points ought to be made in regard to Fukuyama's statement: (1) in fact, there are not many examples of militarily executed preemptions by the United States, especially when it comes to major wars of the order of Iraq; (2) in launching the Iraq invasion, the Bush administration implemented, in fact, a preventive-war strategy, attacking a country that was not an imminent threat to the United States; (3) it is very difficult, indeed impossible, to justify preventive war either legally or morally, since it endangers the legitimacy of American action if and when it is carried out. In general, when compared to preemption, preventive war "ought properly to be used in a far more restricted number of cases";[70] alternatively, it might not be used at all.

Using preventive war against a relatively minor country such as Iraq has proven extremely risky and costly for the United States, the Middle East, and even world stability. It elevated preventive war to a new status in overall US policy and was the sort of bold but risky strategy that came to characterize the foreign policy of Bush in general. While a preventive war could have been justified against, say, Nazi Germany in 1936 and 1937, in view of the real danger that it posed, launching an attack on a minor country has proven difficult to justify. But beyond Iraq, the use of preventive war shook up the very foundations of traditional US policy. It indicated to many that the United States was bound on establishing *Pax Americana* by using unilateral military force.

In launching a preventive war, Bush in effect extended most radically the notion of self-defense beyond its traditional, confined use. The Bush Doctrine amounts to an extension of the right of self-defense to include not merely preemption, where it sometimes could be justified, but also prevention, where it cannot possibly be justified by the norms and principles of contemporary international law. The ultimate meaning of such an extension—unilateral, militaristic, and unlimited—is to *vacate the notion of genuine self-defense of its concrete and highly limited content.*

Above all, the Bush Doctrine reflected the desire of the president, his assistants, and supporters outside the administration to use military force heavily and emphasize the *dominance* of the United States in international affairs. It is interesting and instructive to compare the Clinton era and the George W. Bush era in this regard. Madeleine Albright, Clinton's second secretary of state, described the United States as the "indispensable power." This was, and was perceived in the world as, a much less ambitious concept than "a dominant power." More important, it reflected a more modest notion of what the United States could and should do despite its military superiority. No such modest claim could be found in the Bush Doctrine.

Another important and substantive goal incorporated into the Bush Doctrine was the democratic transformation of the world and particularly the Middle East. Supporters of the president's ambitions in this regard argued repeatedly that democracies do not fight each other and that democratizing the Middle East would make it less prone to terrorism, especially anti-American terrorism. In the words of one Bush supporter: "President Bush is not the first president to want to make the world safe for democracy. He is, however, the first to use democracy to make the world safe for America."[71] It is important to note in this regard that (1) Bush was, by and large, unsuccessful in democratizing the Middle East; (2) those countries or regions that became more democratic (by conducting, for example, elections) did not become less prone to terrorism (e.g., Lebanon, the Palestinian territories); and (3) for all intents and purposes, the Bush administration deserted its democratizing ambitions as it drew to an end. In general, the argument that democracy cannot be imposed from the outside has been proven, as expected, correct.[72] Democracy has to emerge from below as part of the culture of a people, their economic and social development, and other factors. Moreover, an invasion and an occupation might encourage nondemocratic forces, as it seemed to do in Iraq.

The *international tools* adopted by the Bush Doctrine to achieve its goals were as strongly rejected by many observers as the substance of the policy itself (fighting state terrorism, adopting preemption/prevention, promoting democratization). The moralistic tone of the Bush Doctrine did not make it more acceptable, either. These tools included a combination of complementary principles: strong preference for *unilateral action* if and when possible (as in Afghanistan in 2001), the establishment of an *ad hoc coalition* if and when advantageous (as in Iraq in 2003), and under no circumstances reliance on international organizations as a necessary condition for promoting what the United States perceived as its interests. This set of principles reflected US military dominance (that is, its ability to act alone), the aversion of many Americans to alliances (part and parcel of traditional exceptionalism[73]), and traditional hostility toward the United Nations. Yet, the Bush administration adopted this set of principles more enthusiastically than any other administration in memory and used the post-9/11 moment to promote its policies with those particular tools.

In its totality, the strong emphasis of the Bush Doctrine on preemption/prevention, combined with its insistence on unilateralism and uninhibited moralistic language, constituted *a strategic innovation of the first order*. While the Bush Doctrine has drawn on previous initiatives of the United States, the policies it actually led to made a long-established imperial tendency much more explicit and even permanent than anything seen before.[74] In many ways the Bush Doctrine constituted the most important change in American strategic policy since 1947 (when the policy of containment came into being). The overall goal of the Bush Doctrine seems to have been the establishment of an American-dominated world. By emphasizing military power, democratization as a justification for intervention, and the right to use force unilaterally in a preemptive and even preventive manner, the president laid down the marker for the future. He adopted a high-risk strategy without really comprehending all the ramifications of that strategy.

The post-9/11 moment, coming against the background of the post–Cold War era and the challenges it presented to US leadership in the world, gave Bush a truly unique opportunity to implement his far-reaching designs by changing the status quo through the use of unilateral force. But the fundamental goals of the Bush administration, as well as the means it chose to achieve them, proved erroneous as well as unachievable and even counterproductive. In the final analysis, the Bush Doctrine, with its central goal of establishing US imperial rule via democratization, did not survive Bush's controversial presidency. He left behind a less stable, less democratic, and more terror-prone world than he found when he ascended to the presidency in 2001. Most important, the legitimacy of the United States was squandered in the process, while the main goal of the antiterror campaign—capturing Osama bin Laden—was not achieved.

The departure of George W. Bush from the White House will enable the United States to change the overall trajectory of his policy. Yet the overreaching of the Bush Doctrine, the president's personal alienation from the world, and the waste of economic and military resources will not be easy to overcome. Like an aircraft carrier, US foreign policy is not only hard to navigate; it is even harder to reverse. Yet, what some have called "the accidental revolution"[75] must be reversed; it simply cannot be sustained.[76] A return to Realism is necessary.

Above everything else, it is essential to restore the American-European relations wrecked by the Bush Doctrine and its policy consequences.[77] The Bush administration alienated the United States from its natural allies. Even Great Britain, America's closest ally, felt uneasy about the Iraq war, according to people closely familiar with the situation.[78]

In its policies, the Bush administration broke numerous norms. Says Pape: "The US conquest of Iraq ... challenges one of the most important norms in international politics—that democracies do not fight preventive wars—and so undermines the assurance that comes from the expectation that democratic institutions can keep a sole superpower from altering the status quo to its advantage."[79]

One of the most serious problems with the Bush Doctrine was that it was seen, correctly, as entirely unilateralist, despite the fact that 9/11 was understood to constitute a challenge to the entire world community. To most people, the public pronouncements of President Bush seemed like diktats to which the traditional allies of the United States were expected to conform.[80] This style of leadership was resented bitterly, especially in Europe.

The Bush Doctrine reflected the president's vision of a new world order dominated completely and unilaterally by the United States. Yet, he was greatly influenced by Vice President Cheney and other hardliners. Cheney promoted the idea of formulating a new, broad, and bold doctrine, and Bush adopted the idea. He decided that in the future the United States would strike preemptively at threats rather than rely on containment or deterrence.[81] In doing so, he proved himself to be extremely unrealistic.

CHAPTER 3

THE NEOCONSERVATIVE REVOLUTION

The Ideological Infrastructure of the Bush Doctrine

The approach adopted by the Bush administration toward the international system—the explicit, bold attempt to unilaterally restructure this system—ought to be understood as part and parcel of one of the truly most significant and far-reaching ideological schemes ever developed in the modern history of the United States. Any attempt to explain Bush's foreign policy separate from its ideological foundations—possibly as a gut reaction, reflexive response to a series of shocking events, the president's personality, or the balance of influence within the decision-making unit around him—is destined to failure and is fundamentally incomplete.

An ideology that many have called Neoconservatism has been the basis of the foreign policy of the Bush administration (although declining in importance toward the end of the administration), and not merely after the September 11, 2001, terrorist assaults or as a direct result of that momentous event.[1] As an ideology, Neoconservatism could be perceived as an *incoherent hybrid of contradictory ideas.* Indeed, it has been developed by many individuals over a long period of time and was applied by even more individuals to a series of international events; thus, it could not be expected to have the degree of coherence that often characterizes a single-authored ideology. Nevertheless, there is a logic, structure, and specific content to Neoconservatism that could and must be uncovered. Most important, there is a strong, inherent link

between Neoconservatism and the Bush Doctrine. This chapter tries to identify this link.

Despite the enormous amount of material written about Neoconservatism,
particularly since many critics have viewed it as singularly responsible for the
Iraq war (which it was not), there are several common errors in describing and
analyzing this ideology that ought to be singled out from the beginning. First,
there is a perception that the Bush administration somehow *misinterpreted*
Neoconservatism or at least some elements of it; in reality, the policy adopted
by the administration (and by the president personally) was extremely loyal to
the Neoconservative ideology and was recognized as such not only by its opponents but also by its supporters. Second, there is often a lack of appreciation of
the depth of Neoconservatism as *a far-reaching, transformative, revisionist* ideology; this analytical error leads some observers to mistakenly look at Neoconservatism as a form of Realism or even conservatism, while in fact, it is a negation
of both. Third, there is often a lack of detail about many different dimensions of
Neoconservatism. A fuller understanding of Neoconservatism requires a de-
construction of it, which breaks the ideology into its constituent components
and then looks at it as a coherent whole.

The *thesis* of this chapter is that what has come to be known as Neoconservatism ought to be viewed first as *a triple revolution:* it is an ideology that tries
to transform not just American conservatism[2] (a good reason for calling it
Neoconservatism), but also US foreign policy and, above all, the very nature of
the international political system. Second, Neoconservatism is an *idealist-*
constructed "dream"[3] and an elaborated value system, not a pragmatic solution
to concrete challenges; it is therefore a mistake to identify it with any kind of
Realism, including even "offensive realism"[4] or "nationalist realism"[5] (despite
the presence of offensive prescriptions and nationalist fervor inherent in this
ideology). Third, Neoconservatism ought to be understood as a *thoroughly revisionist set of revolutionary ideas fundamentally opposed to the status quo;* it already
was such during the Cold War (when some of its intellectual founding fathers[6]
opposed Mutual Assured Destruction, détente, and bipolarity itself), through
the period of what might be called restrained unipolarism (under Bush-41 and
Bill Clinton, 1989–2001), and throughout the presidency of George W. Bush.
Neoconservatism cannot be understood but as a call for the complete *desertion*

of the American tradition of self-restraint, moderation, and close cooperation with other nations and the adoption of a limitless hegemonic ambition.[7] Fourth, there is a significant amount of evidence to indicate that President Bush himself adopted the most important tenets of Neoconservatism after 9/11, as recognized triumphantly by the most prominent Neoconservatives themselves.[8]

The overall argument of this chapter is, then, that what is generally known as Neoconservatism constitutes, despite its name, an *alternative ideology* not only to what is viewed as American liberalism but also to American conservatism, both of which it rejects with similar fervor and disdain.[9] Most important, Neoconservatism is an inherently radical ideology, based on the idea of constant, relentless struggle for power—a *permanent revolution* of a sort—in which traditional American strategies such as containment and deterrence (as well as older, European strategies such as balance of power) ought to be rejected in favor of the establishment of an American, worldwide hegemony. While Neoconservatism reflects old American ideas—including Manifest Destiny and exceptionalism in general—it has been able to carry those ideas further than most other ideologies in this country's history, due to America's dominant position in the post–Cold War world. Moreover, most of those identified as Neoconservatives (or often self-identified as such) believe in the complete, radical restructuring of the global society and politics.

Some commentators have noticed the prominent role of Jewish intellectuals among Neoconservatives. Jacob Heilbrunn, for example, argues that Neoconservatism is a "Jewish mindset" that was shaped by the Jewish immigrant experience, the Holocaust, and the twentieth-century struggle against totalitarianism.[10] According to this explanation, many Jews came to Neoconservatism by opposing irresolute liberalism. While some Neoconservatives might indeed be "explainable" by those factors, surely not all are. Moreover, many Neoconservatives are non-Jews. Daniel Patrick Moynihan, Jeane Kirkpatrick, and Michael Novak, for example, came from a Catholic background. Moreover, numerous Jews who went through the experiences Heilbrunn notes never became Neoconservatives. In general, it is probably more useful to focus on the ideology of Neoconservatism than on its sociology. This is the approach taken by this chapter.

The Principles of Neoconservatism:
Different Perspectives

It is practically impossible to fully and satisfactorily summarize the Neoconservative belief system in a single chapter (if at all). Yet we can gain insight into Neoconservatism by focusing on the most important ideas that constitute this ideology, as these are viewed from different perspectives: by the supporters and inventors of this ideology, by disappointed critics (sometimes former Neoconservatives themselves), and by this ideology's opponents and critics.

Irving Kristol, often referred to as the godfather of Neoconservatism, identifies some of the following principles of Neoconservatism: (1) It is designed to *convert American conservatism* and the Republican Party. In other words, Kristol views Neoconservatism as an ideology opposing the status quo and particularly conservatism. (2) It is a hopeful, forward-looking, and cheerful ideology, according to Kristol. I would argue that Neoconservatism is, in fact, thoroughly pessimistic (see below). (3) "Patriotism is a natural and healthy sentiment that should be encouraged by both private and public institutions," says Kristol. The promotion of American patriotism is clearly a fundamental Neoconservative principle, although often carried to an extreme, according to the opponents of this ideology. (4) "World government is a terrible idea since it can lead to world tyranny," argues Kristol, but he does not explain who supports this terrible idea of world government. (5) "Statesmen should, above all, have the ability to distinguish friends from enemies." (Again, the relevance of this statement is unclear; it is a truism.) (6) Finally and maybe most important, Kristol says, "For a great power, the 'national interest' is *not a geographical term. . . .* A smaller nation might appropriately feel that its national interest *begins and ends at its borders,* and that its foreign policy is almost always in a *defensive mode.* A larger nation has more extensive interests. And large nations, whose *identity is ideological,* like the Soviet Union of yesteryear and the United States of today, inevitably have *ideological interests in addition to more material concerns* [emphasis added]."[11]

The theoretical distinctions offered by Kristol are extremely interesting in view of the significant impact (although never full control, as alleged by their opponents) of Neoconservatism during the Bush administration's tenure in Washington. Kristol makes a distinction between great powers and smaller nations, between defensive and presumably offensive modes of operation, and between material and ideological interests. One may safely assume that Kristol, along with other Neoconservatives, believes that the United States is a great power (many Neocons go much further and believe it is unique and exceptional), that it ought to purse an offensive mode of operation, and that it has ideological interests in addition to its material interests. His subtle language sounds as if he supports what some might see as imperial foreign policy.

If the language of the elderly Irving Kristol is somewhat subtle, subdued, and in need of interpretation as to its real meaning, his son William Kristol and his colleague Robert Kagan, cofounders of the Project for the New American Century and possibly the most prominent second-generation Neoconservatives, have tended to be blunter than Irving Kristol.[12] These writers and many others have called for the maximal use of American power abroad (particularly in the Middle East), promoting it as good not only for America but for the world at large. "Benevolent hegemony" has become a slogan on behalf of global domination, beginning with the Iraq war as a supreme case of America's resolve. Since the hegemonic recommendation precedes September 11, 2001, by several years (or more), it is quite clear that it has little to do with the terrorist assaults on America. At most, it might be argued, 9/11 fortified the thinking of some of the most radical Neoconservatives; it surely gave them an opportunity to push their ideological convictions and turn them into actual policies.

Francis Fukuyama, at one time very close to the Neoconservatives (both ideologically and personally) and later a critic of their position, has a take on the Neoconservative ideology that's different from either first-generation or second-generation Neoconservatives.[13] Writing in the era after the invasion of Iraq and therefore with a broader perspective, Fukuyama sees four fundamental ideas in Neoconservatism: (1) Proponents are concerned with democracy and human rights and the internal policies of states in general. Here one must ask whether the Neoconservatives have *genuine* interest in democracy and human rights or in the imposition of American dominion on other countries. On the other hand, there can be no question that the Neoconservatives are genuinely concerned with the internal policies of other states, a feature that sharply separates them from conservatives and Realists alike and allows them to promote an extensive interventionist foreign policy on behalf of the United States. The vast literature written by self-identified Neoconservatives actually says that much. (2) They believe that US power can be used for moral purposes. While there can be no question that the Neoconservatives like to promote the extensive use of military power, their many critics doubt that their "purposes" are genuinely moral. (3) Neoconservatives are skeptical about international law and institutions. They are indeed unilateralists and global militarists, and as such have no use for international law and institutions that might hinder, limit, or restrain the dominant military power of the United States. (4) They oppose social engineering. While this is a principle of Neoconservatism in regard to US domestic policy, the Neoconservatives do support the engineering of societies and politics in other countries.

Fukuyama argues that the Bush administration applied these fundamental ideas in a biased manner by overestimating the threat to the United States from radical Islam, the conflation of a variety of phenomena (terrorism, weapons of mass destruction, Iraq, proliferation of nuclear weapons and/or technology, etc.), a failure to anticipate the global reaction to the imposition of benevolent hegemony, presenting an overly optimistic view, and so forth. In other words, for Fukuyama the problem is not with the conceptual framework of Neoconservatism but with the way it was interpreted and applied.

This volume rejects Fukuyama's arguments. The *Bush administration applied faithfully* the Neoconservative ideology (although other factors influenced it as well). The administration made the argument, promoted for years by the Neoconservatives, that it needed to fix Iraq's and other countries' internal policies and that those countries must be democratized; both the Neoconservatives and the Bush administration parted company with the conservatives and the Realists over this specific issue. Moreover, the Bush administration, particularly the president himself, moralized the war policy and sold it to the country as a struggle between good and evil, precisely in a *Neoconservative mode of thinking and argumentation*. In doing so, the United States ignored legal and institutional restraints, as well as world public opinion, and followed the prescriptions offered by the Neoconservatives. The Iraq war fits extremely well with the ideological positions of the Neoconservative ideology. The critique offered by Fukuyama refers to specific policy errors of the administration, not the ideological positions taken by it.

Stefan Halper and Jonathan Clarke, both self-identified conservative critics of Neoconservatism, pinpoint the following components of that ideology:

(1) a perception of politics as a choice between good and evil and analyzing international issues in black-and-white categories reflective of moral arrogance;[14] (2) a strong emphasis on military power and even "fascination with war";[15] (3) Hobbesian pessimism; (4) a disdain for conventional diplomacy, pragmatism, multilateral institutions; and (5) a focus on the Middle East and global Islam. In general, this conservative critique is quite accurate, although it often reveals the emotional bitterness of many conservatives and their resentment toward the Neoconservative claim on the Right's agenda and policies. The one place where the conservatives' depiction might be somewhat inaccurate is in the argument that the Neoconservative position reflects "Hobbesian pessimism." In fact, the Neoconservative position is a more complex mixture of pessimism about the nature of international politics and optimism about the prospect of change resulting from America's actions. This point is elaborated on and expanded below.

Neoconservatism: An Analytical Approach

Having summed up the positions of different authors and, in fact, different ideological camps in regard to what they perceive as Neoconservatism, the following analysis is based on what Neoconservatives themselves have written and said about their belief system in general and the opinions they have expressed about a variety of political phenomena.[16] Emphasis is placed on identifying the ideological components of the Neoconservative ideology, their link to the Bush Doctrine and the administration's policies (particularly in the first term), and the manner in which they form a coherent whole.

Neoconservatism is based on several major ideas that will be covered here in some detail: (1) assertive nationalism (or patriotism); (2) radicalism (reflected in complete rejection of the status quo); (3) militarism, especially in terms of switching from a defensive posture of deterrence and containment to an offensive posture of preemption and prevention; (4) exceptionalism; (5) a mixture of optimism and Hobbesian pessimism; (6) imperial universalism in the name of two different but connected ideas, democratization and benevolent hegemony; (7) evangelism; and (8) unilateralism. Those elements will be covered here systematically, highlighting their interconnectedness.

Patriotic and Nationalist Philosophy

First, in the most general terms, Neoconservatism reflects a *patriotic and nationalist philosophy*. In fact, this position has evolved as a reaction to what was perceived as the counterculture of the 1960s that the founding fathers of the movement (especially Irving Kristol, Jeane Kirkpatrick, and Norman Podhoretz) saw as anti-American and unpatriotic. In regard to this patriotic bent, Neoconservatives represent an antithesis to postnationalist European public opinion and to some left-of-center, liberal elements within the American society itself.

The patriotism of the Neoconservatives has been reflected in their consistent support for any and all wars and conflicts the United States has been involved in for the past fifty years or so: the Soviet-American conflict (in which Neoconservatism's founding fathers took a radical position, following such analysts as Albert Wohlstetter, 1913–1997), the wars in the former Yugoslavia (where many Neoconservatives urged American involvement), and the two wars against Iraq. In regard to the USSR, the Neocons opposed détente (even though this policy was adopted by a conservative administration), applauded Ronald Reagan's "Evil Empire" rhetoric toward the Soviet Union but accused him of appeasement once he began arms-control negotiations with the Soviets,[17] and so forth. While the implosion of the USSR seems to have moderated several Neoconservatives, particularly older ones, the majority of them remain highly nationalistic, radical, and militant in their position toward any external conflict.[18] No significant cognitive dissonance seems to have developed among most Neocons despite the disappearance of the Soviet Union from the scene.

An element that might explain the Neoconservatives' unrestrained patriotism is their belief in the uniqueness of the American experience and destiny, a notion directly connected to the belief in American exceptionalism as well as in the absolute superiority of American military power (see below). Patriotism, exceptionalism, and militarism have led some of the most prominent Neocons to support unabashedly *a strategy of American intervention* against tyrannical and anti-American regimes.[19] Interestingly, tyrannical or undemocratic but pro-American regimes were not targeted by the Neoconservatives, suggesting that their ideology is not as committed to democracy as it is to nationalism.

Radicalism

A second characteristic of the Neoconservative philosophy is its *strong tendency toward radicalism.* This radicalism has been reflected in complete and total *rejection of the status quo in world politics* (and to some extent in domestic American politics), as well as in the *ambitious, far-reaching plans* of the Neoconservatives. It was a somewhat surprising position in view of America's strong, advantageous position in the world and the frequent assumption among analysts of international politics that nations benefiting from the status quo would ordinarily like to maintain it. On the other hand, John Mearsheimer has argued convincingly that great powers often pursue global hegemony as a way of increasing their security and freedom of action.[20] The Mearsheimer thesis has been validated to some extent during the Bush administration, and some analysts suggested that even before.[21]

More specifically, among the Neoconservatives the radical approach to political problems has been reflected in an unmatched will to use military means to overthrow the status quo and pursue global hegemony, even in the face of complete opposition by the outside world (which many Neoconservatives have considered unworthy, dismissing it out of hand). Furthermore, Neoconservatism has been truly revolutionary in terms of the deeper philosophical contents of its beliefs,[22] both in terms of its recommendations for operational policies[23] and in terms of its aggressive, argumentative style. Andrew J. Bacevich has argued that "the ultimate purpose" of the Neoconservatives and the Bush administration was to "transform a huge swath of the Islamic world stretching from Morocco all the way through Pakistan and Central Asia to Indonesia and the southern Philippines."[24] Iraq was but the first installment of that ambitious plan.

Although the radicalism of Neoconservatism has been in evidence in the past—especially during the Cold War 1960s—this radicalism has continued unabashed in the contemporary era. Thus, Neoconservatives have tended to label as appeasers all those seeking middle-of-the-road positions to political problems, accommodation with rivals, and consultations with friends and allies, as well as working within the existing international system. Theirs has always been the politics of power, domination, coercion, and noncompromise. In this regard, Neoconservatism has been out of the confines of normal democratic politics, making its ideal of democratization a strange, unnatural, and unconvincing element of their own philosophy.

In view of the fundamental revolutionary temperament of Neoconservatism, it is no wonder that its adherents tended to be vehemently against traditional American conservatism,[25] in many ways their only competitors on the Right. At the same time, American conservatives have tended to reject what they have viewed as the Neoconservative credo; they have seen it as both misleading and unrepresentative.[26] Their position has been reflected in the stance taken toward important issues, such as the Iraq invasion, by central figures in the shaping of American foreign policy.[27] The rift between Neoconservatives and traditional conservatives in America (both the realpolitik and the semi-isolationist types) brings into sharper relief the radical nature of the Neoconservative movement. On all foreign policy issues, the Neocons have taken a more militant, radical view than the other branches of the American Right.

In dealing with this conflict within the American Right, it is essential to recognize that the Neoconservatives *have succeeded in establishing their revolutionary views* on America's role in the world as the *dominant norm* within the American Right. Many traditionally conservative think tanks, publications, and institutions have fallen under the control of Neoconservatism. This has become the intellectual infrastructure for the foreign policy of the Bush administration and has enabled it to carry out its own brand of radical politics.

Militarism

Third, Neoconservatism has been characterized by its *strong endorsement of military instruments* for the promotion of what has been viewed as the national interest of the United States and even the interest of humanity at large. The temptation to heavily rely on military power is easily understood if one remembers that the United States has enjoyed enormous military supremacy in the post–Cold War period, that the Neoconservative ideological position has been in favor of an almost *unlimited expansion* of US influence around the world, and that other countries, significantly weaker than the United States, have been actively opposed to the Neoconservative designs. Taking all these factors into account, it seems reasonable to argue that only through military power could the United States have hoped to implement the Neoconservative agenda; this has been precisely the argument on the part of the Neoconservatives.

The militaristic push by the Neoconservatives reveals the *fundamental goals* of their movement: spreading democracy throughout the world (in reality, however, only to countries in opposition to the United States), effecting regime change in several countries, and establishing American global hegemony. In more specific, practical terms, those basic goals have translated to *the rejection of traditional American defensive postures in favor of offensive ones,* particularly in moving away from deterrence and containment to preemption and prevention. Within Neoconservative thought, militarism ought to be seen as merely the instrument through which hegemonic goals might be achieved.

It is important to realize that while the ascendance of George W. Bush to the presidency and the events of September 11, 2001, enabled the Neoconservatives to implement their goals via military means, the goals themselves had been formulated years before the arrival of Bush-43 at the White House. The Neoconservative ideas were espoused in the writings of people like Irving Kristol and Norman Podhoretz in the 1960s and 1970s (although often ignored by Republican administrations as late as the 1980s and early 1990s). The ideas had also appeared in internal but highly important documents such as the 1992 Pentagon study prepared by then secretary of defense Dick Cheney and his undersecretary for policy, Paul Wolfowitz. This remarkable document, a possible predictor of what was to come, argued that in the post–Cold War period the United States should transform the unipolar moment into a unipolar era by precluding "the emergence of any potential future global competitor."[28] The document reflects the strong hegemonic proclivity of some of the Neoconservatives, particularly Wolfowitz (a student of Wohlstetter, a man critical of traditional deterrence and positive toward first-strike nuclear strategy). The fundamental philosophy of the Project for the New American Century, formulated in 1997, was identical to the 1992 Cheney-Wolfowitz document.[29]

The militaristic enthusiasm of the Neoconservatives is quite rational. Since Neoconservatives are convinced that their truth is absolute, they rarely show any reluctance to use military means to promote their ideas. In this regard, the character of Neoconservatism is totalitarian. Absolute truths lead to radical, violent means for their implementation. And, indeed, in the case of Neoconservatism there has been a strong, even inevitable military bent in the promotion of the movement's goals. Moreover, the writings of prominent Neoconservatives show that many of them believe that military power determines national destiny. So-called soft power, as well as international law, norms, and institutions, is entirely unimportant in their minds. No wonder that by the end of the Bush administration the legitimacy of the United States in the world hit rock bottom. Said Halper and Clarke, bona fide conservatives and Realists, about the Neoconservatives: they "treat power—raw, military power—as the alpha and omega of American interaction with the world."[30]

While the vast majority of the Neoconservatives have leaned toward endorsing militaristic means as tools for achieving imperial ambitions of which they approve, the younger generation of Neoconservatives has been even more aggressive in its militarism than the older generation. Max Boot is a perfect example of the younger Neoconservatives' enthusiastic support for constant military conflict.[31] Boot believes that the United States should unambiguously embrace its imperial role, has speculated on the possibility that the United States would occupy the Saudi oil fields, and once bemoaned that too few Americans have died in Afghanistan.

Although the main reason for the Neoconservative enthusiasm for military solutions has been ideological, to at least some degree it might be looked upon as opportunistic. The dominance of the United States in several recent wars— particularly the first Gulf War (1990 to 1991), the bombing at Kosovo (1999), and the war in Afghanistan (beginning in 2001)—has been such that it emboldened the armchair Neoconservatives and generated more aggressive strategies. Suddenly it looked as if the United States could do all it wanted to do. The temptation was too great to pass on for the grandiose thinking of many of the Neoconservatives. In George W. Bush they found a president willing to go along with their ideological designs.

Four interesting phenomena ought to be mentioned in regard to the Neoconservative inclination to recommend the use of military means for the promotion of US interests. First, in general, the Neocons have tended to *de-emphasize traditional methods of influence,* such as diplomacy and economic pressure, in favor of military instruments.[32] Second, the Neocons have rarely paid significant attention to the *moral and ethical implications* of the extensive use of force by the United States. Third, there seems to be an assumption in the Neoconservative set of recommendations for America's foreign policy that anything that promotes *US interests* is, by definition, moral and ethical. Kristol and Kagan, for example, argue in their remarkable 1996 *Foreign Affairs* article that

"[America's] moral goals and its fundamental national interests are almost always in harmony."[33] Fourth, the Neocons seriously contend that the world's major powers welcome US global involvement and prefer America's benevolent hegemony to its alternatives.[34] All of these four phenomena are highly controversial, particularly when considered together.

The Neoconservatives are nothing if unaware of the controversial nature of their own actions and voluminous writings. Most interesting, they recognize their own proclivity to recommend the use of military force. For example, Kagan, a leading Neoconservative, writes approvingly that "the US resorts to force more quickly and, compared with Europe, is less patient with diplomacy. *Americans generally favor policies of coercion rather than persuasion* [emphasis added]."[35] Many Neocons seem to cherish the use of arms. Irving Kristol, for example, emphasizes triumphantly America's incredible global military superiority. He then endorses the use of that superiority to fulfill US responsibilities abroad, pointing out that he does not believe in the rule of law in the international arena.[36]

Exceptionalism

Fourth, the Neoconservatives have continuously presented a strong American exceptionalist position. Exceptionalism is the belief that America is not merely special but truly unique and even superior to other nations of the world, because of its historical experience, inherent social values (such as equality), and political institutions (especially its vibrant democracy).[37] Many Americans are convinced that the United States represents a unique historical force in the world, a force destined to improve the global society through all means at its disposal, particularly military power. This strong conviction, inherent in all stripes of the Neoconservative movement, has been there from the very beginning, but it seems to have become stronger with time and was used very effectively after 9/11.

Exceptionalism in present-day America is a strange mix of beliefs, particularly when it comes to Neoconservatism. While this mix was present in the past, it appears more radically today under the influence of the Neoconservatives than it has in most historical eras. What might look like a serious contradiction is quite evident in the case of the Neoconservative movement. On the one hand, the exceptionalist belief system reflects the ultimate commitment of the

Neoconservatives to America's soft power, particularly its vibrant democracy and capitalist economic system. On the other hand, rather than allowing these values to impact the world by *attracting* it to the United States as a source of soft power,[38] the Neoconservatives support imposing these values via America's superior coercive force—that is, through America's *ultimate hard power*.

Of course, it must be recognized that the strong sense of exceptionalism reflected in the Neoconservative philosophy has been part of the American cultural DNA for generations. This infrastructural culture has been used by the Neoconservatives to the fullest. In the short history of the United States—even before the United States came into being as a sovereign nation—the notion emerged that America is "unique in history, an entirely new and progressive society based on eternal, transcendent values, which is the country's destiny and duty to spread to the rest of the world."[39]

It should be noted that exceptionalism in America is common to all or almost all political persuasions, on all sides of the political spectrum. As such, it is an extremely powerful political tool, capable of producing wide-ranging coalitions of the type that produced, for example, the Iraq war in 2003.[40] The idea of exceptionalism has been used by the liberal Left by leaders such as former president Jimmy Carter,[41] among liberal internationalists such as former president Woodrow Wilson,[42] and among many right-wingers such as former president Ronald Reagan. During the presidency of George W. Bush the idea of exceptionalism was heavily used by the Neoconservatives.

Fukuyama, himself an ex-Neocon, has identified *the inherent link between the idea of American exceptionalism in the Neoconservative ideology and Bush's foreign policy*. Fukuyama emphasizes that the notion of benevolent hegemony—a concept introduced into the political discourse by the Neoconservatives prior to Bush's rise to power—was "premised on American exceptionalism, the idea that America could use its power in instances where others could not *because it was more virtuous than other countries* [emphasis added]."[43] Moreover, Fukuyama adds that "more than any other group, it was the neoconservatives both inside and outside the Bush administration who pushed for democratizing Iraq and the broader Middle East,"[44] a clear-cut exceptionalist idea that America has an obligation to "do good in the world."

The impact of the Neocon exceptionalist language and policy recommendations on President Bush has been enormous, although the definitive, comprehensive account of its extent has yet to be written. Thus, the president has adopted not merely the policy of invading Iraq, a project for which the Neoconservatives lobbied for years, but he has heavily used their exceptionalist rationale and language to justify it. Terms such as *axis of evil* clearly reflected Neoconservative ideology. In his second inaugural address (January 2005) Bush declared that the United States was committed to seeking the growth of democratic institutions all over the world with the ultimate goal of ending tyranny in the world.[45] This "democratization" idea has been at the very center of the Neoconservative ideology for a long time, clearly marking their unique, distinct approach to American foreign policy.

In making their case for an exceptionalist America, the Neoconservatives, cleverly, have emphasized that their position has deep historical roots.[46] And indeed, already in the early days of the Republic, President George Washington proclaimed that the United States should follow a different foreign policy than other nations.[47] As early as 1831, the brilliant French commentator Alexis de Tocqueville coined the term "American exceptionalism."[48] Several American presidents emphasized the uniqueness of the United States, arguing for the global spread of democracy and self-determination (Wilson) or human rights and peace (Carter). It should be noted, however, that while several Neocons have tried to create the impression that they were true Wilsonians, the basis of their democratization project rests on force and coercion, Wilson's on the promotion of international organizations and law. The Neocons' endorsement of military interventionism negates completely the notion of self-determination so heavily emphasized by President Wilson.[49] Similarly, Carter was a true believer in human rights and world peace; the essence of Neoconservatism, on the other hand, has been the promotion of American hegemony through confrontation, coercion, and even war.

An interesting essay with a sympathetic view of Neoconservatism defines American exceptionalism as "a revolutionary or messianic ethos that rises periodically to push the United States into global intervention in the name of individual liberty and freedom." In trying to justify the Neoconservative philosophy, Zachary Seldin argues that this interventionist ethos is but *a natural outgrowth* of American political development, and thus difficult for Europeans and others to understand.[50] Although it is true that the United States has indeed carried out, from time to time, interventionist policy, it is hard to imagine more radical policy than that recommended by the Neoconservative camp, particularly in a world already dominated by the United States. Seldin's attempt to rehabilitate the Neocon policy in the name of the American "messianic ethos" has been, generally speaking, unsuccessful.

For the Neocons, since the United States is exceptional, it should be guided in the conduct of its foreign policy by different standards than other countries. This means, however, that the United States has not only special rights but also *unique responsibilities*. The uniqueness of the American political experiment demands that the United States accepts those responsibilities abroad and fulfills, in effect, a morally superior purpose.

In the final analysis, although Bush reaffirmed American exceptionalism in everything he did after 9/11, exploiting this concept in justifying military action, in effect he subverted it.[51]

Optimism and Pessimism

Fifth, among the Neoconservatives one finds an interesting combination of deep pessimism about the nature of the international system but, at the same time, the optimistic conviction that America will eventually prevail and be able to make the world in its own image. On the one hand, Neoconservatives have always shown a deep skepticism about social engineering, reflecting their opposition to the liberalism of the 1960s (as well as to Soviet communism), but on the other hand, they have expressed their strong belief that American power can and will change the world. The rise of George W. Bush, and the closeness to him achieved by the Neoconservatives, is an indication of the power of the optimistic worldview, although the results of the administration's actions are not.

Once again, one cannot possibly understand Neoconservatism without a deeper understanding of American culture. The American tends to be an optimist. In the words of Gabriel Almond, "The riches of his heritage and the mobility of his social order have produced a generally euphoric tendency, that is, the expectation that one can by effort and good will achieve or approximate one's goals."[52] This overall optimistic inclination, a "we cannot fail" attitude, has characterized the proponents of Manifest Destiny[53] and other such movements, but it has also been evident among most Neoconservative ideologues.

In the past, American optimism has typically been accompanied by a pragmatic attitude toward the possibility of finding peaceful solutions to world problems and particularly to conflicts. Optimism and pragmatism have gone to-gether, hand in hand. Interestingly, this pragmatism has not prevailed among most Neoconservatives. Rather, in approaching conflict most of them have shown a lack of pragmatic flexibility, an overly ideological or doctrinaire ap-proach, and a lack of openness toward the outside, non-American world. In dealing with domestic opponents, as well as with countries with diverse atti-tudes on the international scene, Neoconservatives, as well as President George W. Bush, have shown an almost complete inability to pragmatically compro-mise, somewhat reminiscent of Wilson's inability to compromise with his op-ponents. When it comes to the Neoconservative ideology and to President Bush's modus operandi, the power of democracy as compromising, organized intelligence,[54] the belief in the infinite power of human rationality through dia-logue, does not work. It has been overwhelmed by the sense of righteousness and pessimism.

Another difference between the traditional optimistic attitude of Americans and the attitude of most of the Neoconservatives is that the traditional attitude has been based, at least in most instances, on the material wealth of America, while the Neoconservative attitude has tended strongly toward military power. America's abundance, reflected in the sheer geographical size of the land[55] or in the enormous economic strength of the country,[56] could serve as good explana-tory factors for the traditional American optimistic attitude. But in the case of the Neoconservatives, particularly over the past two decades, the military power of the United States has been emphasized a lot more than the country's economic might.

While the Neoconservatives often describe their own belief system as hope-ful, optimistic, and forward-looking,[57] sometimes in contrasting it with Euro-pean conservatism, even cursory reading in the vast literature produced by the Neoconservatives reveals that it is actually based on a highly pessimistic view of the world. Almost all Neoconservatives see the world as an extremely danger-ous, threatening, out of control environment. In this jungle of war of all against all, raw military power is perceived as the only guarantor of survival. The Neo-conservatives, thus, view the world as Hobbesian to the core. It is interesting to note in that context that Thomas Hobbes's solution to the anarchic state of nature—establishing law and order through government—is apparently not the solution for international chaos recommended by the Neoconservatives. In fact, the Neoconservatives are highly suspicious of any governmental solution to conflict that, on the international level, should come through international organizations. The Neoconservatives specifically and adamantly reject the possibility of close cooperation among nations on the international level. For the Neoconservatives, the solution is to be found in unilateral American hegemony.

So if the world is chaotic and anarchic, what is the source of Neoconservative optimism? It is their assumption, or at least their argument, that (1) the American model of democracy and capitalist economy is the ultimately preferable model for an established government, and (2) that the United States will eventually be able to convert the rest of the world and create it in its own image. In other words, hegemonism is the source of Neoconservative optimism even though their analysis of the nature of the world is highly pessimistic.

In comparing different perspectives on the world, the Neoconservatives are clearly closer to Hobbes and his view of the state of nature than to Immanuel Kant's perpetual peace and shared world citizenship.[58] In a chaotic situation of war of all against all, which they pessimistically assume, only American unilateral action might introduce a measure of order.

The sense of optimism among the Neoconservatives, despite their fundamental philosophical pessimism, is to a large extent a function of contemporary politics. Given the surprising conclusion of the Cold War, with the implosion of the USSR and the resulting unipolar American dominance, the Neocons further developed their belief system that the future of the world rests with the global spread of democracy. Moreover, many of them believed that the result was already decided, predestined by the end of the Cold War. A leading Neoconservative at the time, Fukuyama argued in his "end of history" thesis that liberal democratic capitalism had prevailed in the contest of ideas throughout history and that no alternative was likely to ever challenge it.[59] For Neoconservatives it was just a matter of being on the right side of history. While Neoconservatives started off in the 1960s with the pessimistic view that there was no beneficial way to produce good social engineering on the national level (that is, in the United States), they ended up with the optimistic position that there are good prospects for global social engineering.

Nowhere else has the unconstrained optimism of the Neoconservatives shown its face more clearly than in the Iraq invasion of 2003. Unrealistic, optimistic predictions were made by practically all the major Neoconservative spokespeople. They foresaw an easy campaign, declared victory prematurely,[60] predicted that the invading forces would be welcomed by the Iraqis as liberators, thought that the oil supply would quickly recover and increase dramatically, and, above all, envisioned that Iraqi democracy would flourish. The optimistic, collective euphoria of the Neoconservatives had no bounds, reflecting hubris and triumphalism, totally unjustified by the conditions of the country and revealing a worrisome lack of connectedness.

It seems that in regard to Iraq and the Middle Eastern democratization project in general, the Neoconservatives and members of the Bush administration, including the president himself, adopted a utopian position,[61] a total negation of Realism. This utopianism, optimistic in its essence, is rooted in the religious-political tradition of America. At the same time, it closely reflects the Neoconservative agenda.

Imperial Universalism

Sixth, Neoconservatism reflects a strong sense of what might be called imperial universalism, sometimes expressed in general philosophical or even theological terms and at other times expressed as a desire to democratize the entire world and to impose on it the specific American model of democratic capitalism. While the Neoconservative ideology has, of course, many antecedents in American history, this volume maintains that the strong emphasis on benevolent hegemony and worldwide democratization, as well as the elevation of these ideas—backed up by the unique military superiority achieved by the United States—to the forefront of American foreign policy, is an innovation, particularly in terms of post-1945 US attitude.[62]

Zbigniew Brzezinski, who served as Carter's national security adviser in the 1970s, argues that universalism, as well as optimism, forms the basis for the *legitimacy* of the American political system.[63] The assumption on the part of many Americans has been that their democratic freedoms and even the specific governmental form of the United States are relevant for all societies, people, and countries. Louis Hartz has characterized this position as American liberal absolutism and noted that its norms are believed to be self-evidently right.[64] The implication of this self-evident absolutism is that there can be no compromise with any competing ideas.[65] Thus, it might be argued, *universalism when combined with superior power leads inevitably to imperial thrust.*

There can be no question that in the specific case of contemporary Neoconservatism, universalism in one of its most aggressive forms has played a major role. Not only have most Neoconservatives believed in the absolute rightness of their position, but they also have been totally committed to the militaristic enforcement of that position abroad. While Brzezinski speaks about legitimacy as linked to universalism and attained by it, the universalist claims of the Neoconservatives and their rather energetic application to American policy abroad led, in fact, to the *significant loss of legitimacy by the United States,* not because of the substance of its ideological goals as much as by the methods adopted by the Bush administration for promoting them. These methods have been supported and even inspired by the Neoconservatives.

In promoting their universalist message, some Neoconservatives have defended their position by referring to the well-known, far-reaching universalism of President Wilson. While it is true that Wilson could have come across as all-knowing and self-righteous, it must be remembered that in terms of substance his goals were totally different than those of the Neoconservatives. In a certain way, Wilson was a true universalist, although a believer in America's unique role in spreading this universalism in the world. The Neoconservatives, on the other hand, ought to be understood as primarily nationalists, aiming at establishing an American global hegemony. Their universalism is in its very essence imperial.

An elaboration on the distinction between Wilson and the Neoconservatives (as well as the Bush administration), especially in relation to American universalism, could be useful in bringing into sharper relief the true nature of the Neoconservative ideology. In general terms, President Wilson was an enthusiastic promoter of idealist internationalism, while the Neoconservatives have always been hegemonic nationalists. While both Wilson and the Neoconservatives spoke about universalist values that are or are presumably American values, in reality, the difference between the way they perceived these values could not have been more pronounced. While both Wilson and the Neocons saw America as a force for bettering the world, and even as a "crusader state,"[66] their formulas are quite different.

Wilson supported several "universalist" ideas, some introduced by him and considered quite original and far-reaching at the time. He insisted on self-determination for all peoples (at a time when a large number of national groups did not enjoy sovereignty), democratic government (reflecting directly an

American value), respect for international law, the establishment of collective security, and a league of nations.[67]

The means chosen by the Neoconservatives for the spreading of the universal American message have been totally different from the ones endorsed by Wilson. While democratic government has been high on the Neoconservative agenda, in fact, while Neoconservatives have talked about liberating people from the rule of their tyrants, they have sought ways to impose America's control. The vast majority of the world, those "liberated" by the Neoconservative intervention and those who merely observed it, thought it had nothing to do with democracy and self-determination.

In the field of international politics the Neocons have deviated even more dramatically from Wilson's prescription. For them, international law has been entirely irrelevant for the conduct of foreign policy and, in fact, an impediment to the promotion of America's interests. As for collective security and international organizations (like the League of Nations or the UN), the Neocons have made it quite clear for years that they do not believe in collective security or in the international institutions that are supposed to promote it. Their solution to issues of security has been a unilateral American action or, if possible, the buildup of "a coalition of the willing" to deal with a specific problem, issue, or crisis. The Neoconservatives have been as committed anti-internationalists as any group in the history of the United States, and surely as any in the post-1945 era.

It is quite surprising that the true nature of Neoconservatism as a nationalist, anti-internationalist group has not been recognized by all analysts, despite the fact that the Neoconservatives themselves have been quite open and honest about their position. The historian David Kennedy, for example, argued in a 2005 essay that every president since Wilson had "embraced the core precepts of Wilsonianism. . . . In the aftermath of 9/11 they have, if anything, taken an even greater vitality."[68] Nothing can be further from the truth when one examines the administration of George W. Bush and the ideology of its Neocon supporters.

Although Wilson was a universalist, he dreamt of a "community of interest" as *a substitute for the selfish national interests* that, in his opinion, drove the Europeans to endless wars. The Neoconservative ideology, on the other hand, is grounded precisely in the values condemned by Wilson, selfish and narrowly defined national interests.

One may correctly identify Wilson's universalism and even condemn it as an "outward-looking and expansive form of American exceptionalism," as was done by Stanley Hoffmann.[69] But it is one thing to argue that the example of democracy is so compelling that others would likely follow it, as former presidents Wilson and Carter did, yet another to coerce other nations to adopt democracy via military invasion, as was done by Bush-43 with the inspirational backing of the Neoconservatives.

What I call imperial universalism has been part of American foreign policy for a long time, but in different eras it has played different roles and with different consequences. The imperial universalism of the United States has been reflected in an effort to export America's values to other parts of the world, a behavior characteristic of numerous nations, particularly strong nations and even more so empires. In many ways, America has become an empire.[70] Yet, the imperial interests as well as the imperial capabilities of the United States in the post–World War II era were restrained by the existence of bipolarity and another empire.

The key for analyzing the American imperial universalism under George W. Bush is to understand that the Neoconservatives, more than any other group in America, have seen the disappearance of the Soviet Union from the international scene as providing a unique opportunity for *unrestrained expansion of America's power, influence, and domination.* In many ways, the Neocon reading of the situation was correct. Yet their radical position, particularly the lobbying on behalf of unilateral military action as the preferred method of exporting America's exceptionalist imperial universalism, has proven to be counterproductive. The willingness of the president to go along with the prescription of the Neoconservatives has been, of course, of critical importance. Ironically, in being as politically successful and influential as they have been, the Neoconservatives have contributed significantly to the sharp decline in the legitimacy of America's unique position. The United States has learned that its exceptionalist message, its imperial universalism, depends after all on the willingness of others to adopt it.

Interestingly, many Americans have been uneasy about accepting the position of the United States as a contemporary empire, as if the concept itself is pejorative. Thus, President Bush himself declared in a press conference: "We are not an imperial power . . . we are a liberating power."[71] Yet the sheer power of the United States, the level of its influence all over the world, and particularly its capacity and willingness to project its military power in various areas of the world make it into a quintessential imperial power.

President Bush, under the influence of the Neoconservatives or on his own, has used language that is clearly reflective of what I call imperial universalism. In remarks for the National Endowment for Democracy, the president said:

> The advance of freedom is the calling of our time; it is the calling of our country. . . . We believe that liberty is the design of nature; we believe that liberty is the direction of history. We believe that human fulfillment and excellence come in the responsible exercise of liberty. And we believe that freedom—the freedom we prize—*is not for* us alone, it is the right and capacity of all mankind.[72]

This kind of messianic, universalistic credo has been continuously expressed by the president and his supporters. Moreover, on many occasions he linked the advance of freedom with the use of American military power, thus giving teeth to the imperial universalism in his message. The key is that Bush and the Neoconservatives have never recognized that freedom and liberty are "American values" that others may or may not want to adopt. For them, America's values are universally right, and the United States has both the right and the duty to spread them around the world, if necessary by the force of arms.

In adopting this type of universalism, Bush and his Neoconservative allies missed an important, crucial point. No matter how important and powerful a country may be, in today's world it cannot export its values by the force of arms alone, especially not in a unilateral fashion. Such an effort is doomed to fail, to generate unbearable costs, and to result in global resentment. This is precisely what happened to President Bush's imperial universalism.[73]

Conversion and Evangelism

Seventh, Neocons are strong, committed evangelists—they want to convert the world into the ways of America. It is not a large step from universalism and optimism to evangelism, from vision to crusade.[74] Neoconservatives believe that the United States has a right and even the duty to convert others, if necessary, by the force of arms. This imperative is not merely because it is in the national interest of the United States to convert others, but because it is morally the right way to act. This evangelical spirit has also been dominant in the Bush administration, particularly since September 11, 2001.

It is impossible to understand the American missionary spirit, so clearly demonstrated by the Neoconservatives and by the Bush administration in rhetoric and action, without returning to the commitment of Americans to "do good in the world."[75] This idea is deeply rooted in Puritanism, the Protestant tradition, and specifically the Great Awakening in the second quarter of the eighteenth century. Historians have documented the close relationship between religion and politics in American society. What was right in the religious sphere was right in politics, thought Henry Adams.[76] Some have suggested that the struggle for religious tolerance in America fostered the development of political liberty and the democratization of the political process.[77]

American Protestants in general, whether in the Puritanism of John Winthrop during the seventeenth century or the Calvinist theology of American Baptists, focused on the salvation of the individual and on the sharp distinction between good and evil. This theology provided strong support for the "belief that the colonies held *a particular responsibility for the success of free government all through the world* [emphasis added]."[78] This historical background, deeply influential in terms of America's political culture, has strongly resonated during the Bush administration.

The Great Awakening and other such movements in the United States represented a claim for America's moral superiority. Years later, Woodrow Wilson argued that the United States was "a superior nation, admirably suited to lead"[79] and, equally important, to make the world safe for democracy. Jimmy Carter echoed similar motifs when he launched his "crusade" for human rights. George W. Bush was surely not the first president to bring religious themes into the White House and apply them with conviction to his policies.

In the area of foreign policy, the American mission has usually tended toward an interventionist posture.[80] The religious, moralistic logic has led the country in that direction. It is not sufficient to serve as a passive example to the world. That example must be promoted by the diplomat who, like the evangelical preacher, converts others to the faith.

These evangelical leanings have clearly been evident in the language used by officials in the Bush administration, particularly by the president himself, as well as by his Neoconservative supporters. They have broadcasted to the world four messages, four "isms": We are different (exceptionalism). We are right (moralism). We shall prevail (optimism). We must convert (evangelism).[81]

In pursuing those principles, the Neocon-inspired Bush administration pursued the war in Iraq in an effort to convert the Middle East into a democratic region. The policy was carried out within the framework of the good-versus-evil analysis offered by the Neocons and adopted by the president and his chief assistants. Their predictions in regard to the future of the Middle East were overly optimistic, but not atypical for the spirit of America.

Not surprisingly, the Bush administration found it extremely difficult to cooperate with other nations as equals in pursuing its goals, even though the goals—defeating international terrorism—were universally accepted. This was a problem for America in the past as well, particularly during the Vietnam War.[82] Now, as then, other nations found America's attitude paternalistic. The belief in the universality of democratic values, as defined authoritatively by the representatives of one nation, is not particularly conducive for international consensus. The tendency to view the world in black-and-white, good-versus-evil terms is not helpful in dealing with political problems.

Unilateralism

Eighth, in view of this ideology, no wonder that Neoconservatism has been highly unilateralist in formulating its positions, announcing them to the world with great fanfare; more important, the Bush administration has acted to implement the Neocons' ideas via military means.[83] The absolutist, moralist nature of Neoconservatism has not allowed its adherents to compromise with others, thus making cooperation impossible.[84]

By virtue of its highly nationalistic policies—acting on the basis of what they have perceived as the American national interest and it alone—the Bush administration and its Neoconservative allies quickly alienated many in the United States and even more abroad. Even before 9/11, "the unilateralists assumed that American global hegemony enables the United States to transform the world; other countries will join the United States (bandwagon), not oppose it."[85] By the time 9/11 happened, merely eight months after assuming power, the Bush administration had already established a full-fledged unilateralist behavioral pattern. Nevertheless, 9/11 generated genuine sympathy for America all over the world, an opportunity to launch a more multilateral foreign policy.

But shortly after September 11, 2001, came the operation against Afghanistan, carried out almost unilaterally by the United States, with some help from the UK, despite some genuine offers of aid by other countries in NATO. A year and a half later, the Iraq war was launched, essentially an American operation with the help of several members of the "coalition of the willing." Thus, two opportunities for a genuine international effort were squandered by the Bush administration.

It is important to realize that unilateralism was not merely a tactical matter for the administration. It was a salient characteristic of both the Neoconservative movement and the Bush administration. Some Neocons have stated repeatedly that as the strongest country in the contemporary world, America simply does not need to cooperate with others in pursuit of its interests. Others have said that as a unique, exceptional country, the United States does not share the same goals or even values with other countries, including Western democracies. According to that logic, the United States must use its superior power to change the world's status quo.[86] Moreover, America needs to do so alone.

In acting unilaterally, administration officials were relentless. For example, John Bolton, the Bush administration's point man on international organizations and for a while the US ambassador to the United Nations, repeatedly denigrated international organizations and called for their abolition. In other times he suggested that the United States should simply ignore such organizations. It was a dramatic departure from the traditional American diplomacy based on broad bipartisan consensus.[87]

In the important introduction to their edited volume, *Present Dangers*, Robert Kagan and William Kristol described the 1990s as a decade of "squandered opportunities" and called for the United States to shoulder its global responsibilities without waiting for others (that is, to act alone).[88] In contrast to this Neoconservative attitude, most American administrations since 1945 have combined policies based on the use of force and multilateral diplomacy, working in most situations in close cooperation with other nations. This overall strategy also was adopted by the two post–Cold War presidents preceding George W. Bush in the White House, George H. W. Bush and Bill Clinton.

The Neoconservative unilateralist prism led the Bush administration to adopt the most unilateralist foreign policy in the modern history of the United States, ignoring not only the United Nations but also NATO and its closest allies. The thesis of this volume is that this unilateralism had little to do with 9/11. From its first days, the Bush administration adopted a rejectionist policy toward a large number of international agreements. This position reflected the strongly held ideological conviction that international agreements and even institutions "limited rather than secured American power."[89] The events of September 11 escalated this unilateralist policy.

ASSESSING THE NEOCONSERVATIVE PARADIGM

The overall impact of this eight-component ideology we call Neoconservatism was enormous within the Bush administration. It apparently also impacted Bush himself. Although not a reader, Bush was surrounded by several bona fide Neoconservatives (such as Paul Wolfowitz and Lewis "Scooter" Libby) and by some of the Neocons' closest political allies (including Cheney and Rumsfeld). There were several areas in which the president seemed to have been influenced by Neoconservative thought. For example, Bush initially rejected the notion of "nation building," the deliberate efforts by the United States to construct national institutions, political and physical, in dysfunctional or failed states. Yet he, in effect, adopted this policy in both Afghanistan and Iraq, as well as in other places.[90] It is doubtful that the Iraq invasion, easily the most important initiative by the Bush administration, would have happened without the Neoconservative influence.

What this chapter calls the Neoconservative ideology is, as could be expected, somewhat of a hybrid—numerous ideas, observations, and positions on political matters (domestic and international) and not necessarily a highly systematic exposition of well-connected propositions. The chapter looked at the Neoconservative ideology as a coherent whole, pointing out the links between the different components of the analysis offered by the Neoconservatives.

Fundamentally, Neoconservatism has challenged two dominant approaches to politics in America.[91] First, it has offered a strong critique of what the Neoconservatives view, with disdain, as American liberalism and the counterculture it produced in the 1960s—lack of patriotism and resolve in foreign policy, social engineering and the Great Society, moral corruption. The second challenge of Neoconservatism was to Realism, an approach to foreign policy adopted by the Republican administration of Richard Nixon and Henry Kissinger, but that Albert Wohlstetter, a major influence on Richard Perle and Paul Wolfowitz, condemned as capitulating to Soviet aggression. So Neoconservatism was not merely a call to reject the Left in its liberal incarnation, including its rejection of the American intervention in Vietnam, but also a call to reject the traditional, centrist Realism, a position that reflected a strong bipartisan Washington consensus.

The refusal of George H. W. Bush to attack Baghdad in 1991, despite America's overwhelming military superiority, reflected the traditional approach of Washington to foreign policy problems—militarily strong but politically moderate, unilateral and multilateral at the same time, calculating and nuanced. This decision broke the back of the cooperative relations between the Washington Realists (the James Bakers and Brent Scowcrofts of the capital) and the ideologues in the Bush-41 administration (Wolfowitz and eventually Cheney). It was followed in short order by the draft Pentagon report "Defense Planning Guidance" in 1992, written for Cheney by Wolfowitz, along with other would-be Neoconservatives (Libby, Zalmay Khalilzad, and Eric Edelman), all future members of the Bush-43 administration.[92]

Although during the Clinton administration that followed (1993 to 2001) the Neoconservatives could not implement their designs for an aggressive, expansionist, militaristic, and unilateral foreign policy, they had finally arrived with the election of George W. Bush to the White House. With Cheney as a sympathetic vice president and an inexperienced and unknowledgeable president in the Oval Office, the Neoconservatives could now provide the Bush administration with a measure of intellectual coherence. Moreover, they could impact specific policies and chart the overall course of America's relations with the world. September 11, then, had given them a unique historical opportunity to do that, over and above their wildest dreams.

In analyzing Neoconservatism, it might be important to theoretically identify a variety of factions within this very loose movement. Gary Dorrien, for example, offers a distinction between *nationalist realists,* those committed to defending American superiority in the world, and *democratic globalists,* those committed to assuming the burdens of Pax Americana.[93] In a similar vein, Dorrien notes that there are significant disagreements among what he calls *Neocons and conservative unipolarists* on how the United States should maintain its global dominance. He specifically distinguishes between *nationalist realists* (a camp that includes, in his opinion, such personalities as the analyst Charles Krauthammer, former secretary of defense Donald Rumsfeld, and John Bolton, who served as US ambassador to the UN) who "want to get out of the peacekeeping business as much as possible," and *democratic globalists,* such as Max Boot, Lawrence Kaplan, and William Kristol, who want the United States to dramatically expand its war-fighting and occupying capacity in order to maintain its benevolent hegemony.[94] While that kind of microanalysis is useful and fascinating, the argument of this chapter has been that within the Bush administration, the differences between nationalistic realists, democratic globalists, and conservative globalists have been altogether negligible, particularly after 9/11. Maybe the greatest achievement of the Neocon movement has been its *ability to bring those different strands of the right wing together and unite them behind the president's policy.*

Several analysts tend to confuse or blur the differences between Neoconservatism and other types of American conservatism. To the extent to which Neoconservatism's main goal is to wreck the status quo in favor of a completely new system, particularly in foreign policy, it is clearly not a conservative ideology at all. Even more common among analysts is the failure to distinguish between Neoconservatism and Realism. Mohammed Nuruzzaman, for example, offers an analytical framework he calls Neoconservative realism,[95] a contradiction in terms. While his analysis of the deviations of the Bush Doctrine from traditional Realism is altogether correct, his insistence on linking it to Realism is not. The notion of exporting American values to other countries and even full regions—and inhospitable regions at that—is a complete and total negation of realism. Even the kind of unilateralism and anti-internationalism envisioned by the Neocons is at odds with traditional realism, including that of the rightist kind.

In analyzing Neoconservatism, it is essential to understand its actual impact on the critical political debate in the United States in the post-9/11 period. However important might have been the impact of the pessimistic outlook of people such as Leo Strauss and Albert Wohlstetter, the key is to analyze the link between the ideology of the Neoconservatives (covered in this chapter) and the actual policy implemented by the Bush administration (see chapter 1). It is important to understand in this context the decision-making process adopted by the Bush White House (see chapter 5) and the inclination of the president himself to go along with the more radical, Neoconservative branch of his administration (chapter 4).

CHAPTER 4

THE PERSONALITY OF GEORGE W. BUSH

The international challenges faced by the United States prior to and following September 11, 2001, and the solutions offered to those challenges by the Neo-conservative ideologues have been covered; this chapter evaluates the place of the personality of George W. Bush in the overall explanation of US foreign policy between 2001 and 2008.

In general, the impact of a single personality (no matter how prominent) on the overall foreign policy of the United States has been somewhat limited. To begin with, the characteristics of individuals are but a few of the numerous factors determining American foreign policy. Other factors, including structural-systemic (covered in this volume in chapter 2) and ideological (chapter 3) ones, could potentially limit the impact of leaders' personal characteristics. While it is true that the president has a unique position in influencing the overall foreign policy of the country, even he has to face limitations on his ability to control foreign policy or influence it decisively (often a source of personal frustrations).

In spite of those inherent impediments on the impact of an individual, in the case of the foreign policy of the United States between 2001 and 2008, the impact of the president's personality seems to have been substantial. A large number of writers have tried to assess the presidency of George W. Bush from this particular perspective.[1] "George Bush and his presidency have been enormously consequential," writes Peggy Noonan, a former speechwriter for

Ronald Reagan.[2] The importance of the Bush presidency is linked particularly to two structural, systemic factors. First, following the assaults of September 11, 2001, the United States faced what most people saw as a crisis situation, in which the president's direct involvement in foreign policy decision making becomes crucial, not unlike the Cuban Missile Crisis under John F. Kennedy. Second, the United States continued to face the challenge of a fundamental transition in the international political system, somewhat similar to the challenge of formulating an overall policy toward the Soviet Union in the formative years of the Cold War, 1946 to 1950. Also, such a transition requires a high level of direct presidential involvement.

The thesis of this chapter has two parts. In the first (and much shorter) part it will be argued that, in comparative terms, George W. Bush may prove to have been *the most influential person* in terms of the formulation and implementation of American foreign policy in the post–World War II era. Second, it will be argued that in terms of his personality traits, Bush was not only unprepared but ill suited to meet the extraordinary challenges that his administration faced. He was inexperienced and lacking in specific knowledge of or interest in international matters; even more important, he did not have the intellectual curiosity essential for an effective presidency at one of the most critical times for the United States and the world. Moreover, Bush brought with him to the White House an extreme Manichean, absolutist mindset, a tendency to view the world as a monumental, moralistic battlefield between good and evil.[3] This attitude made him into a nonreflective, closed-minded, inflexible, and rigid "decider," incapable of admitting (publicly, privately, and probably even to himself) any mistakes and, therefore, constitutionally incapable of seriously considering a change of course. Although by nature a charismatic leader with considerable political and interpersonal gifts, Bush led the country and the world by acting on his instincts, as he himself proudly said on numerous occasions; he rarely led by engaging members of his administration, let alone the wider public, in intensive dialogue and rational analysis of different options or by offering impassioned, fact-based argumentation. All in all, Bush's personality fit quite well what James David Barber calls an active-negative president,[4] although some analysts have classified him as active-positive. His personality and actions resemble those of former presidents Woodrow Wilson, Lyndon Baines Johnson, and Richard Nixon, leaders whose presidencies ended badly. In his core, Bush was a believer in American exceptionalism, an assertive nationalist. His nationalism reflected three tributaries: the Neoconservative belief in "regime change" and "benevolent hegemony" (under the banner of democratization), the hard-nosed superhawkishness of Dick Cheney and Donald Rumsfeld, and the messianic evangelism that he brought with him to the White House. Bush's personality, along with several world events and the Neocon ideology, made an endless war unavoidable. It was a perfect example of a self-fulfilling prophecy of potentially disastrous proportions.

Bush's Unique Historical Challenge

Three systemic factors determined the unique importance of Bush as a revolutionary shaper of contemporary American foreign policy beyond his own personality traits. First, the genuine *crisis situation* created by the September 11 terrorist attacks produced a practically unanimous feeling in America that the government of the United States (that is, the president) needed to react quickly, comprehensively, and decisively in order to protect America against the threat to its highest values.[5] This dominant position within the United States, and even in many countries beyond America, gave President Bush a truly unusual leeway in initiating fundamental, long-term changes in American foreign policy. It allowed him to dominate the process through which the response to 9/11 was formulated, working hand in hand with the Neoconservatives who offered him a template fitting his temperament.[6]

Second, the fact that Bush faced prior to and even more after 9/11 a complicated *transitional situation* in the international system destined him to become a uniquely important decision maker in the field of foreign policy. As demonstrated by, among others, Woodrow Wilson and Harry S. Truman, transitional periods give presidents unique opportunities to shape world politics for generations to come. With Bush this was even more the case than it was in regard to Wilson and Truman. Bush became president at the time that the United States was the recognizable global hyperpower, easily the single most dominant country in the world. While the United States had to deal with an increasingly diverse, polyarchic world,[7] its dominance has provided it with an opportunity to guide the world toward new horizons. That dominance put the man in the White House in a unique position of influence.

Third, the fact that September 11 constituted in the minds of most professional observers, and the public at large, a new, ambiguous, and unusually complex situation in which the United States was challenged by a nonstate representing an ill-defined ideology and unspecified demands allowed the White House, more than any other American institution (such as Congress), to *define the situation* and *implement a solution*. More than any other event in memory, 9/11 threw the ball into the president's court: it was an event that gave the president of the United States as much power as any leader ever had in reshaping the world.

Those three factors, in combination, facilitated the Bush revolution in foreign policy. But the specific shape that this revolution took was determined by the personality of the president, the interactions that he had with his closest advisers, the decision-making process that he created within his administration, and the ideological messages that he chose to absorb, adopt, and implement. It is to the president's personality that we now turn.

Classifying Bush

George W. Bush has become one of America's most controversial presidents ever. He is now in a league with Richard Nixon. Writes Noonan: "Americans don't really know, deep in their heads, whether this president, in his post-9/11 decisions, is a great man or a catastrophe, a visionary or wholly out of his depth."[8] In order to take the measure of Bush we need to look deeper into the *type of leadership* he provided during his time in office. That is, we need to classify him so that he may be compared to other presidents.

Political scientists, historians, journalists, and others have been trying to classify presidents for many years. While the assessment of presidents is somewhat of a national sport, particularly since the position became so prominent domestically and internationally, the real importance of a classification is in its ability to identify the critical personality traits that shape the character of a president and determine his behavior in office. In principle, of course, every classification is to some extent arbitrary; that is, the traits that might be important to its inventor might not be important to others. Moreover, once a classificatory system is established and adopted, it might be applied in different ways by different analysts. In the social sciences, a classification is but a tool for analyzing behavioral patterns.

Among the better-known and more useful classifications of American presidents is the one developed by Duke University political science professor James David Barber. Barber argues that presidents ought to be understood not merely in terms of their worldviews—that is, what substantive beliefs they have[9]—but also and especially in terms of their character. Two particular dimensions of character are chosen by Barber as critical for classifying presidents: (1) the energy presidents put into their job, or whether they are *active or passive*; and (2) their personal satisfaction with their presidential duties, or whether their attitude toward their job is *negative or positive*. Active presidents are engaged, eager to lead, and ready to formulate new policies, while passive presidents prefer to maintain the status quo and avoid conflict. In terms of satisfaction derived from the job, Barber maintains that while positive presidents enjoy the job, negative presidents look at it as a duty and a chore. Barber observed that such negativity might be rooted in childhood experiences; while those men of high achievement might accept their powerful position, they do not necessarily enjoy it.

This dual distinction leads Barber to identify four types of American presidents: (1) The active-positive president is results oriented: he thoroughly enjoys the job and wants to use it to introduce the changes he believes in (most historians would include Franklin Delano Roosevelt, Harry S. Truman, Gerald Ford, and George H. W. Bush in this category). (2) Active-negative presidents want to get power, keep it, and even expand it, but they do not really derive satisfaction from the job (Barber and many others would include in this category the most dangerous of all presidential groups, Democrats Woodrow Wilson and Lyndon Johnson and Republicans Herbert Hoover and Richard Nixon). (3) While passive-positive presidents enjoy their job, they tend to seek popularity and avoid rocking the boat (William Taft and Warren Harding are often thought to fit this category well). (4) Negative-passive presidents carry their presidential obligations dutifully, but they do not push forward any particular political agenda (Calvin Coolidge is surely included in this category; more debatable is the inclusion of Dwight Eisenhower).

An assessment of the presidency of George W. Bush reveals a president who was, for the most part, the very model of an active-negative character. Although prior to 9/11 he was somewhat passive, after the terrorist attacks on America he became energetically engaged in carrying out his obligations and displayed extreme assertiveness in pushing for a fundamental change in the status quo.[10] This position reflected the active side of Bush's character. Throughout the years, Bush has shown that he is firm and resolute, and able to make tough decisions. Yet, there were indications that Bush was incapable of deriving personal satisfaction from the presidency itself.[11] For him, it seems, the most important rewards of the presidency were the status, the prestige, and the recognition that came with the job—"I am the decider!"[12]—because those benefits emphasized his importance, enabled him to sustain the positions he had taken (regardless of the facts), and reaffirmed his authority. Bush resembled negative presidents, such as Johnson and Nixon, in his unwillingness and inability to learn from his mistakes; like them, his capabilities of change, growth, and flexibility were severely limited.

Numerous historical examples are relevant and instructive in understanding Bush, although none of them fits him precisely. Woodrow Wilson, albeit a true intellectual (unlike Bush), was also deeply committed to his brand of evangelical religiosity and was similarly incapable of compromising. This intransigence would not allow Wilson to seek accommodation with his opponents in the Senate, leaving the United States out of the League of Nations. Lyndon Johnson, a genius as a political operator, stuck to his guns in Vietnam and was, in effect, forced out of office by his own party. Richard Nixon, Johnson's successor in the White House, while one of the most talented of all modern presidents in the field of foreign affairs, was obsessed with power and control, leading eventually to his self-destruction.

George W. Bush revealed tendencies similar to those of his predecessors. Like Wilson, for the most part, Bush was not capable of pragmatic compromising with his rivals. He stuck to his guns in Iraq, as Johnson did in Vietnam (although, in view of 9/11, the country gave Bush a lot more leeway). Bush's obsession with power and control—having run one of the tightest and most secretive operations in the history of the White House—was similar in character to Nixon's. Yet, under the veneer of strength and infallibility, there were serious and consequential psychological weaknesses and vulnerabilities in Bush's presidency. His bravado, shown in his talk and even in his walk, reflected lack of self-confidence and self-esteem. It was a façade covering up the real person.[13]

It is interesting to note that even some professional analysts have failed to identify George W. Bush as an active-negative, although lack of historical perspective and sufficient documentation might have been responsible for that shortsightedness. One explanation for that failure is that at the beginning of his presidency, Bush looked very much like a typical passive-negative president, a latter-day Calvin Coolidge. Thus, not only has Bush delegated huge responsibilities to his aides and adopted a CEO presidential model (see chapter 5), but he also let it be known that he did not read newspapers and did not feel the need to do so. Moreover, in the first seven to eight months of his presidency, Bush spent nearly half his time away from the White House,[14] often vacationing on his ranch in Crawford, Texas, spending considerable effort on clearing the dead brush. Bush gave the impression that he was an "accidental president."[15] Some of Bush's personal characteristics (see below) and the unique circumstances of his arrival at the White House strengthened the impression that the United States was about to experience one or two terms of a passive, uninterested president.

Some observers thought that Bush was an active-positive president,[16] particularly after 9/11 when his performance in public looked impressively engaging, caring, and focused. In hindsight and from a larger historical perspective, it could be argued that reading Bush as positive (in the sense of Barber's classification) was a serious misdiagnosis of his personality type. Those who chose this line of analysis emphasized Bush's willingness to surround himself with high-quality, formidable advisers without fear that they would outshine him; they brought this as evidence of the president's self-confidence and openness. Yet, we know now that some of those high-quality advisers (most notably Colin Powell) were purposely marginalized, often ignored, and eventually fired. Some of the analysts even argued that Bush "embraced the views of the liberal multilateralists,"[17] a conclusion entirely unsupported by the facts. Bush actually has negated all the assumptions and undermined all the policies of the liberal-multilateral camp; after 9/11 in particular he moved very much in the direction of the Neoconservatives. Above all, Bush's adoption of a Manichean, black-and-white perspective on the world fits his active-negative character a lot more than it fits an active-positive posture.

Barber's theory is that presidents must be understood in terms of their past—their childhoods and formative years hold the key to their behavior as presidents. Bush's childhood suggests serious problems in terms of his self-esteem.

He was raised by a father who had an almost perfect American life: a Yale graduate with a Phi Beta Kappa distinction, an all-American baseball star in college, a heroic combat pilot in World War II, a pursuer of a successful career in business and in politics. For many years, George W. Bush could not have possibly measured up to his accomplished father: he was an unaccomplished student, was a cheerleader for his university's basketball team, served in the Air National Guard as a pilot, ran unsuccessfully for Congress, failed in business (an oil company), and by his own admission drank too much. In contrast to his father and others in his family, he demonstrated little or no interest in public affairs and completely ignored the intense public debate over the Vietnam War, the biggest issue on the agenda during his college days.

Many have suggested that the unavoidable comparison with his father generated *strong resentment* in George W. Bush, a rather reasonable thesis. Bush, for example, once told Dick Armey, a prominent House Republican: "I am more like Ronald Reagan than my dad,"[18] a remarkable comment in which "W" replaced his father with someone else. He also liked to emphasize the fact that although his father was raised in the East, he was raised in Texas, drawing attention to the contrasts between them. The same goes for comparisons with his younger brother Jeb, considered by many as much smarter than George W.

There is no question that the younger Bush saw himself forever in *competition* with the older Bush. Pursuing a political career and eventually running for president, in and of itself, could be seen as a competitive move by the younger Bush. Invading Iraq was yet another such move. Bush-43 must have felt good in removing Saddam from power and convincingly winning reelection, two feats unachieved by his nemesis, his father.

These psychological explanations, one focused on resentment and the other on competition, are, of course, not mutually exclusive. In fact, they complement each other rather well. Powerful resentment could lead naturally to competitiveness. It seems that in the case of George W. Bush, both sets of feelings were important in shaping his character.

John Dean, a former assistant to Richard Nixon, has correctly identified George W. Bush as an active-negative president.[19] Like Dean's previous boss, Bush above all emphasized secrecy, loyalty, and control in the White House. Like Nixon, he divided the world into "enemies" and "friends" and pursued an unpopular war.

Beyond the Nixon comparison, all active-negative presidents tend to have *split personalities*. While on the one hand these presidents have been able to achieve great things—establishing the League of Nations (Wilson), the Great Society (Johnson), or the opening to China (Nixon)—they have also displayed great failures. Those failures have often been the result of the president's personality, his inability to do what was realistically possible and acceptable, his inability to compromise with others in the domestic or international political arena, and ultimately his inability to resolve internal psychological contradictions.

The case of George W. Bush seems to be a classic. His administration had a split personality from the very beginning, but this condition escalated especially after 9/11. The Bush White House was torn between two forces—the need to fight terrorism and its determination to do so by promoting democracy.[20] The split personality characterized both the president[21] and his administration, including his closest decision-making unit. One side of the split personality was reflected in classic Realism—a cold, calculated foreign policy, resting on efforts to build consensus at home and cooperation abroad. The chief promoter of such Realism was Colin Powell, who handled successfully the crisis with China before 9/11 and the crisis with Pakistan following 9/11, using in both cases a traditional combination of force and diplomacy. But the split personality had a second part—the idealistic one, later known as Neoconservative.

How did George W. Bush handle this split? He gradually moved in the idealistic, Neoconservative direction and eventually adopted it completely as the overarching policy of his administration. But, interestingly, the idealistic policy of democratization was used very unevenly. Toward countries such as Pakistan, China, and Russia, the Bush administration carried out Realist policy. Toward Iraq and the Palestinian territories the policy adopted was democratization. Moreover, while the overall rhetoric of the administration emphasized democracy, close allies of the United States—Egypt, Saudi Arabia, and Jordan, for example—were given a reprieve from American pressure.

Knowledge, Experience, and Interest

A comprehensive look at the record of President Bush, based on the testimonies of his associates and an examination of his policies and speeches, reveals that his most important characteristics as a policy maker were his tendency to adopt a Manichean outlook toward the challenges he faced, his pessimistic and conflictual view of the world, his closed-mindedness toward alternative views on issues of substance, and his lack of flexibility in reexamining his own political positions.

But before we turn to those central characteristics of President Bush's personality that impacted his attitudes toward substantive issues of foreign policy, it is important to look at some of his more fundamental traits. There are several of these that characterized Bush: lack of foreign policy *experience*, minimal *knowledge* of or *interest* in international affairs (or public affairs in general), and the absence of *intellectual curiosity* are among them. On the other hand, it is also important to recognize some of Bush's traits as a leader: great confidence in his own *intuition*, a *charismatic personality*, and great *interpersonal skills*.

Experience and Knowledge

When George W. Bush declared his intention of running for the presidency, numerous observers noticed his complete lack of experience in or knowledge of the field of foreign policy. In responding to what was identified as a problem, Bush adopted a remarkably nondefensive approach. "He freely admitted that he had much to learn about world affairs,"[22] reflecting his already well-known self-confidence. The issue of experience and knowledge was particularly sensitive, at least potentially, in view of the fact that the candidate's father, ex-president George H. W. Bush, was considered to be highly knowledgeable, experienced, and successful in the field of foreign policy. Comparisons between father and son were unavoidable, potentially influencing the son's behavior once he assumed the presidency.[23]

In devising a response to the experience and knowledge problem, Bush emphasized his intention to rely on the advice of people with great experience in the area of foreign affairs, including several of his father's associates. Bush also proceeded by asking Dick Cheney, a former congressman, White House chief of staff, and secretary of defense, to be his running mate, a move perceived in the country as giving him a cover against the accusation of lack of experience and knowledge.

It is interesting to note in this context that, once he got elected, Bush indeed appointed a great number of well-known foreign policy experts to his administration; yet many have thought that he still lacked the judgment to distinguish between good and bad advice and that due to his minimal knowledge and experience he became too dependent on his aides' advice. Similar dependency relationships developed between the president and Vice President Cheney,[24] one of the most experienced Washington hands in the field of security matters. Those dependencies became more severe and more consequential after September 11, 2001, because the stakes became so much higher.

In general, Bush's 2000 presidential campaign did not seriously address foreign policy issues. This fact, as well as several public comments by candidate Bush on matters of foreign policy, "betrayed a basic ignorance of world affairs,"[25] lack of preparation that was particularly disturbing in contrast to his two immediate predecessors. Although after the election and the January 2001 inauguration the issue of knowledge and experience was off the agenda, it would come back to dominate the discussion after September 11, 2001.

The lack of basic knowledge remained a problem with Bush. So in December 2002, after almost two years in the White House, Bush met with a few senators and members of the House. The discussion focused on the relationships between the Israelis and the Palestinians. Tom Lantos, a California Democrat, mentioned that if there was going to be a peacekeeping force in the West Bank and the Gaza Strip, Sweden might be able to lead it. "I don't know why you are talking about Sweden," responded Bush. "They're the neutral one. They don't have an army." When Lantos responded that it was Switzerland that was neutral, Bush insisted: "No, no, it's Sweden that has no army." Although several weeks later, at a Christmas party, Bush admitted his mistake, the impression was that once it came to foreign affairs, he simply was out of his depth. The story, reported by Ron Suskind in the *New York Times Magazine* (October 17, 2004), was one of many similar ones, leaving the impression that the president lacked important knowledge in regard to foreign policy.

Interest

Many presidential candidates in America lack knowledge of or experience in foreign affairs. Historically, US governors have been highly successful in pursuing the presidency (more so than the holders of other offices, such as senators). Yet, most of them had little or no experience in foreign affairs.

Nevertheless, despite lack of experience, many candidates for the presidency have shown genuine interest in foreign affairs, let alone in public affairs in general. Good examples are Jimmy Carter and Bill Clinton, both former governors of southern states. In this sense, George W. Bush was quite unique. In addition to having little background in and knowledge of foreign affairs, he gave the feeling to many observers that he had absolutely no interest in the subject. Robert Jervis observes that prior to 9/11 "the president did not have deeply rooted views about foreign policy."[26] In fact, he had little interest in it.

This lack of interest in foreign affairs on the part of candidate Bush was seen as part and parcel of a more general problem: Bush's general lack of intellectual curiosity. In fact, one might easily argue that George W. Bush went out of his way to display, openly and publicly, an anti-intellectual attitude.[27] He projected himself as acting on the basis of gut instincts and morality (reflected in his religion), not intellect. This combination created a clear impression that in the Bush White House there was no room for deliberation and analysis, let alone dialogue and debate. There was a "decider" and those who facilitated and implemented his decisions.[28]

The characteristic anti-intellectual profile of Bush's personality was exhibited in his biography. Thus, before his ascendance to the presidency, Bush had hardly ever traveled abroad, despite the fact that he could have easily done so. Moreover, there is a strong impression that anti-intellectualism was a fixture in Bush's character, a fundamental attitude. It therefore continued in the White House. Daalder and Lindsay, commenting on Bush's development, have observed that "there was no evidence that Bush's interest in world affairs deepened as he aged."[29] After Bush's assumption of power, leaders interacting with him remained disappointed by what they saw as lack of interest and curiosity about many issues, particularly international ones.[30]

Interestingly, this lack of interest, or at least the impression of lack of interest, was particularly noticeable until September 11, 2001. Fred Greenstein, a renowned political psychologist who wrote an article sympathetic to the Bush presidency after September 11, 2001, nevertheless concluded that on a number of instances in the pre-9/11 period it seemed evident that Bush "needed to dig deeper into policy content than had been his wont."[31] On a number of occasions he made rookie mistakes, indicating lack of interest as well as lack of fundamental knowledge.[32]

Whatever one might think about George W. Bush's knowledge of and interest in foreign affairs, it became quite clear during the campaign and following the assumption of the presidency that he simply lacked the level of fascination with public policy that characterized Bill Clinton[33] or the level of knowledge and experience that characterized his own father. These comparisons are of great relevance in view of the fact that Bush-41 and Bill Clinton were the only two presidents of the post–Cold War era.[34]

It seems that Bush's creative interest in the international world, and genuine openness toward it, remained unusually low. Thus, he tended to gravitate toward books that confirmed what he already "knew" or, better yet, what he chose to know, books that confirmed his ideology. Among the volumes that generated Bush's praise over the past few years are, for example, Andrew Roberts's *A History of the English-Speaking Peoples Since 1900* (2006) and Natan Sharansky's *A Case for Democracy* (2004). The overtly anti-intellectual Bush invited those authors to the White House.

EVANGELICAL MANICHEAN RADICALISM

In terms of the substance as well as the structure of his belief system, President Bush presented a rather similar outlook to the one presented by many of the better-known Neoconservatives. While there were surely significant biographical differences between Bush, a self-described born-again Christian, and many of the Neocons, for the most part secular intellectuals, in terms of the content of the belief systems, the similarities were clearly more prominent than the differences. The belief system that united Bush and the Neocons might be called Evangelical Manichean Radicalism. This belief system might be reduced to three major attitudinal components: (1) The world is divided into good versus evil forces (the forces of light versus the forces of darkness in biblical language). (2) The forces of light must (and will) defeat the forces of darkness. (3) The path to victory over "evil" is through a military confrontation. Those three components were assumed to be true by definition; they have rarely been examined empirically. In fact, as articles of faith they are not even given to an empirical examination.

The most important characteristic of Bush's attitude to life in general and to politics in particular—*his core belief*—has been his tendency to look at the world as a stage for a clash between good and evil, right and wrong. For Bush, the world presented binary choices. His reaction to 9/11 was simple—"either you are with us, or you are with the terrorists," he famously stated to America and to the world.[35] In terms of Bush's personality, it is important to realize that, for him, his approach to the issues on the agenda was not merely a policy matter, but an internalized moral and religious conviction. Approaching all issues from the perspective of personal faith, the implementation of his policies looked to him like a matter of determination and resolve, not of data and facts.

A sign of things to come was given already during one of the debates between Republican presidential candidates when Bush, along with the other candidates, was asked who was the most important political philosopher or thinker he most identified with. With no hesitation Bush said, "Christ, because he changed my heart." Bush believed that by finding Jesus he discovered the absolute truth and that he had been commanded to spread the truth to others. On at least one occasion (speaking to Pennsylvania Amish) Bush stated, "I trust that God speaks through me"; many other statements indicate that he actually believed it, even if he did not express it in so many words. His reaction to 9/11 was as straightforward as it was simplistic and decisive: the United States, and he as its president, were obliged to eradicate the evil that the terrorists represented. The most important part of his approach, however, was that he chose to define that "evil" in the broadest possible manner. Rather than limiting it to the people who actually carried out the assaults or were factually connected to it, he included individual leaders and regimes that opposed the United States. In doing so, the president antagonized most of the world. Moreover, he made permanent war unavoidable.

The way in which Bush defined evil, and went about fighting it, coincided with the prescriptions offered to the United States by the Neoconservatives for years. At the center of his definition were countries unfriendly to America, among them Iraq, Iran, and North Korea. His plan was simple: defeat those countries militarily and thereby establish a global American hegemony in the world, all of it under the banner of eradicating evil.

While it remains unknown whether Bush actually read the Neoconservative writings, several of his top policy associates—notably Cheney, Rumsfeld, and

Wolfowitz—were closely connected to Neoconservative positions for years. What is important is that "simpleminded Manichean dogmatism,"[36] in either its religious or secular formulations, became in effect the *agreed-upon ideological infrastructure of the administration*, uniting the president, his authoritative vice president, and key governmental officials.

In the case of the president himself, his faith was so strong that it made analysis unnecessary. If one believes that he is on a mission from God, and that he truly knows what this mission is, careful examination of the facts, comparison of alternative explanations and options, and other activities that fall under "analysis" become utterly unimportant and even blasphemous. Empiricism has no place in the mind of the believer. Certitude and religious convictions dominate. Observes Jervis: "Bush is prone to look for missions that give his life and his country meaning, to see the world in terms of good and evil, and to believe in the possibility and efficacy of transformation."[37] In Bush's missionary world, analytical focus was secondary at best, if it exists at all.

It is interesting to note in this context that Michael Gerson ultimately became one of the truly close advisers to Bush. Gerson graduated from a religious institution of higher learning, Wheaton College in Illinois, worked for Watergate-felon-turned-evangelist Charles Colson, and was interviewed by candidate Bush in 1999 and hired on the spot as a speechwriter. Already during the 2000 campaign Gerson wrote for Bush speeches that anticipated the president's second inaugural address five years hence,[38] although those themes were still relatively peripheral in Bush's message. Gerson's thinking and its impact on the president became more central, even dominant, after 9/11. "Gerson was the vehicle through which Bush maneuvered alongside the neocon agenda, by linking its expansionist impulses with explicitly moral imperative."[39] In fact, in practical terms there was no real difference between the Neocon endorsement of benevolent hegemony, the nationalist, hawkish position of Cheney and Rumsfeld, and the Bush-Gerson religious logic. While there was a high degree of convergence between those different strands, in terms of his own inclinations, it seems as if Bush felt most comfortable with the Gerson approach. In July 2002 Bush appointed Gerson as a policy adviser, in addition to being his speechwriter.

Andrew Bacevich and Elizabeth Prodromou suggest that "in the aftermath of 9/11, conceptions of justice, largely evangelical in their origin, became fused with a set of policy prescriptions aimed at transforming US national security strategy. Religion has been rendered *an instrument* used to provide *moral justification for what is, in effect, a strategy of empire* (emphasis added)."[40] It is extremely difficult to know to what extent Bush really believed or chose to simply use religion as an instrument for promoting his foreign policy agenda, although there seems to be plenty of evidence to indicate that the president was a genuine believer. Be that as it may, Bush used religious terminology quite often and couched his entire foreign policy in religious terms. What is most important politically is that "Bush's religious worldview coincided with the neocons' secular worldview."[41] Those two belief systems, along with the "nationalist assertiveness" of people like Cheney and Rumsfeld, complemented each other very well.

Richard Shweder calls the president's stance "missionary moral progressivism."[42] It is a belief that there are non-negotiable demands grounded in universal moral truths for the design of any decent society, and that the United States should lead the world toward that ideal.[43] A famous earlier version of such "progressivism" was the nineteenth-century British understanding of the "White man's burden."[44] In promoting this mission, Bush used both religious and secular language, mixing up the idea that the United States needed to fight against "evil" and "evildoers" (concepts with religious connotations) and, at the same time, to promote such values as democracy, freedom, and liberty (that is, a secular agenda). In doing so, Bush followed in the footsteps of other American presidents, particularly Woodrow Wilson and Jimmy Carter.[45]

What is particularly interesting to note is that those two other evangelical presidents of the modern era had a very different substantive mission than the one promoted by George W. Bush. Both were committed internationalists and saw themselves as leading peacemakers in an overly conflictual world. Like Wilson, Bush aspired to remake, reinvent the world. Like Carter, he saw himself as a promoter of human rights. While in terms of the structure of their belief system the three presidents were surprisingly similar—thus, none of the three could separate his faith from politics—the substance of their message could not have been more different.

Bush displayed the personality of a crusader, in John Stoessinger's terms.[46] Although he promised during the 2000 campaign a humble foreign policy, after he took office, and particularly since 9/11, his policy was *the most ambitious foreign policy in the history of the United States*. It aimed at remaking the world in the image of the United States while using religious language to justify this project. Yet, while Bush often spoke to the United States and to the world in religious terms, he worked tirelessly toward the enhancement of America's unilateral power.

NATIONALIST CONFLICTUAL PESSIMISM

The foreign policy of George W. Bush had three tributaries, all leading to the very same river. The first was the Neoconservative thinking of people like the Kristols, the Podhoretzs, and the Kagans, and represented in the administration by Deputy Secretary of Defense Paul Wolfowitz; it promoted the idea of democratizing the world through military action and establishing the benevolent hegemony of the United States.[47] The second was the power-politics super-hawkishness of Cheney and Rumsfeld, trying to extend US influence and domination as far as possible. The third was the religious messianism of Gerson and other evangelicals. They all united around the Iraq invasion. More important, they all agreed that American nationalism was the carrier of their ultimate designs.

Jervis argues that three principles informed US foreign policy under Bush—democratization of other states, prevention (including preventive war), and transformation of the international system.[48] Those three principles were translated by Bush into both his nationalist and his theological language, his evangelical Christianity, and his belief in America's mission. On a certain level of abstraction, those principles were perceived as the good and their opposition as evil, from the perspectives of both nationalism and Christianity. Bush became totally committed to expanding the good and destroying evil under the banner of those three ideas. His ideological commitments amounted to a rejection of Realism and its bias toward maintaining the status quo.

Like the Neocons, Bush saw the world as a jungle-like, conflictual place. This was a reflection of his combative personality. The family he was raised in was highly competitive, and this experience left its mark on the president. Many observers had the impression that Bush was not open to a dialogue based on the analysis of facts, the presentation of alternative opinions, and some kind of rational decision making. Like his chief foreign policy advisers—Cheney and Rumsfeld—Bush was a superhawk. He has already demonstrated his approach in the first eight months of his administration in regard to missile defense, the

International Criminal Court, the Kyoto Protocol, and many other issues. And, in a most general way, he brought with him to the White House a deeply religious, messianic-evangelical attitude. But all three of those belief systems focused on the centrality of the United States as an agent of change in the world. In the center of Bush's world was his identity as an American. While he presented to the world a model of liberation, in reality it meant for him an action by the United States against other nations.

There is no evidence that Bush was a Neoconservative prior to his arrival at the White House. Yet, there is plenty of evidence that the story of his life, as he himself perceived it and relayed it to others, was about faith. He found Christ. But the key point is that for Bush, faith and nationalism were linked: he saw the United States as implementing the faith. If everything is based on faith, and the fundamental belief is that your nation represents all that is good while others represent evil, the only option open is conflict and the establishment of domination.

LACK OF OPENNESS AND FLEXIBILITY

The title of Robert Draper's book, *Dead Certain*, captures the nature of the personality of George W. Bush more than most books on America's forty-third president. Bush was a man hardly capable of changing his position on any issue, and he was even less likely to admit to others that he had changed his position. If and when he changed his stance, as in approving the "surge" in Iraq or letting Donald Rumsfeld go after the 2006 election, this change came only after several years of proven, utterly failing policies. Moreover, even when "changing," Bush insisted on the wisdom and correctness of his original policies. There is no evidence at all that Bush was open to new ideas or that he ever made an effort to learn from his or his administration's mistakes.

In fact, the single most important initiative taken by the Bush administration, the Iraq war, confirmed that Bush was completely incapable of admitting mistakes, let alone changing his behavior. He stuck to his position on Iraq after the March 2003 invasion and supported the appointees charged with implementing his decision—even those responsible for grave errors—for years, sometimes at a significant political cost to himself. While his loyalty could be praised, it is his lack of an open mind, extreme rigidity, and lack of flexibility that are more evident and politically more relevant. It seems that in Bush's mind, loyalty to his people was equated with loyalty to the cause he chose to promote.

Interestingly, the inflexibility and lack of openness on the part of Bush often were presented by the president's supporters, particularly the Neocons, in positive terms.[49] Bush has been described by his supporters as a firm, resolute leader, ready to make whatever tough, unpopular, and controversial decisions had to be made. Moreover, Bush himself seemed to believe that the display of confidence can create facts, change reality, and achieve results. In a country shocked and bewildered by 9/11, Bush's determination and confidence might indeed have achieved results that in other circumstances would not be possible.

Maybe the real explanation for Bush's rigidity is his unshaken ideology, rooted in his religious convictions. Religion is, almost by definition, not open to compromises, changes, and growth. If a president believes that he represents the universal truth, or God, the likelihood for a change in his position is rather limited. In the specific case of George W. Bush, inflexibility seemed to be inevitable and the content of the belief system was extremely Manichean.

Arrogance

Bush himself, more than most other presidents, spoke often about his personal characteristics as a leader. He claimed to govern the country without paying any attention to the polls or to public opinion, even though his own spokesman, Scott McClellan, described the Bush White House as being in a permanent campaign mode.[50]

Bush went out of his way to show that he was his own man, independent, resolute, acting on the basis of his personal understanding of what ought to be done. But, beyond Bush's personality traits, there was his Manichean mindset, the content of his belief system. The sharp distinction drawn between good and evil leads those who adopt that position to view themselves—personally and as part of a collective—as being on the side of the absolute good, fighting to eradicate the evil of their real or imagined rivals. This approach is invariably characterized by unshakeable certitude, unrestrained aggression, and unmitigated arrogance. Another consequence of this mindset is lack of openness. There are many indications that President Bush perceived himself to be the "commander in chief of a righteous crusade"[51] and that many of his supporters saw him in the same vein.

Jackson Lears offers an interesting comparison between the Vietnam War and the Iraq war, Bush's most important initiative, through the eyes of Senator J. William Fulbright and particularly his book, *The Arrogance of Power*.[52] Fulbright saw America's Vietnam involvement as arrogant. This arrogance was sustained by religious fervor, the illusion of omnipotence and messianic spirit, all cloaked in the robes of righteousness.[53] The similarities between Vietnam and Iraq are amazing; the personality of President Bush accentuated those similarities.

Arrogance and inflexibility are two sides of the same coin. The lack of openness in Bush often showed itself in the form of a large number of arrogant statements. On one occasion the president reminded everyone that he was the "decider" (even though the situation, the war in Iraq, was clearly one that involved others, including Congress). On another occasion Bush stated: "I am the commander. . . . I do not need to explain why I say things."[54]

It could be argued that the arrogance of George W. Bush was merely a reflection of his weakness. It is mere overcompensatory behavior on the part of a person who described himself as an underachiever. The more besieged Bush became, the more arrogant and aggressive his attitude. For example, after the 2006 midterm elections, reflecting the great dissatisfaction of the public with the Iraq war and its chief proponent, George W. Bush decided to escalate the war in Iraq.

The arrogance shown by the president could easily be understood if we perceive his presidency to be, in the final analysis, a test of his personal power. As president, he worked tirelessly to expand presidential power—his power—both domestically and internationally. The weaker he felt, the more aggressive, blatant, and arrogant became his attitude, particularly toward those whom he identified as challenging him (including radical Muslims, liberal critics in the United States, old allies like Gerhardt Schroeder, and even conservatives or Realists in America).

September 11, 2001, was, for Bush, the ultimate personal challenge. The United States was exposed as vulnerable. He had to react by seeking ultimate power—global hegemony. The only ideology available to him at this moment, in addition to his deep religious belief system, was the Neoconservative one. It offered a recipe, a justification, and a rationale for American hegemony.

INSTINCT

Part of Bush's arrogance was his constant refrain that he made decisions on the basis of intuition and gut reaction. The message, or so it seemed, was clear: "I, George Bush, do not have to *know* anything, because my intuition will lead me to the right decision." This attitude puts Bush ahead of other people who presumably do not have such instinct to guide them. The country was treated to the president's gut when he met Putin in June 2001 for the first time. Said Bush about the president of Russia: "I looked the man in the eye. I found him to be very straightforward and trustworthy. . . . I was able to get a sense of his soul."[55] Interestingly, Putin later disappointed Bush (who never admitted it) and others. Bush's gut proved wrong. This inclination of the president to act on intuition was referred to by none other than Colin Powell, his Realist secretary of state, as Bush's "cowboy instincts."[56]

The arrogant position of the president affected people around him (as is often happening in other administrations) in a profound way. In fact, it changed the way US foreign policy was made, often resulting in policy based on *faith* rather than *facts and analysis*. One senior Bush aide, for example, dismissed criticism of the administration from what he himself called the "reality-based community," which he defined as people who believe that solutions emerge from "judicious study of discernable reality." In a truly amazing statement, this official elaborated: "That's not the way the world works anymore. . . . We are an empire now, and when we act, we create our own reality." And more on the difference between the new White House modus operandi and the outside world: "We are history's actors . . . and you, all of you, will be left to just study what we do."[57] Zbigniew Brzezinski, an old foreign policy hand, accurately described it as an "astonishing pronouncement."[58]

A much more important gut reaction by Bush was his response to the events of September 11, 2001. Even Laura Bush said that "George is pretty impulsive and does pretty much everything to excess."[59] It seems that Bush's fundamental decisions on 9/11 resulted not from careful analysis or extensive consultations but from gut reaction. Said Brzezinski, "The events of 9/11 were an epiphany for Bush. After a single day's seclusion, the new president emerged transformed."[60]

ASSESSING THE IMPACT

This chapter has identified several personality traits of George W. Bush. The impact of those character traits of the forty-third president on the policies adopted eventually by the United States during his administration was devastating. People in the White House and other parts of the administration were reluctant to confront Bush with alternative opinions to those promoted by the White House or even present unpleasant truths, having witnessed "disdain for contemplation and deliberation, a retreat from empiricism, and sometimes bullying impatience with doubters and even friendly questioners."[61] Those who did present alternative thoughts, notably secretaries Paul O'Neill and Colin Powell, as well as Environmental Protection Agency administrator Christine Todd Whitman, were marginalized and eventually shown the door. O'Neill, Bush's first treasury secretary, has famously characterized Bush's leadership style as "a blind man in a room full of deaf people."[62] Because of his closed-mindedness and rigidity, Bush showed from the very beginning a tendency to control, marginalize, disregard, and eventually silence moderate voices in his administration. Most important in terms of foreign policy, Colin Powell, Bush's highly respected, Realist secretary of state, was neutralized from day one by the presence and the immense influence of superhawks such as Cheney, Rumsfeld, and Wolfowitz. While Powell was used by the White House to sell the WMD story to the world, and particularly to American public opinion, he was unceremoniously let go at the beginning of the second Bush administration, along with his deputy Richard Armitage.

The main problem with Bush's faith-based attitude was that it impacted directly not only the way in which the president approached foreign policy decisions but also the manner in which he "demanded unquestioning faith from his followers, his staff, his senior aides and his kindred in the Republican party. Once he makes a decision—often swiftly, based on creed or moral position—he expects complete faith in its rightness," testified people closely familiar with Bush's White House.[63]

Yet, one cannot understand Bush's ability to implement his agenda, and sustain it in the face of huge public opposition, without the Neoconservative factor. The Neocons gave Bush assurances that his policies were the right ones, despite the fact that these policies lost the support of American public opinion once they faltered. One example would suffice. On February 28, 2007, Bush hosted a "literary luncheon" in the White House, honoring Andrew Roberts's book, *A History of the English-Speaking Peoples Since 1900*.[64] In addition to Roberts, a conservative Brit, some of the most important Neocon intellectuals were in attendance, among them Irving Kristol, Norman Podhoretz, Irwin Stelzer, and Michael Novak.[65] Roberts, whose book was severely criticized by many, offered his "lessons" from the Iraq war.

The combination of Neocon imperialistic push and Bush's uncritical decisiveness produced a furious search for what one author (quoting John Quincy Adams) called "monsters to destroy,"[66] leading the United States toward unnecessary confrontations in which it lost its legitimacy as the recognized, responsible, and rational leader of the world community. The president's decisive attitude was merely an extension of his Christian belief system, buttressed by the Neoconservative ideology. For Bush, punishing "evildoers" was not merely a right but an obligation.[67]

The negative aspects of Bush's personality, as well as their impact on the quality of his decision making, deteriorated with time, particularly after September 11. Although the tendency toward rigidity was inherent in Bush's personality when he assumed office, his intolerance toward those who doubted him escalated significantly after the terrorist attacks. At the beginning of his run for the presidency, several people noted that although Bush did not have a lot of knowledge of international matters, he was interested in learning and showed an open mind. Even superhawk Richard Perle shared this opinion, a fact that attracted him to Bush. To whatever extent Bush had an open mind and willingness to learn, it seemed to evaporate.

Interestingly, in some presidencies the quality of crisis management has tended to increase over time, especially in terms of the openness of the president (which was enhanced) and his closeness to others in the decision-making unit (which has increased).[68] The opposite was the case with George W. Bush personally and his administration in general. Rather than having more nuanced analysis in government councils and more fact-based argumentation toward the outside world, the Bush administration became more rigid, less deliberative, and less contemplative over time. The message to the world became more and more detached, unrealistic, and evangelical.[69]

While the final historical account of the Bush administration has not yet been written, there is a strong impression that those characteristics of the decision-making process reflected, above all, the ideological preferences and the personality of the president. Ron Suskind summarized the dynamic process within the administration well: "The executive's balance between analysis and resolution, between contemplation and action, was being tipped by the pull of righteous faith."[70] Rather than using his increasing knowledge of foreign policy for opening up the process, Bush seemed to close it off. In his faith-based administration, there was no room for analysis, let alone alternative faiths. Powell, a "lone pragmatist in a sea of ideologues,"[71] was marginalized.

As the Bush presidency drew to an end, it became clear that the president's vision for America and the world would come to naught: (1) terrorism was not defeated in Afghanistan, Iraq, Pakistan, or other places; (2) real democracy was not established in the Middle East or, specifically, in Iraq, and in some countries radicals came to power under the guise of democracy; and (3) America's legitimacy and reputation in the world declined. As we seek a fundamental reason for Bush's failure, it seems that the president's vision and the means adopted by him for its implementation had nothing to do with the real challenges faced by America and the world. The vision and the instruments adopted by the president did not reflect "the art of the possible" but the ideal, missionary, and evangelical truth of George W. Bush. Put differently, there was a clear disconnect between reality and vision, challenge and response.

In trying to sell his policies to the country Bush argued that America's ideals, which he described as spreading freedom and democracy, were identical to American interests. This argumentation was hardly proven. In fact, in promoting America's interests, the Bush administration supported highly undemocratic countries such as Saudi Arabia, Egypt, Pakistan, and Jordan. Bush never recognized the contradiction. It was reflective of his inability to look at reality in a critical manner.

CHAPTER 5

THE DECISION-MAKING PROCESS

In every American administration, the decision-making process brings together several crucial components that determine the country's ultimate course of action in foreign policy. Three elements are of particular importance: the real and perceived challenges presented by the international system, the essential ideology or belief system of the decision makers, and the personality of the president (covered in this volume in chapters 2, 3, and 4, respectively). The relationships between these three elements determine, in the final analysis, the actual policy adopted by the country.

In the decision-making process in the administration of George W. Bush, the challenges faced by the United States, albeit serious and real, were largely misconstrued, misread, and misperceived by those involved in determining the American reaction to them: the president and his most influential advisers. The misperception of the challenges was the result of the ideological biases of the top presidential advisers and the willingness of the president to go along with them.

Alternative Models and Personality/Ideological Thesis

Several alternative models have been suggested for dealing with American foreign policy decision making. While all of them have some relevance for understanding the decision-making process under George W. Bush, as will be explained in this chapter, none is entirely satisfactory for capturing what looks like the uniqueness of that presidency.

In a seminal book, Richard Johnson[1] has identified three alternative models for foreign policy decision making: (1) a *formalistic model,* in which decision making is centralized and managed through hierarchical structures; (2) a *competitive model,* in which governmental agencies, bureaus, and departments, but also individuals, compete for the attention of the president; (3) a *collegial model,* in which there are debates within small circles of competing policy advocates.[2] None of these models neatly applies to the Bush White House. In the formalistic model, used by Harry S. Truman, procedures must be followed. In the case of the Bush administration's decision making, Vice President Dick Cheney, an official with no formal foreign policy responsibility, had considerable influence, exercised through both the creation of new bureaucratic entities (see below) and his uniquely close personal relationship with the president. Other deviations from the formalistic model, such as directly pressuring the intelligence agencies to respond to the political needs of the administration, also violated existing procedures.

The competitive model (used heavily by Franklin Delano Roosevelt) is somewhat more similar to the Bush administration's than the formalistic model, yet not entirely so. The model is more parallel to the early and late periods in the Bush administration, but not to the crucial middle period (when the fateful decisions were made about the Iraq war). The competitive model fosters open discussion and debate between competing actors trying to influence the policy outcome. The Bush White House did not allow such competition. In the words of one analyst, "neither the president nor the secretary of defense relied on structured debate and disciplined dissent to aid his decision making. Under their leadership, both the White House and the Pentagon used management models that emphasized inspiration and guidance from above and loyalty and compliance from below."[3] On the issue of Iraq, for example, the president made his opinion known early and strongly; there was never a real, competitive exchange on the wisdom of invading Iraq, merely on how it ought to be done. Even on the modalities of policy implementation the "debate" was limited.

The collegial model (used intensively by both John F. Kennedy and Bill Clinton) emphasizes teamwork, a situation in which debate among partners is allowed and even encouraged. Such a model was never really employed in the Bush White House, an organization split from the beginning into competing ideological camps, Realists versus Neoconservatives (see below). From the start, appointments in the fields of security and foreign policy were made on the basis of ideological positions and interpersonal relationships. Collegiality was lost in the process.

Graham Allison's work explores the way in which large governmental bureaucracies or, alternatively, organizational political "games" determine foreign policy.[4] While Allison's insights are useful, particularly in challenging the traditional assumptions of rational decision making, they are only marginally useful in penetrating the decision-making process in the Bush administration, where ideological convictions and the president's personality seem to have played more important roles than the relative weight of the bureaucracies or even the political machinations of individual actors.

While each one of these institutional models (and surely all of them in combination) highlight important aspects of the decision-making process under George W. Bush, none of them truly captures the essence of the process. What was this "essence"? In the Bush administration, the president (who referred to himself as "the decider") made important decisions, giving limited attention to the substantive arguments or the careful, methodical analysis of these arguments.[5] In all probability the president decided after a close consultation with his vice president (a possible codecider?),[6] while both of them were deeply and increasingly influenced by Neoconservatism, a belief system heavily represented in the decision-making unit and in the foreign policy and security bureaucracies at large.[7] The decision-making process in the Bush administration was, thus, driven by two main factors, ideology and personality,[8] which determined the way the president and people around him defined a situation and formulated the appropriate response to it.[9] Most important, the decision-making process in regard to Iraq (and in general) was not "a dialectical process of structured debate,"[10] which could have created immeasurably better results.

Several arguments will be made in the development of this thesis, emphasizing that decision making in the Bush White House rested on the *combined effect* of the president's personality and the Neoconservative ideology. First, in comparative terms it will be argued that the role of the president as an individual decision maker was unusually central for American foreign policy between 2001 and 2008. The best and most important example is, of course, the decision of President Bush to take the country to war in Iraq and use all the powers at his disposal to convince Congress and the American people to support him.[11] There is no question that the president dominated the political process in regard to Iraq and that none of the existing decision-making, institutional models can explain what happened without reference to his crucial role. While the president was surrounded by a large number of foreign-policy and security advisers, and the interaction among and between them was important, his personal role in shaping every aspect of the Iraq decision was more important. The same might be said about the tense relationships between a variety of bureaucratic organizations within the American government, particularly the Pentagon and the CIA, the Pentagon and the State Department, and the CIA and the Office of the Vice President. While these relations were undoubtedly important, they were never as crucial as the decisions made and the actions taken by the president. In the post-9/11 period, Bush demonstrated the ability of the occupant of the Oval Office to lead the country into war even against massive opposition. Personal factors have proven to be more important than institutional factors, although these personal factors were deeply impacted by the ideological constructs offered by the Neoconservatives.

How was Bush capable of achieving such a level of control? While it might be too early to provide a full explanation, three elements seem to be crucial: first, the enormous power concentration in the modern White House,[12] which in the case of the Bush administration included not only the National Security Council but also the Office of the Vice President and its foreign policy operation (see below); second, Bush's own dogged determination and political skills, intimately connected to his religious weltanschauung; and third, the unique atmosphere in the country after 9/11, an atmosphere that weakened the opposition to Bush's foreign policy initiatives. Patrick Haney has explained the decision to invade Iraq as reflecting a "puzzling mix of porous policy environment alongside a strikingly powerful president."[13] Within this porous environment, argues Haney, the president was "able to act with great unilateral and relatively unchecked power."[14] The key for comprehensively explaining the decision-making process in the Bush administration, and its remarkable effectiveness (as well as its colossal failures), is in combining the Bush personality with the environmental factors, including the ideological ones.

The dominant role of George W. Bush and his ability to control American foreign policy (especially in regard to the Iraq war) reflected his position as what James Pfiffner has called "the nation's first MBA president."[15] As such, Bush achieved "significant policy victories through secrecy, speed, and tight control of the executive branch." Adopting a "top-down control" system, he also found a way of effectively delegating "the implementation [of his policies] to his vice president (arguably his chief operating officer) and his loyal staff team."[16] At the same time, and very important in understanding the failures of the administration, Bush's style included "a tendency to act without sufficient deliberation, an unwillingness to admit the complexity of many policy issues, and a tendency to consider only a narrow range of alternatives."[17] Many sources have reported that the Bush White House lacked serious, detailed deliberation and a coherent decision-making process in regard to both domestic issues and, worse, foreign policy.[18] So, in terms of the decision-making process, the Bush administration left a *mixed, dualistic,* and *contradictory* record: while President Bush had the ability to decide on his own and force the implementation of his decisions, the process adopted by him proved, in the final analysis, very costly in terms of the quality of the decisions that it led to. Decisions such as invading Iraq, dispatching insufficient forces for the invasion, and dissolving the Iraqi security forces[19] were the result of a *poor-quality decision-making process* in a system that rested on the personal capabilities of a single "decider" within the ideological structure of the Neoconservatives.

Stephen Skowronek captures well Bush's character, his dominance over the decision-making process, and the consequences of this dominance for the president's policy process and policy choices. He suggests that Bush "elevated the value of definition in presidential leadership and made it central to his political stance" and that this focus on what it meant to be a presidential leader "was a reflection of the man's innate character."[20] Put differently, Skowronek seems to argue that with Bush everything was about him as a leader, a conclusion reached in this volume in chapter 4. The result of this type of presidential character, says the author, is that "it places *severe limits on open engagement with others in search of solutions,* and when real world events are approached as so many opportunities to affirm one's priors, considerations of prudence and plausibility are easily crowded out. . . . Definition will work to *narrow options, to lock the leader into his chosen course, to inhibit serious readjustments to unexpected turns* and heighten susceptibility to authority-indicting events [emphasis added]."[21] Here lies the paradox of Bush's leadership in the field of foreign policy: while he was surely the leader (and quite gifted at being recognized as such), the solutions for problems reached under his leadership were fundamentally flawed due to the type of leadership he provided.

Bush's leadership style, his insistence on the role of the president as a single "decider," brought about a serious constitutional debate, intensified by the nature of the terrorist threat to America and the world. Bush's imperious modus operandi as head of the executive branch was given legal, constitutional justification by a number of scholars, although criticized by many others.[22] In the aftermath of 9/11, John Yoo, for example, has argued for the functional superiority of the executive branch over Congress and the need for "flexibility." Yoo has maintained that authority has to be vested in the single hands of the commander in chief in order to fight terrorism effectively.[23] This type of argument has provided legitimacy not merely to the executive branch in general but also to Bush's individualized decision-making style. Steven Calabresi has gone even further by arguing for *a unitarian vision* in which the president speaks for the people and the Congress,[24] *a clear deviation from the ideals of separation of power*. Although those constitutional debates have not been resolved, Bush governed, indeed, as if the unitarian vision was the universally accepted law of the land.

CIRCLES OF DECISION MAKING IN THE BUSH ADMINISTRATION

The analysis offered in this chapter will deal with the decision-making process in the Bush administration as it occurred in several different environments or *several ever-widening circles*. It will apply the thesis about the single foreign-policy decider, deeply influenced by ideological considerations, mostly within the first two circles, where the decider as head of the executive branch had the most influence; these are also the two most important circles for this chapter.

The thesis is that *five specific circles* were of particular relevance for the foreign policy of the Bush administration, especially but not exclusively in relation to its decision to invade Iraq in 2003: first, the decision-making unit (DMU) within the White House; second, the foreign policy, defense, and intelligence bureaucracy; third, the wider political class in the United States, and particularly the Congress and the mass media; fourth, American public opinion (or what is sometimes referred to as the American people); and fifth, world public opinion (or public opinion outside the United States). Only minimal consideration will be given to the fifth circle since it was of relatively low relevance, particularly in relation to the decision to invade Iraq.

Particularly in regard to the Iraq invasion: (1) Those "decision-making circles" did not balance each other in the way they were supposed to[25] or in a way that would have been functional, useful, and productive. Put differently, the policy path charted by the decision-making unit (circle 1) easily prevailed within the bureaucracy (circle 2), the political class (circle 3), and among the American people (circle 4) and was never seriously balanced by any of those circles. (2) Each one of these circles, but particularly circles 1 (the DMU) and 2 (the bureaucracy), was greatly flawed in and of itself. (3) Circle 5 (world public opinion) was too weak to have any real influence on the final decision, reflecting the dominance of the United States in world politics.[26] The net result of this situation was disastrous, leading to a fundamentally flawed decision-making process in the Bush administration.

THE DECISION-MAKING UNIT

In many ways the decision-making unit in the Bush administration was never truly a coherent unit. Moreover, in regard to certain important decisions, particularly the controversial invasion of Iraq, the decision-making process that the DMU was supposed to be engaged in was never truly a process.[27] Within the DMU, there was a "decider" (George W. Bush), an unusually influential "code-cider" (Vice President Dick Cheney), their few ideologically identical supporters (limited for the most part to implementing, explaining, and propagating the decisions), and even fewer, muted independent and largely marginalized voices.

In general terms, the decision-making unit was split into a hawkish in-group dominated by the Cheney-Rumsfeld axis (and including Paul Wolfowitz, Lewis "Scooter" Libby, and eventually even Condoleezza Rice, Stephen Hadley, and George Tenet) and a much more moderate, dovish, Realist out-group led by Secretary of State Colin Powell, a group that included also Richard Armitage and possibly Richard Haass.[28] The overwhelmingly crucial fact was that after 9/11 the president clearly and increasingly sided with the larger in-group, although on the way to the Iraq invasion in March 2003 he sometimes ruled in favor of the Realists (e.g., the early decision to act diplomatically toward China on the plane issue, the decision to begin military operations in Afghanistan before going to Iraq, the decision to seek a second UN resolution before the Iraq invasion).

By and large, it could be persuasively argued that by temperament and ideology (that is, by personality type and belief system), President Bush tilted toward the in-group, although tactically he chose on occasion to go with the out-group. As a political actor of significant natural talents, Bush understood the benefits of using the talents of the moderates, particularly Powell, in producing American public opinion on behalf of his real political goals. In a broader strategic sense, however, Bush became closer and closer to the hardline, Neoconservative camp within his administration.

Historical Roots

The struggle between the two political camps within the Bush administration, camps that most accurately could be called Realist and Neoconservative, had important, identifiable historical roots. Those roots could clearly be found in the form of policy debates during the last phase of the first Iraq war in early 1991, although they could be found in even deeper ideological terms in the strong objections of the Neoconservatives to American foreign policy in the 1970s.[29]

More specifically, one needs to examine some of the policy disagreements within the administration of Bush-41 in order to understand the severe infighting within the administration of George W. Bush.[30] Several decisions at the time of George H. W. Bush (clearly a Realist with strong multilateral inclinations) gave birth to what John Davis has called the anti-Powell faction.[31] The first decision by Bush-41 that raised Neoconservative objections was to end the Iraq war without actually destroying the Iraqi army, marching on Baghdad, or deposing Saddam Hussein. This decision by the president was based on the February 27, 1991, recommendation of generals Colin Powell (then chairman of the Joint Chiefs of Staff) and Norman Schwarzkopf, the head of the coalition forces in the Gulf War. In terms of this study of decision making under Bush-43, it is of note that Paul Wolfowitz, then undersecretary of defense for policy, strongly opposed this decision on political, strategic, and, most important, moral grounds. Interestingly, the position taken by Wolfowitz was not shared at the time by his immediate boss, Secretary of Defense Dick Cheney.[32] In some ways, it might be argued that this event gave birth to the Neoconservative, radical, anti-Powell faction within the administration of George W. Bush. Wolfowitz and others were totally committed in the post–Bush-41 era to put Iraq back on the agenda in the future, if and when the opportunity arose.

The decision by Bush-41 to terminate hostilities was followed by the signing of a cease-fire agreement between the coalition forces and the Iraqis at Safwan. This decision, a natural outgrowth of the previous decision, was also bitterly opposed by Wolfowitz.[33] The Safwan agreement allowed the Saddam Hussein regime to survive, although Bush and his advisers believed that it would collapse under the weight of its military defeat in early 1991. Wolfowitz saw Powell and his approach as responsible for Saddam's survival. Yet, he was too isolated within the administration and too low on the administration's totem pole to affect the results. Worse yet, from a Neoconservative perspective, the Clinton administration, which succeeded the Bush-41 administration, adopted a similar pragmatic and Realist policy toward the Iraqi regime of Saddam Hussein.

When George W. Bush was declared the president-elect in late 2000, the Neoconservatives were determined to revisit the Iraq issue under the new administration and to guarantee that this time they would emerge victorious. The Iraq "obsession" remained central in Neoconservative thinking, although merely as a model for the larger hegemonic project. In order to control American policy toward Iraq and US foreign policy in general, the Neoconservatives were determined to have as many of their representatives as possible in top policy positions within the new administration. They were extraordinarily successful in achieving this goal, particularly due to the fact that Vice President–elect Cheney headed Bush's transition team and, as such, was deeply involved in appointments for the incoming administration. Several key decisions in the Bush administration, and the entire direction of US foreign policy, were greatly impacted by those appointments.

As the Bush administration was organized, the main goal of the Neoconservatives was to *counterbalance the influence of the incoming secretary of state, Colin Powell.* The new president, George W. Bush, was apparently receptive to that particular goal, although that fact cannot be conclusively proven yet. The strategy of neutralizing Powell included the surprise nomination of the veteran Donald Rumsfeld as secretary of defense, installing Powell's long-time opponent Paul Wolfowitz as deputy secretary of defense, and appointing several lesser but nevertheless important individuals. Those included Douglas Feith in the Department of Defense, John Bolton at the Department of State (over the objections of Secretary Powell), Elliott Abrams at the National Security Council, and Scooter Libby as chief of staff for Cheney.[34] Those are but some examples of the unprecedented focused efforts to *control foreign policy via appointments*. It is almost inconceivable that George W. Bush, the incoming president, was unaware of this flood of Neoconservative appointees. One might argue that this trend was to his liking.

Conflict was soon emerging between the Powell faction and the determined Neocons in the new administration. The issue, as expected, was Iraq. The Neoconservatives in the administration promoted from the very beginning the argument that the sanctions against the Hussein regime were ineffective and that, in general, containment did not achieve its intended results.[35] This argument was part and parcel of the Neoconservative philosophy; Iraq was merely a test case. The reaction of the Realists, Powell and his supporters, was that the United States ought to adopt "smart sanctions" in order to limit the technology for weapons of mass destruction from arriving in Iraq while easing the pain inflicted on the Iraqi people.

While the main combatants in this intense internal debate during the opening months of the Bush-43 administration were Powell's deputy Richard Armitage and Rumsfeld's deputy Paul Wolfowitz, those two represented two different philosophies on the right foreign policy for the United States, Realism and Neoconservatism. Wolfowitz demanded a regime change in Iraq, even without any clear-cut, new provocation on the part of Saddam Hussein. Powell, forever the moderate Realist, asserted that containment and sanctions had worked.[36] In Powell's favor was the simple fact that sanctions had been institutionalized by the two most recent American administrations, one Republican and the other Democratic (Bush-41's and Clinton's), and that regime change was difficult to achieve. So, at the end of the day, prior to 9/11 President Bush supported his pragmatic Realist secretary of state.

The events of September 11, 2001, changed the political balance of power between the Realists and the Neoconservatives within the Bush administration, and Iraq quickly emerged as the central battlefield. The Neoconservatives argued immediately following the terrorist attacks that the United States must focus on Iraq as the main culprit. They first succeeded in convincing the president that the United States ought to fight not merely terrorist organizations (namely al-Qaeda, which was clearly responsible for 9/11) but also states that support or harbor terrorism. Afghanistan was an obvious target since al-Qaeda was allowed to operate there by the Taliban regime, but the Neocons argued that Iraq ought to be added to the list. In the absence of any evidence whatsoever to tie Saddam Hussein to 9/11, the Realists won the first round: military operations against Afghanistan, but not against Iraq, were approved by the president and commenced several weeks after September 11, 2001.

Nevertheless, the Neocons and what some have called assertive nationalists (people such as Cheney and Rumsfeld) were determined to solve the Iraq issue on their terms once and for all. September 11 provided them with the unique political opening they needed.[37] The president, until then appearing neutral in the battle royal within his administration (allowing, in effect, the competitive model to operate quite effectively), began moving their way, and fast. He demanded that Richard Clarke, the National Security Council's chief counterterrorism adviser, seek evidence for Iraqi involvement in the attacks of September 11. Despite the fact that such evidence was not found, the president gave the Pentagon the green light to start preparations for an Iraq invasion.

To some extent, Powell's Realists might have misjudged the new situation: they and many others underestimated the resolve and the effectiveness of the Neocons, the unique opportunity that 9/11 provided the Neocons to push their radical agenda, and particularly the dangers inherent in the personality of President Bush. In the struggle between the Realists, focusing exclusively on Afghanistan, and the Neocons, pushing toward an Iraq invasion, George W. Bush had most of the cards in his hands. The decision to invade Iraq was his alone, although reflective of the recommendations of the Neocons within his administration. For reasons that were probably deeply rooted in his personality, Bush decided to join the war party.

Analyzing the Decision-Making Unit

Led by Colin Powell, the Realist faction was increasingly marginalized within the overall Bush foreign policy machinery following 9/11, especially in regard to the large, strategic decisions, including the decision to invade Iraq. On occasion, this faction was supported publicly by very important outside forces, including the traditional Realist establishment of the Republican Party and the

British government of Tony Blair (e.g., on the issue of obtaining a second UN resolution from the Security Council). But those outside forces were usually ignored, marginalized, or prevailed upon by members of the dominant in-group. Thus, for example, Representative Dick Armey, House majority leader (1995 to 2003) and a lifelong right-wing Republican, came to believe that President Bush and other administration officials overreacted to the country's post-9/11 fears. When Armey expressed this opinion, however, he was quickly urged by Vice President Cheney "not to dissent from the president's position in public."[38] Regardless of the weaknesses of the case presented by the White House in regard to the Iraq war, there was powerful pressure to support it, particularly on Republicans.

All in all, the leader of the out-group, Colin Powell, stood by Bush despite his deep reservations about and discomfort with the Iraq invasion. Some observers thought that this was out of loyalty and Powell's "background as a soldier."[39] But Powell's utter inability to emerge as an effective challenger to the policy of the in-group, and eventually that of the president, had deeper and more numerous reasons. First, Powell's relations with the president were never particularly warm; thus, in the post-9/11 period his influence was inherently limited. Second, Powell had a distant relationship with the president's chief confidante, Dick Cheney,[40] especially as Cheney was moving to the Right after the first Iraq war. Third, several Neoconservatives, including Paul Wolfowitz, viewed Powell as a major ideological enemy. Fourth, Bush and Cheney suspected from the very beginning that Powell could be too independent, and their suspicions were validated after September 11; so it seems that Powell was frozen out by the two top people within the administration after the terrorist assaults. Fifth, Powell was isolated within the group of the top advisers; he was simply not close to any of the other top advisers (in fact, within the government Powell had only two close allies, Armitage and Haass).[41] Sixth, and maybe most important, Powell was a Realist serving in an administration that had become increasingly Neoconservative. All of these factors were central in regard to the decision to invade Iraq, a decision Powell did not participate in.

The most important fact about the decision-making unit around President Bush, insofar as the Iraq decision was concerned but also in terms of the general attitude toward foreign policy, was that the decision-making unit was a deeply divided group.[42] The dominant part within the DMU was uncompromisingly hawkish, philosophically Neoconservative, and militaristic in its outlook, even though its leaders had no personal military experience. The weaker group was moderate and pragmatic, although never really dovish; it was Realist to its very core, and diplomatic rather than militaristic in its approach, even though its leaders (such as Powell and Armitage inside the administration and Scowcroft on the outside) were for the most part military men. Institutionally, the out-group was located in the Department of State; consequently the entire department was marginalized.[43] The head of the moderate faction, Colin Powell, was "the odd man out in the Bush administration."[44]

Several specific points ought to be made about the decision-making unit in the Bush administration, particularly but not exclusively in relation to the Iraq war. First, the president avoided anything that even *resembled* collective decision making, especially on crucial issues such as whether to execute the Iraq invasion; to the extent that there were discussions between the president and his advisers, they could be described as segmented in that members of the DMU were not asked for their analysis of the options or bottom-line recommendations on important issues,[45] especially not in a forum in which they could be challenged by others to explain their opinions and defend them.[46] Bush's mode of operation was not to discuss issues or analyze them with his advisers in a collective forum, but to *inform* them on what he had decided, and to do so *early and prematurely* in a way that closed off debate, analysis, and even exchange and consultation. Thus, as early as September 16, 2001, a mere five days after the attacks, Bush told Rice, "We won't do Iraq *now*. We're putting Iraq off. But eventually we'll have to *return* to that question [emphasis added]."[47] By November 2001 Bush spoke *confidentially* (rather than collectively or collegially) to Rice and Rumsfeld, but tellingly not to Powell, about Iraq as "a possible next step in the war on terror."[48] Most important, on November 21, 2001, President Bush met privately with Rumsfeld and instructed him to develop a plan for invading Iraq.[49]

Second, the decision-making process was *fundamentally flawed*. The DMU was not involved in vigorously analyzing whether an invasion of Iraq was the best option. While the decision was made early and prematurely by the president, subsequent discussions were devoted only to the *implementation* of the president's decision and to getting public support. Presidential scholar John Burke concludes on the basis of all the material published about Iraq that "at no point is there evidence of *a thorough and sustained debate about the merits* of the case against Iraq and the *evidence and assumptions underlying it* [emphasis added]."[50] James Fallows quotes one administration official as saying that "there was absolutely no debate in the normal sense" about Iraq.[51]

Third, to the extent to which Bush consulted with or spoke to other individuals, ideological commitments dominated those "discussions" and alternative perspectives were ignored, marginalized, or totally dismissed. In general terms, some elements of the process could be characterized by what Irving Janis called groupthink.[52] Thus, for example, a strong *ideological bias* prevailed throughout the process authorizing the Iraq invasion, and it was dominated by what was previously described as a Neoconservative mindset (see chapter 3). Professionals in the different areas of security (such as military officers and CIA analysts), foreign affairs (State Department employees), and Iraq specialists (e.g., members of the Iraq Study Group) were almost entirely ignored.

While the decision to invade Iraq had *many characteristics of groupthink*, it was only partially a classic groupthink situation. The fundamental split within the DMU meant that the type of esprit de corps and amicability that might characterize a genuine, classic groupthink was never established in Bush's DMU. On the other hand, the Neoconservative in-group has demonstrated many of the characteristics of groupthink: there seemed to be strong cohesion among its members and often personal friendships lasting for decades; they had a sense of superior morality (as many Neocon writings demonstrate in abundance); they examined few alternatives to their preferred option (war in Iraq); they ignored information that did not support their position; they had a follow-the-leader behavioral pattern (the leader of the in-group was clearly Dick Cheney); and they had a damn-the-outside-world attitude that characterizes all groupthink situations. On the other hand, not everyone in the DMU joined the groupthink situation, although, most significant, the president himself did. As the groupthink theory would predict, those who did not join were penalized severely. Powell, for example, "paid a price in being excluded or ignored on most major decisions."[53] General Eric Shinseki was publicly humiliated when he questioned the decision of Rumsfeld and Wolfowitz (and ultimately President Bush) to send a relatively small number of troops into Iraq. Assistant to the President for Economic Affairs Lawrence Lindsay was also shown the door when his predictions of the costs of the Iraq war deviated from those of the dominant group.

While the DMU per se could never be characterized as a genuinely group-think group, in a more general way the very style of Bush's decision-making technique constituted *institutionalized groupthink* in its most pervasive form. The president would ordinarily (as in the fundamental reaction to 9/11) make decisions quickly, early, and decisively, forcing others within the DMU to follow or be marginalized. This top-down style prevented any serious, critical analysis of options. The personal consequences of opposition to the presidential will as experienced by such a diverse group of people as Eric Shinseki, Paul O'Neill, Lawrence Lindsay, and Colin Powell sent a chilling message in regard to independence of thought within the Bush administration.

The groupthink in the Bush White House, albeit incomplete, was evident particularly when compared with the decision-making style adopted by his predecessor, Bill Clinton. Under Clinton, intense discussion and forceful disagreements were common as the DMU struggled to reach the best possible solution. Stanley Hoffmann, a long-time observer of foreign policy decision making in the United States and in Europe, notes that "the sort of men and women who defined foreign policy around Bill Clinton, and Clinton himself, were, as de Gaulle had said of John F. Kennedy, 'Europeans' with whom one could discuss and with whom one could disagree, but who, despite the difference of power, were actually partners."[54]

This collegial style totally disappeared under Bush. Give-and-take discussion was incompatible with Bush's personality, leadership style, and even ideology. Groupthink affected his administration's use of intelligence reports; reports that contradicted the politically desirable outcome were simply disregarded. "Bush and his aides were looking for intelligence not to guide their policy on Iraq but to market it,"[55] conclude two observers of the Washington scene.

At the center of the DMU was, as usual, the president. But the role of President Bush was not only very significant but also highly negative from the perspective of encouraging and providing an open-ended, deliberative decision-making process, possibly the most important role of the leader facing a complex situation. While the media described Bush as a puppet, all indications are that he actually dominated the process and that he turned himself into a force for radical reaction rather than moderation, harsh rather than reflective action. Thus, immediately after 9/11, Bush, acting on the basis of instinct rather than analysis, pushed his assistants to think about Iraq as the culprit in spite of evidence to the contrary. When Wolfowitz began pushing for the invasion of Iraq, immediately following 9/11, Bush took him aside and told him, "Keep it up, keep it up."[56] Moreover, rather than removing himself from the deliberations and allowing the process to take its course so as to maximize the likelihood of the best possible option or options to emerge, Bush inserted himself into the decision-making process in a highly personalized manner. The president quickly became identified with the most radical position possible, making a real open, deliberative process impossible. For all intents and purposes, a moderate reaction to 9/11 was unthinkable.

Bush's inclination to "go radical" rhetorically rather than reacting in a thoughtful manner was revealed in numerous pronouncements he made, some of them spontaneously and others introduced by his speechwriters. "You are either with us or with the terrorists" (September 2001 to Congress) and "You are either with us or against us" (press conference with French president Jacques Chirac, November 6, 2001) were pronouncements he uttered several times, "using rhetoric that hearkened back to Christ himself in the New Testament— 'He who is not with me is against me.'"[57] The president vowed to take Osama bin Laden "dead or alive," used the term "axis of evil," and so forth. Bravado became a hallmark of the administration.

Bush and his main assistants routinely ignored the professionals who worked for them, thus not merely creating a morale problem among those professionals but also harming the quality of the decisions made. Maybe no other example is more glaring than the debate over the number of troops needed to occupy Iraq. Realists and many top generals favored four hundred thousand or so, but Secretary of Defense Rumsfeld thought seventy-five thousand would be sufficient.[58]

THE BUREAUCRACY

The second circle that needs examination in terms of assessing the foreign policy of the Bush administration is the huge foreign policy, defense, and intelligence bureaucracy in Washington. Inherent in the presidency itself is a major problem stemming from the sheer size of the American bureaucracy, its complexity, and the diversity of opinion on various issues. Every modern president has to struggle with the question of how to exert decisive influence, let alone control, over the large bureaucracy.

In the case of George W. Bush, one might argue that in general two patterns emerged: (1) while President Bush was quite successful in executing his most important decision—the invasion of Iraq—he failed miserably in regard to the effectiveness of some of the major organizations under his control, particularly the Department of Defense and the armed forces, in establishing US rule over Iraq and the intelligence community (especially the CIA) in making a correct call in regard to weapons of mass destruction in Iraq; (2) to the extent to which Bush succeeded in running the bureaucracy, it was done by applying differentiated treatment to different departments or agencies within the bureaucracy, a treatment often determined by the relationships between the president and the particular head of that unit and the ideological congruence between the president and the people running the various departments.[59]

Several patterns could be identified in regard to the bureaucracy and the way it was managed by the Bush White House. Despite some successes, such as bringing down the Saddam regime quickly, there seem to be numerous failures, reflective of a highly flawed process.

The Intelligence Community

From the perspective of an orderly, responsible decision-making process, it is important to note that the intelligence community in the United States, and particularly many at the Central Intelligence Agency, felt totally manipulated, controlled, and intimidated by the Bush White House. This was particularly the feeling in regard to the justification for the Iraq invasion where many CIA officers felt that they were pressured to produce intelligence reports that would fit the political goals of the administration. There is an enormous amount of information and analysis, much of it produced by people directly involved with intelligence work (the type of individuals who rarely express reservations in public), indicating that this perception was unusually widespread. Paul R. Pillar, who was the CIA senior analyst for the Near East and South Asia, wrote a devastating article in the March–April 2006 issue of *Foreign Affairs* in which he accused the Bush administration of "cherry-picking" intelligence to justify the Iraq war.

Pillar argued that the administration went to war without requesting or being influenced by any strategic intelligence assessments on any aspect of the Iraq situation. Decisions on Iraq simply did not rely on intelligence work. In fact, argued Pillar, "intelligence was misused publicly to *justify decisions already made* (emphasis added)."[60] Pillar's arguments justify the conclusion that the Iraq war was ideologically and politically motivated, not based on real security considerations, such as a genuine, imminent threat to the United States.

Eventually the Bush administration and many of its supporters made the CIA and its director, George Tenet, personally the fall guy for Iraq. The argument, which has some validity, was that Tenet was "overconfident, too eager to be a team player" within the Bush administration,[61] a posture that led him to assure the president that there were indeed weapons of mass destruction in Iraq. Ironically, at least one of the leading Neocons, Paul Wolfowitz, admitted publicly that the WMD issue was not the real reason for invading Iraq. Be that as it may, George Tenet, like everyone else, was under enormous pressure to come up with the "right answers" in responding to his political masters. He apparently did.

The worst aspect of the problem was that the intelligence agencies were not allowed to collect the necessary information or to offer their analysis as they saw fit. The White House constantly interfered with the work of the CIA, pressuring it to come up with the "right answers" and produce reports that would support its political preferences on a variety of critical issues: the existence of weapons of mass destruction in Iraq, the link between Saddam Hussein and al-Qaeda, and so on.

The level and intensity of politically motivated pressure on the intelligence agencies were unprecedented, completely destroying the possibility of producing a good decision-making process based on facts rather than political motives.

In order to undermine the ability of the CIA to fulfill its function, the Department of Defense under Rumsfeld established its own intelligence arm in the Pentagon. This unit operated under the leadership of Douglas Feith, one of the most committed Neoconservatives in the US government.

The Department of State

The Department of State has seen two remarkably different periods during the Bush administration. In the first term, when Colin Powell was the secretary of state, the department was generally marginalized, although sometimes it was used for specific purposes (most notably in solving the plane crisis with China in 2001, producing Pakistan after September 11, and justifying to the world the forthcoming Iraq invasion in early 2003). The marginalization of the Department of State was reflected, for example, in two important ways: (1) Of all the top advisers in the field of security and foreign policy (Cheney, Powell, Rumsfeld, Rice), only Powell was systematically kept out of the president's "loop"; only on January 13, 2003, was Powell informed (but not consulted), in a brief, twelve-minute meeting (!), that the president had decided to go to war;[62] even this short meeting occurred only after Rice urged the president to have it.[63] (2) The control of post-Saddam Iraq was given to the Pentagon despite the huge preparatory work done by the Iraq Study Group prior to the invasion.

In looking for the fundamental reasons for the treatment of the Department of State, personal relations and ideological differences come to mind. First, President Bush did not like Powell, a man who enjoyed higher popularity than the president (with the exception of the immediate post-9/11 period). The personal tensions, possibly due to Powell's undiminished popularity, were exacerbated due to Powell's independence and his strong tilt toward Realism and pragmatism. Thus, after September 11, when some Neoconservatives talked publicly about the possible involvement of Iraq in the traumatic events of that day, Powell abruptly contradicted them and did so publicly. The increasingly Neoconservative White House did not look kindly on Powell, and he was eventually let go—in effect fired—when the first term of the Bush presidency came to an end. The Bush-Powell relationship was a typical case for the Bush administration, explainable in straightforward personal and ideological terms.

The relationships between the White House, and Bush personally, and the Department of State became much closer during the second term, when Condoleezza Rice took over as secretary of state. Once again it was demonstrated that with George W. Bush everything was personal. Unlike Powell, Rice was a friend of the president, his foreign policy "tutor," and by no means an independent actor. Although Rice assumed an increasingly Realist foreign policy on a variety of issues, such as recommending negotiations with North Korea,[64] her influence with the president remained significant.

While the treatment of the Department of State was mostly personal (especially when Colin Powell served as secretary) and somewhat ideological, it had a bureaucratic aspect to it as well. In an administration that took a clear militaristic attitude to international affairs, the Department of Defense had to be regarded by the White House as the single most important bureaucratic tool. Under the assertive Donald Rumsfeld, a close friend of Vice President Cheney, it was. President Bush consulted often and early with Rumsfeld, in contrast with his lack of consultations with Rumsfeld's State Department rival, Colin Powell. Bush kept Rumsfeld on the job for as long as he could, despite the widespread perception (shared by many Republicans) that the Pentagon performed unsatisfactorily in Iraq.

To keep an eye on what the independent Powell was doing, the radical anti-internationalist John Bolton was appointed by the Bush White House as undersecretary of state for arms control and international security, a position he occupied until 2005.

Department of Defense

Given the inclination of the Neoconservatives to use military tools, and the solid and increasing support of that group in the highest echelon of the White House, it is no surprise that the Department of Defense was treated so favorably from the very beginning of the Bush administration. This was reflected in the special relationships between Secretary Rumsfeld and Vice President Cheney, the unofficial "czar" of foreign and security policy within the administration, the generous allocations of funds for the Department of Defense,[65] the approval of pet projects like missile defense, and so forth. This favoritism intensified after 9/11.

The most important project for the Pentagon in the first term of George W. Bush (and, in effect, throughout the Bush-43 presidency) was the 2003 Iraq invasion and the ensuing occupation of that country. While the CIA was highly involved in the operation in Afghanistan and performed quite well in deposing the Taliban from power in Kabul, control over the Iraq operation, including postwar reconstruction, was given to the Department of Defense. This was done, and continued, despite the department's enormous failure in establishing law and order in Iraq. Michael O'Hanlon sums it up from a broad historical perspective in the following words: "The post-invasion phase of the Iraq mission has been the least well-planned American military mission since Somalia in

1993, if not Lebanon in 1983, and its consequences for the nation have been far worse than any set of military mistakes since Vietnam."[66] While O'Hanlon emphasizes the partial responsibility of the uniformed officers, there can be no doubt that the ultimate responsibility lies with their civilian chiefs, particularly Rumsfeld and Wolfowitz, and through them, with Bush himself. One aspect that O'Hanlon does not deal with in sufficient detail is the overly optimistic nature of the planning for the Iraq war, rooted in self-righteousness, a sense of moral superiority, and a we-cannot-fail attitude, all characteristics of what Janis identified as groupthink. Those aspects of the Iraq war were also reflective of the fundamental assumptions of Neoconservatism and, particularly, its belief in American hegemony via coercion. Iraq was merely a test case.

Interestingly, even those who supported the Iraq invasion, notably Republican senator John McCain, thought that the implementation of the war by the highest civilian echelons of the Pentagon, particularly Rumsfeld, Wolfowitz, and Feith, revealed an almost unprecedented level of incompetence. While the White House and its Department of Defense allies accused the CIA of being mistaken on the issue of WMD, there was no question that the Pentagon failed to plan for the post-Saddam era by sending a minimal force to Iraq (and that was despite private and public warnings). O'Hanlon describes the planning by the Office of Undersecretary of Defense Douglas Feith, the Pentagon unit responsible for that planning, as "unfocused, shallow, and too dependent on optimistic scenarios that saw Ahmed Chalabi (or perhaps some of Saddam's more moderate generals) taking charge without the need for a strong US role in the stabilization mission."[67]

Nevertheless, despite the enormous failure of the Pentagon in executing the war effectively, it took President Bush over three and a half years to let Rumsfeld go. This was an indication of the president's management style, where personal loyalty and ideological congruence ranked higher than the accomplishment of stated goals.

The decision-making process and leadership style within the DOD was flawed, resembling the decision-making process in the White House. Thus, Rumsfeld behaved in an extremely imperious manner toward his subordinates, including high-ranking generals. Anybody expressing a position incompatible with that of the civilian heads of the department endangered their career and reputation. General Eric Shinseki, the respected army chief of staff, was, in effect, fired after expressing his professional opinion about the size of the forces needed for an effective war in Iraq, an opinion that was eventually proven right. Shinseki was publicly berated and humiliated by his civilian superiors, both Rumsfeld and Wolfowitz. This type of treatment sends chills down the spine of subordinates and guarantees that they will not give their best advice to their superiors.

Maybe the worst part of the Pentagon performance in regard to the Iraq war was *the complete politicization of the campaign.* In order to sell the war to the public, Pentagon officials and outside Neocon pundits minimized the size of the armed forces needed to take Iraq and rule it, the monetary cost of the war, the expected Iraqi opposition to the invading force, the difficulty of bringing up oil production, and so forth. The campaign to convince the public of the necessity of the war and its potential benefit to America and the world was truly unprecedented. The explanation of this behavior, says O'Hanlon, includes "the administration's desire to portray the Iraq war as a relatively easy undertaking in order to assure domestic and international support, the administration's disdain for nation-building, and the Pentagon's unrealistic hope that Ahmed Chalabi and the rather small Iraqi National Congress might somehow assume control of the country after Saddam fell."[68]

While all of these factors might have played a role, the deeper explanation is rooted in the commitment of the top Pentagon leadership (that is, Rumsfeld, Wolfowitz, Feith, and others) to the Neoconservative hegemonic dream and their assumption that such dominance can easily be achieved. Whether President Bush shared this dream from the beginning of his administration or was converted into it after the assaults of September 11, by the time of the Iraq invasion he completely bought into it.

New Bureaucratic Actors

One characteristic of the Bush administration was that it allowed several new or at least irregular actors to be highly involved, and in some cases even control, the foreign policy process. These organizations included the vice president's office (never before exercising the level of influence achieved under Bush), Douglas Feith's intelligence operation in the Department of Defense, and even

Ahmed Chalabi's Iraqi National Congress, deeply connected to important Neoconservatives (such as Richard Perle, Paul Wolfowitz, and others).

Of these organizations, easily the most important was the Office of the Vice President. Under the authoritative, secretive Dick Cheney, this office emerged as the crucial link in the decision-making chain, reflecting once again the close personal and ideological link between President Bush and Vice President Cheney. Some people even came to believe that Cheney was in charge of American foreign policy,[69] although there is no solid evidence to substantiate this claim. Larry Wilkerson, who served as Colin Powell's chief of staff, thought that "the Iraq war was produced by an almost parallel foreign policy apparatus run not by the National Security Council but by the extraordinarily influential Office of the Vice President."[70] Whether this was the case or not, what one can say with confidence is that the vice president enjoyed enormous influence with George W. Bush and that he was at the very center of the group that pushed for the invasion of Iraq in 2003. In doing so, the vice president and his assistants were relentless, arguing that such action was necessary in terms of both weapons of mass destruction and a link to international terrorism, while ignoring the worldwide opposition to the impending operation.

A large staff of professionals, including some key Neocons such as Scooter Libby (Cheney's chief of staff) and David Wurmser (Cheney's Middle East adviser), were among the most active members of this new governmental unit established around the vice president. By creating what looked like a mini–National Security Council in his office, with a dozen national security specialists of unusually high caliber, Cheney was able to achieve enormous influence.[71] Not only was he, by the power of his official position and close personal relations with Bush, the chief counselor to the president, but he had at his fingertips a bureaucratic machinery pushing his ideas in the highest echelons of the US government. By any measure, the power given to the vice president in the Bush administration was without precedent in American history. The events of September 11, 2001, allowed the vice president to make full use of that power.

The main goal of the vice president and people working for him following 9/11 was to initiate the Iraq invasion. To achieve this goal, certain evidence had to be produced: that Saddam had weapons of mass destruction and that he had substantial links with the al-Qaeda terrorist network. If those "facts" could be established, Saddam's regime could have been presented as an imminent threat to the United States, thus justifying a preemptive strike. The problem was that those "facts" were invented. The CIA could not substantiate those claims. Therefore, in the period leading to Iraq, Cheney made frequent visits to CIA headquarters in Langley, Virginia, demanding answers on Iraq's weapon programs and the country's ties to terrorists. Both Cheney and Wolfowitz were preoccupied, even obsessed, with Iraq.[72] There is no evidence that Bush was trying to stop them; in fact, all indications are that he shared their view that an invasion of Iraq was necessary.

It seems that in the prelude to the invasion of Iraq, the machinery of US foreign policy broke down. The in-group in the White House, quarterbacked by Cheney, was determined to go to war with Iraq. Yet, the data collected by the CIA—particularly in regard to weapons of mass destruction and links to terrorism—did not support the conclusion that war was justified and necessary. Two alternative interpretations are possible. First, Cheney, Rumsfeld, and Wolfowitz did not trust the CIA's intelligence-gathering capabilities.[73] Second, members of the "war party" in Washington understood that they could not produce the CIA and, thus, did everything in their power to reduce the agency's power. The second interpretation is more convincing. "Cheney and Rumsfeld were men used to getting their way, even if it meant trampling over colleagues."[74]

The vice president's office was involved in the controversial outing of Valerie Plame Wilson, a CIA operative on weapons of mass destruction.[75] It was part and parcel of a huge operation designed to mislead the public on the issue of these weapons.

THE POLITICAL CLASS

Beyond the decision-making unit (circle 1) and the bureaucratic structures (circle 2), in order to convince the country to go to war against Iraq and to adopt other planks of its foreign policy, the Bush administration needed to get substantial support from what one might call America's political class. This political class—organizations and individuals actively interested in foreign policy issues—included at least three primary elements: elected officials (and particularly members of the Senate and the House of Representatives), the mass media (and primarily the main news organizations, either electronic or printed), and think tanks around the country (but primarily in Washington).

Congress

As argued in this chapter, the events of September 11, 2001, have created anomalies in the decision-making process within the Bush administration. Yet anomalies were created in other places within the American political system as well. One crucial organization that seemed to change under the impact of the terrorist attacks was the US Congress. In the post-9/11 era, Congress became unusually supportive of the White House.

Without going into a detailed analysis of congressional politics in the post-9/11 era, it is interesting to note that, in effect, the US Congress gave the president a blank check in terms of going to war in Iraq. While this was not the first blank check ever issued by Congress, it was quite remarkable in view of several facts: (1) There was no real, hard evidence that Iraq posed an imminent threat to the United States. (2) Unlike Vietnam, when a blank check was given to President Lyndon Johnson, the Iraqi regime was not supported by any hostile country posing a threat to the United States, and surely not by any major country (though North Vietnam was supported by the Soviet Union and China). (3) Bush's reputation with many people in Congress was questionable, although his popularity soared after September 11. (4) World public opinion was united against war in Iraq. The congressional support for the Iraq war was bipartisan, while the support for the first Gulf War was mostly limited to the Republicans. It is interesting to note in this context that the relatively limited military interventions on the part of the Clinton administration (in Somalia, Haiti, Bosnia, Kosovo) also received limited support.

The willingness of Congress to follow rather than to lead in the area of foreign policy and defense was quite compatible with the Neoconservative "belief that foreign affairs are the prerogative of the executive branch and that Congress and the public should be only minimally involved and selectively informed."[76] The Neoconservatives' roots in the Vietnam War were crucial in determining their position on the desired marginality of Congress and the public in regard to initiatives taken by the Bush administration.

So why did Congress act as it did, authorizing in a bipartisan vote (October 11, 2002) the use of force? Because of the fear of senators and representatives of the wrath of the public if they acted against the will of the president. It is interesting to note in this context that the vote was scheduled to take place about three weeks prior to the midterm elections.

In general terms, it could be argued that the events of September 11 simply paralyzed the Congress, practically neutralizing the foundational constitutional idea of checks and balances.

The Media

When it comes to the decision to invade Iraq, and other decisions claimed by the Bush administration as part of the War on Terrorism, the American media was exceptionally nonaggressive and nonprobing in questioning the administration's decisions. The intimidation factor of 9/11 was substantial; among many journalists there was a feeling that questioning the administration's motives or modus operandi would be unpatriotic or perceived as such. Even ex–White House spokesman Scott McClellan commented in his recent book on this phenomenon, maintaining that the press corps was too accepting of the administration's perspective on the Iraq war.[77]

When the magnitude of the Iraq debacle became clear, the media began to shift toward a more critical view of the war and the overall decision-making process of the Bush administration. Self-criticism came from the *New York Times*, which in many of its prewar stories (e.g., those written by Judith Miller) bought the government's line on weapons of mass destruction in Iraq, the link between Saddam Hussein and al-Qaeda, and so forth. Even Bob Woodward, the most famous journalist at the *Washington Post*, "acknowledged that he was part of the 'groupthink' that helped sell the war," and famed reporter and anchorman Dan Rather of CBS "admitted that there was no excuse for his own performance in this regard."[78]

Think Tanks

Supporters of the Iraq war and the Neoconservative foreign policy line in general were exceptionally well endowed with the support of think tanks in the nation's capital and beyond. Among their more prominent supporters one can find such important Washington-based institutions as the Heritage Foundation, the American Enterprise Institute, and the Hudson Institute, the 1997-established Project for the New American Century that was organized by Neoconservative leaders Bill Kristol and Robert Kagan, the Center for Security Policy, and many others (including the Hoover Institution in California). Moreover, the administration's policies were powerfully supported by numerous publications such as the *National Interest,* Norman Podhoretz's *Commentary,* Bill Kristol's the *Weekly Standard,* the establishmentarian *Wall Street Journal,* the *Washington Times,* and so forth.

AMERICAN AND WORLD PUBLIC OPINION

By and large, the Bush administration succeeded in convincing most Americans that the Iraq invasion was urgently necessary and justified. The arguments used by the administration—Saddam Hussein's violations of UN resolutions with regard to weapon inspections inside Iraq, his ambition to possess weapons of mass destruction or his actual possession of them, and his aid or potential aid to terrorists—persuaded most Americans to go along with President Bush. The fears generated by 9/11 created a hospitable environment for the Neoconservative rationale. "The United States went into Iraq with a higher level of domestic support for war than at almost any time in its history,"[79] a political environment that was skillfully produced by the administration.

Several factors worked in favor of broad public support for the Iraq invasion in addition to the fear factor. Public officials—including Bush and Cheney, Rumsfeld and Rice—spoke often and strongly about the alleged imminent danger posed by the Iraqi regime, some of them using the powerful imagery of a nuclear attack on the United States in order to persuade public opinion to move their way. Of particular importance in this regard was the presentation of Secretary of State Colin Powell to the United Nations Security Council; while it might not have convinced world public opinion to support the impending invasion, it surely clinched such support from the American people.

Another reason for the public support for the invasion was that both administration officials and Neocon supporters outside the administration argued that toppling Saddam Hussein, occupying Iraq, and installing a pro-American regime in Baghdad would be an easy task, accomplished with small investment of resources. One proponent of the invasion twice described the invasion as a "cakewalk,"[80] the postinvasion reconstruction cost was envisioned as insignificant, and projections for the expected and huge revenues of Iraqi oil were publicly made.[81] Although those rosy depictions of the forthcoming war were based on the ease of winning the first Gulf War (1990 to 1991) and the Kosovo War in the former Yugoslavia, they were grossly inaccurate with regard to Iraq in 2003. Be that as it may, circle 4 was secured for the administration's decision to go into Iraq.

Securing the support of world public opinion proved a lot tougher. In fact, it failed miserably. When Bush left the White House in January 2009, his popularity in the world was as low as that of any American president. Although non-Americans are, of course, not part of the American political system, informally they are an important constituency that any US president has to take into account.

Members of the Bush administration almost went out of their way to ignore and sometimes insult non-Americans, particularly but not exclusively in the context of the Iraq war (thus, the Kyoto decision and the one on the International Criminal Court were as offensive to Europeans as the Iraq decision). The unilateral use of American military power has been part of the ideology of Neoconservatism. Yet, in the Iraq war, and particularly following the occupation of Iraq, this ideological position came to damage the reputation of the United States and undermine its legitimacy.

CHAPTER 6

LESSONS FOR FUTURE
PRESIDENTS

America and the World Beyond Bush and Neoconservatism

By the end of 2008, on the eve of President Bush's departure from the White House, the foreign policy of the United States was somewhat in disarray. The War on Terror was inconclusive in Iraq and deteriorating in Afghanistan and in neighboring Pakistan. America's financial debt increased as its economy declined. Peace between Israelis and Palestinians looked as far away as ever. Above all, since 2001 the United States had lost incalculably in terms of its reputation for responsible leadership, prestige, and legitimacy. When presidential candidate Barack Obama traveled to Germany, France, and the United Kingdom in the summer of 2008, he was met with hundreds of thousands of enthusiastic citizens and scores of politicians. The subliminal message of the Europeans was unmistakable—let the Bush presidency end so that a new agenda for the United States and the world could be adopted.

Interestingly, the foreign policy of the Bush administration began to change toward the end of the administration's tenure in office. The closer to the finish line, the more consultative, cooperationist, and multilateral the administration became. These changes were demonstrated in policies toward Iran (sending an American negotiator to Europe), Iraq (accepting the notion of a "time horizon" for eventual withdrawal), North Korea (reaching a negotiated deal with the regime), the Israeli-Palestinian issue (pushing for an agreement), and so forth. These initiatives reflected several possible changes: (1) a real understanding by the administration or elements within it of the mistakes committed;[1] (2) the decline of the Neoconservative faction within the administration and especially out of the administration and the strengthening of the Realists under Secretary of State Condoleezza Rice;[2] (3) a cold, calculated look by George W. Bush at his historical legacy and his determination to have at least some concrete achievements before he departed Washington.

This chapter will attempt to draw lessons from the Bush administration's tenure in office and particularly from its early, vigorous adoption and application of the Neoconservative philosophy to American foreign policy. While those lessons will touch on all levels of analysis—the international system (chapter 2), the individual level (chapter 4), and the decision-making level (chapter 5)—most of the analysis in the first half of this chapter will focus on the ideological characteristics of Neoconservatism and the extent to which those ought to be reaffirmed or rejected in the future.

As a political philosophy, Neoconservatism has been at the center of American foreign policy since George W. Bush's ascendance to the presidency. Like other right-wing crusades in American history, such as Joseph McCarthy's anti-communist campaign of the 1950s, Neoconservatism did not come under close or extensive scrutiny until it began to falter politically.[3] It is important to note that many of the people associated with the Neoconservative ideology have continued to offer positive commentary about the fundamentals of the movement and its implications for the future, as might indeed be expected.[4] On the other hand, public analyses by such Neoconservatives as Francis Fukuyama,[5] Robert Kagan,[6] and Ben Wattenberg[7] have tended to reflect a different tone, sometimes implicitly apologetic and on occasion openly critical of that movement.

Among the Neoconservatives, one of the most interesting individuals has been Francis Fukuyama, an influential commentator with a rich Neoconservative past.[8] In 1989, as the Cold War came to an end, Fukuyama published an important article[9] and then a book (1992),[10] both titled "The End of History." In those heavily quoted works he offered an altogether positive, even triumphalist assessment of the victory of Western, capitalist, liberal democracy. Moreover, during the 1990s Fukuyama was clearly identified with the Neoconservatives, supportive of such important events for the movement as the establishment of the Project for the New American Century (1997) and the publication of the Iraq letter to President Clinton (1998). Fukuyama continued to support a hard line after 9/11, signing the public letter to President George W. Bush on September 20, 2001, which endorsed action against the Saddam regime.

But beginning in 2002, as the Bush administration unmistakably started to push the United States toward the Iraq invasion, Fukuyama had an ideological change of heart. He became increasingly critical of the foreign policy of the Bush administration, particularly its unilateralist and militaristic bent, and of the position taken by his fellow Neoconservatives in support of that policy.

Most important, in his book *America at the Crossroads*, Fukuyama argues that in its invasion of Iraq, the Bush administration misinterpreted the Neoconservative legacy. This is a strange argument, in view of the fact that the invasion of Iraq seemed to respond quite precisely to the demands of the Neoconservatives and that numerous Neoconservatives actually served in prominent positions in the Bush administration.[11]

It is important to note that Fukuyama's disagreement with the Neoconservatives and the policies of the Bush administration was not primarily over the incompetence of the implementation of the war plans in Iraq, although he was critical of these as well. Rather, Fukuyama's bone of contention with Bush and the Neocons was a *principled disagreement* with the policies themselves. Fukuyama was particularly critical of the strategic doctrine of preemption that he viewed as, in fact, a preventive war. This policy shift was at the very center of the Bush Doctrine, as well as at the center of the Neoconservative ideology of regime change. Fukuyama was also critical of what he viewed as the "obsession" of the Neocons with regime change in Iraq, with the unilateral nature of American action, with the promotion of the notion of benevolent hegemony, and with other key elements of Neoconservatism as applied by the Bush administration.

Fukuyama eventually reached the conclusion that the Iraq invasion discredited "the entire Neoconservative agenda" and restored authority to the Realists.[12] His powerful analysis reflects a deep sense of frustration and self-doubt within the movement. If foreign policy prescription can be judged by its results, then Neoconservatism has been a huge failure.

NEOCONSERVATISM UNDER THE MICROSCOPE FOR A BETTER FUTURE

Chapter 3 of this volume offers a detailed analysis of Neoconservatism in terms of eight of its more pronounced components. It could be useful to now offer an assessment of the future of American foreign policy in terms of each of those ideological components.

Patriotic and Nationalist Philosophy

One the most notable characteristics of all Neoconservative writings has been its patriotic, nationalist flavor. Already in the 1960s, despite their early emphasis on domestic politics and policies, would-be Neoconservatives (not yet known by that name) condemned the anti-Vietnam movement as anti-American, lacking in patriotism and love of country.[13] The Bush administration adopted a similar line when it came to power and carried it forward throughout its eight-year tenure in Washington. This commitment to what was sometimes defined as the "American interest" was reflected in the interventionist policy against regimes considered tyrannical and anti-American. Tyrannical and pro-American regimes such as Egypt and Saudi Arabia, or even nondemocratic but somewhat neutral regimes such as China and Russia, were not targeted for intervention.

It is important to understand that the Neoconservatives have always been, above all, "men of power"[14] but that, above all, they saw power as an instrument for imposing America's will on the world. That is to say, even though some Neocons started as revolutionaries on behalf of cosmopolitan ideologies, by the 1960s they were already committed American nationalists. Nationalism was evident in the positions taken by the Neocons during the Bush administration.

As for the future of American foreign policy, it is generally *unwise* to define US goals in *purely patriotic and nationalist goals*. Several of America's closest allies, particularly countries in western and northern Europe, all thriving democracies, no longer define their interests in pure nationalistic terms. A narrow definition of "US interests" of the type represented by both the Neoconservatives and the Bush administration is simply not "marketable" anymore, nor is it acceptable by most Europeans as a basis for the US leadership position. Ironically, while both the Bush administration and its Neocon supporters pushed the narrow definition of US national interest and justified it in patriotic terms, such a definition is greatly dysfunctional for the sole remaining superpower. Thus, the rationale used by Bush and the Neoconservatives was self-defeating and is likely to remain so in the future.

The foundational rationale for American foreign policy, particularly in regard to key political decisions, ought to be more general so as to appeal to people in the West and beyond. The definition and development of such a rationale is necessary for the American "escape" from the kind of ideological isolation that the country suffered as a result of the Iraq war.

Radicalism

The Neoconservative philosophy and rhetoric, and the policy of the Bush administration carried on the basis of that philosophy and confrontational style, smacked of radical politics.[15] Incrementalism, compromise, gradualism, pragmatism—part and parcel of much of the American political tradition—were rejected in favor of fundamentalism, confrontation, and above all the deep rejection of the status quo. Although Bush revealed only a limited tendency to support the Neoconservative attitude prior to 9/11, that tendency became an overwhelming avalanche following the terrorist attacks.

The continuation of such radicalism could be detrimental for the interests of the United States in the future. With the United States as the natural leader of the West, the democratic-capitalist world, and the transatlantic alliance, most people in the world look for *American moderation and deliberative rationality*. This was particularly the attitude among Europeans after 9/11. In fighting against those who saw it as reflecting a radical image, the Bush administration defined its opponents as "Old Europe" versus the allegedly pro-American "New Europe." In reality, however, in all parts of Europe, the vast majority of the people opposed what they clearly identified as American radicalism. Another verbal trick by Neoconservatives and, more specifically, supporters of the Iraq war was to accuse their opponents of being appeasers or even disloyal traitors. The historical analogies and extreme confrontational language used by the Neocons—a technique that had for a long time characterized magazines such as *Commentary*, the *National Interest*, and the *Weekly Standard*—strengthened their radical image and that of their allies in the Bush administration.

The ultimate failure of such debate tactics and the policies they promoted ought to be a warning for the future. By sheer size, inventive ingenuity, and openness America is destined to lead the world, but if and only if it can project itself as a thoughtful, deliberative, well-informed, and above all moderate leader. The fundamentally revolutionary character of Neoconservatism did not allow the Bush administration to lead by moderation, but in the post-Bush era the United States might be able to revive this model.

At the same time, it seems as if during the second Bush term, his administration began to move away from the radicalism of the first term. Thus, for example, regime change through preventive war was sidelined.[16] More cooperation with allies and even negotiations with rivals (North Korea) were also notable. Although the reputation of the United States was seriously damaged, those changes were well received.

Militarism

Of all the ideological movements in the post–World War II era, Neoconservatism was the strongest, most enthusiastic supporter of the widespread, frequent use of America's superior military power. Many Neocons argued for the use of power as an instrument of spreading democracy (as was done by the French Republic after the Revolution); others argued for the promotion of American security through the disarming of dangerous rivals. The Bush administration used, interchangeably, all of these rationales. Moreover, it revised the traditional defensive posture of a status quo–oriented America to a fundamentally offensive stance of a revolutionary America in search of global hegemony.

The overuse of the military option backfired. While in the past, limited military intervention in places like Bosnia and Kosovo, or even Somalia and Haiti, was marginally acceptable to many people (often despite vocal complaints), power projection via massive invasion of a country that did not attack the United States and had no capacity to do so was clearly unacceptable to many. The Bush Doctrine of not only preemption but, in fact, prevention—while promoted in theory by the Neocons for years—met with almost unanimous global rejection. Moreover, the Bush administration also negated the Caspar Weinberger–Colin Powell doctrine (developed under Republican administrations) that required the use of American power only under highly restrictive conditions as a last resort, the use of overwhelming military force, a clear-cut exit strategy, well-defined military objectives, and strong support by the American people and Congress.[17] The Iraq war violated all of these provisions.

It is possible, as well as necessary, for a future president to *reverse the highly militaristic Bush Doctrine and to adopt a much more restrictive use of the military option than the one deployed by the forty-third president and his associates.* The de-militarization of American defense and foreign policy could be achieved via the reaffirmation of the American commitment to fight international terrorism (al-beit in close cooperation with other countries) and the reassertion of the right of the United States to defend itself against an armed attack[18] and even to pre-empt such an attack in certain situations. At the same time, the United States should declare that it has no intention of launching preventive strikes against, let alone invading, other countries, and surely not for the sake of regime change and democratization. While Neoconservative writings and the policies of the Bush administration reflect strong preference for the use of America's military might, future administrations must reaffirm the country's commitment to inter-national law, international organizations, and nonaggression. Such a policy shift is likely to gain the United States at least some of the legitimacy it lost during the Bush years.

In George W. Bush the Neoconservatives found a president willing to use the enormously powerful armed forces of the United States for their ideologi-cal, imperial goals. Although previous Republican presidents—including Nixon and Ford, Reagan and George H. W. Bush—were reluctant to use and overuse America's power projection capabilities, such reluctance was not evi-dent during the years of Bush-43 in the White House.

Future presidents of any party might well want to consider a shift from an emphasis on the use of military force to alternative methods of influence—that is, diplomatic and economic modes of influence. Such a shift is likely to be more acceptable and more legitimate to the rest of the world, thus increasing Amer-ica's impact on world politics. The Neoconservatives and many in the Bush ad-ministration had a tendency to "treat power—raw, military power—as the alpha and omega of American interaction with the world;"[19] future administra-tions will need to significantly expand the American repertoire.

Exceptionalism

Neoconservative writers based much of their analyses of American foreign pol-icy, and specifically their recommendations in regard to that foreign policy, on the notion of US exceptionalism. Like many others before them, they tended to argue that America was unique and superior to other nations, particularly because of its democratic values, social and economic freedoms, and so forth. Exceptionalist arguments came to dominate Bush's policies after 9/11 and the justification for those policies. The so-called War on Terror, the military intervention in Afghanistan, and the Iraq invasion were justified primarily not as necessary in terms of US national interest and security needs but, equally important, as reflecting America's fundamental values. Bush's crusade was designed to create a new world in America's image, the ultimate exceptionalist dream.

The language of exceptionalism employed by the Bush administration proved to be an unreliable crutch for US foreign policy, an important lesson for the future. First, one cannot coerce other societies to adopt America's values, including democracy; if those values are to be adopted by other societies, it might happen gradually and from "below," not abruptly and from "above" (let alone dictated from the "outside"). Second, many of the key countries for America's national interest (such as Egypt, Jordan, and Saudi Arabia) are far from reflecting America's values; pressuring them publicly to do so might backfire, as it already did. Third, presenting America as exceptional and superior is the ultimate turnoff, weakening the country's soft power rather than strengthening it. Fourth, the marriage of idealist exceptionalism—that is, the selling of American values—and coercive military action, which has been the ultimate formula offered to the world by both the Neoconservatives and the Bush administration, looked to many observers to be fundamentally dishonest and hypocritical. The perception was that the United States was pushing its national interest, particularly in terms of military presence and control over oil, while using "values" to cover up its real intentions.

Future administrations will need to rethink both the rationale and the presentation of "exceptionalism" as promoted by the Bush administration and its Neocon supporters. "President Bush and his senior political advisers added to the problems faced by the United States by miscalculating the appeal of American exceptionalism and democracy to other countries."[20] Moreover, the president and his advisers never learned from experience and never changed their views. The Neoconservatives in particular pushed the envelope as far as it could be pushed by arguing for the establishment of global benevolent hegemony, combining America's dominance with its presumed benefits for the dominated.

One way of presenting a more genuine and attractive model to the world is by separating as much as possible the American governmental ideal—democracy, equality, social and economic freedoms—from its foreign policy, and to commit to the principle that the domestic ideal will not dictate the international agenda and behavior.

Global interventionism based on messianic exceptionalism, even if presented in the name of promoting freedom, is a recipe for endless conflict and strife, surely not the real promotion of democracy. It is reflective of arrogance and is viewed by the world as arrogant.[21] While Bush's policies were based on exceptionalist rationale, there is no evidence that they were effective in either promoting American values or US material interests. A new administration will need to desert both the language and the attitude adopted by the Bush administration.

Optimism and Pessimism

The vast Neoconservative literature has presented an interesting mixture of pessimism and optimism; this mixture was fully reflected in the rhetoric and behavior of the Bush administration. This hybrid, sometimes surprising combination needs to be replaced in the future with a more realistic, pragmatic position.

On the one hand most Neoconservative ideologues and many Bush administration officials tended to look at the international political system very pessimistically—a war of all against all with no possibility for genuine cooperation, the necessity of using military force to promote one's interests, the uselessness and irrelevance of international law, and so forth. On the other hand, both the Neoconservatives and Bush administration officials, including the president himself, believed optimistically that eventually the United States would prevail by converting the world to its own, superior ways.

Interestingly, while in the past American optimism, rooted deeply in the country's sense of exceptionalism, was often (although not always) accompanied by a pragmatic approach to complex international conflicts,[22] such pragmatism could hardly be found in the Bush administration's approach to foreign policy. In fact, in most cases the president and his top officials demonstrated lack of pragmatic flexibility and openness, as well as a tendency to stick to their strong ideological positions. If pragmatism is characterized by the willingness to accept compromise with long-term rivals, then the Bush administration was most of the time nonpragmatic. While the administration talked an optimistic language, it was guided most of the time by a highly pessimistic, Hobbesian attitude toward the world. In the mind of the president and his Neoconservative supporters, military power was the ultimate arbiter of the relations between countries.

As for the future, any American administration will have to desert the pessimistic view of the Neocons and their allies in the Bush administration in order to promote the real interests of the United States in the international arena. Close cooperation among nations of the world, particularly among those who share similar political values and a similar level of economic development, is not only possible but necessary and mutually beneficial. Yet such cooperation must be based on a measure of trust and a fundamentally more optimistic perspective than the one presented by the Bush administration.

To the extent that Neoconservatives expressed a sense of optimism about the world, and specifically about achieving the goals of American foreign policy, such sentiment was reflective of the triumphalist attitude of the post–Cold War era. Francis Fukuyama's thesis that liberal democracy had prevailed in the contest of ideas and that no ideological alternative to it was likely to develop[23] was fully accepted by the Neoconservatives. Moreover, it was applied, somewhat indiscriminately, to the rest of the world. The invasion of Iraq became a sort of test case, with the Neoconservatives justifying it in ideological terms as an exercise in "democracy-spreading." But not only was the Iraq case a generalized case of overoptimistic zealotry, but it was accompanied by numerous overly optimistic predictions on the part of both the Neocons and Bush administration officials. The collective euphoria of both groups came to be symbolized by the "Mission Accomplished" speech (May 1, 2003) by the president while standing on the deck of the aircraft carrier *Abraham Lincoln*.

This desertion of traditional, pragmatic realism in favor of overly optimistic utopianism[24] or alternatively undue pessimism will need to be changed by future American presidents. Foreign policy must be carefully calibrated to avoid strict ideological fixtures that are devoid of any reality.

Imperial Universalism

The second inaugural address by President Bush, delivered in January 2005, reflected what might be called imperial universalism, the idea that the United States has a universal message and that this message has unlimited, global, imperial application. Many Neoconservatives and Bush administration officials "argued that the United States should actively deploy its overwhelming military, economic, and political might to remake the world in its image, and that doing so would serve the interests of other countries as well as the United States,"[25] thus expressing openly the imperial universalist credo. Neoconservatism has believed in that particular "truth" for decades, and President Bush seemed not only to have bought this message but even to have given it theological validation. The intensity of Bush's adoption of America's imperial mission was something of an innovation.

Universalism has been, of course, part and parcel of America's self-perception for generations, in many ways even legitimizing the American political system itself.[26] Yet it was carried further by the Bush administration than by any other administration, because under Bush the sense of imperial universalism—the belief that the American model is universally applicable—was combined with the superior military power of the United States. It is interesting to note in that context that both Bush-41 and Bill Clinton resisted the calls to promote the American imperial universalism as far as it could go, despite the fact that also during their presidencies the United States enjoyed enormous military dominance. Such was not the case under George W. Bush.

This comparison suggests that future presidents should be able to resist the temptation of imperial universalism despite America's continued military advantage. The loss of a substantial amount of legitimacy under Bush-43, particularly as a consequence of the 2003 Iraq invasion, might serve as an impetus for future presidents to avoid the overuse of America's imperial universalism.

While the promotion of democracy under Bush was not all that different from its promotion under other presidents, the means chosen by the forty-third president were very different. Woodrow Wilson, for example, was committed to the democratization project but, at the same time, promoted self-determination, the League of Nations, and international law, ideals that were as far from George W. Bush's as possible. The means chosen by Bush were the use of military force, supported by the so-called coalition of the willing, and in direct opposition to international law and organizations. While Wilson (as well as Jimmy Carter) were internationalists, Bush represented a nationalist strand among American universalists, somewhat of a contradiction in terms.

In promoting a narrow American interest under the banner of universalism, Bush and his Neoconservative ideological supporters revealed a fundamental lack of understanding of the current international system. It is a system that resists the imperial thrust of Great Powers and makes them pay a heavy price—in terms of legitimacy—if and when they decide to use their power anyway. It is not a system that allows the exportation of values through military force, and surely not unilateral force. Future presidents will ignore these lessons at their peril.

Conversion and Evangelism

Members of the Bush administration, including the president himself as well as his Neoconservative supporters, have carried the universalistic, imperial message one logical step further—trying to convert others to the American message. Neoconservatives have always believed that others have to be converted to what they regard as a universal truth, even by the force of arms. For Wolfowitz and others the message of US foreign policy has never been merely or even mainly about narrow, material American national interest but about morality. After September 11 the president picked up this same line, explaining his policies in terms of values more than in terms of interests. He often injected religious themes into his speeches.

As argued in chapter 3, the president and his supporters focused on four messages, all linked logically to one another: America is different (exceptionalism); it is right (moralism); it shall prevail (optimism); it must covert others to its ways (evangelism).[27] The war in Iraq serves as a good example for this type of logic. Two observers of the Washington scene called this "a faith-based war."[28] The Bush administration executed this war not merely to eliminate a challenger to America's predominant position but also in order to convert Iraq, and then the rest of the Middle East, into a democratic region. The president himself framed the campaign as a morality play of good versus evil, and the defeat of Iraq was supposed to begin the conversion of the entire Muslim world.

The next president of the United States will need to revisit and reframe this particular morality play. While defeating international terrorism has been a universal goal shared by all nations, the vast majority of world public opinion has resented the religious language of the Bush administration and its paternalistic tone. The support for democratic values is enormous, but for those to be exported, the evangelical rhetoric needs to be deserted. Future leaders of the United States will need to resist what Walter Lippman called "the persistent evangel in Americanism."[29]

Unilateralism

The administration of George W. Bush possibly was the most unilateralist administration in the history of the United States, implementing important new initiatives with no serious consultation with America's allies. While many observers linked this attitude to the trauma of 9/11, a full-fledged unilateral style was already established during the preceding eight months. "Even before the attacks of September 11, 2001, the administration revealed deep suspicion of international law,"[30] viewing it as limiting the ability of the United States to use force as it saw fit. While, in fact, the 2001 terrorist attacks actually would have enabled the administration to establish new, more cooperative relationships with other countries, this route was never fully explored as an idea, let alone taken.

It is in the area of cooperation with other nations that a new president might want to introduce the most dramatic changes in American foreign policy. The Neocon position that America simply does not need to cooperate with others since it is the strongest country in the world proved dysfunctional. The tasks on the agenda of the United States and the world are simply too enormous to be carried out by America alone, particularly given the nature of the contemporary international system.[31]

The only logic for the continuation of unilateralism is if the United States wants to maintain the pursuit of change in the world's status quo, as it did during the Bush administration.[32] If, on the other hand, a new grand strategy is to be adopted (see below), and if its goals are to enhance stability in an inherently unstable world, then American unilateralism ought to be given a public burial.

The Neoconservatives were by ideology and nature radical unilateralists. Their attitude found a fertile ground in the Bush administration—so much so that they have not merely been able to steer the country in a unilateralist direction, but were successful in gaining appointments for their ideological brothers, even for sensitive positions that required close cooperation with other nations. Maybe the best example for that kind of "achievement" was the nomination of John Bolton as the American ambassador to the United Nations, an appointment that was made after a long period of damaging unilateralism.

The ideological position of the Neocons in regard to cooperation with other nations was multifaceted; as such, it impacted the policies of the Bush administration in many areas. Thus, in regard to military interventions, the administration's unilateral position reigned supreme, as demonstrated in both the cases of Afghanistan (despite the willingness of allies to assist America) and Iraq. A similar position was adopted in regard to international agreements and institutions. The Neoconservatives and members of the Bush administration viewed those as limiting rather than securing American power.[33] It is interesting to note in this context that the 9/11 experience strengthened unilateralism rather than weakening it.

A new administration in Washington will have to look particularly closely at relations with allies in the post-Bush era. The Bush-43 administration showed disdain toward traditional European allies, and it looked to punish them for not going along with America's plans.[34] It was a clear deviation from the policies of Bush-41 and Bill Clinton, the other two post–Cold War presidents.[35] A return to the level of cooperation during those presidents' tenure ought to be reestablished.

A New Grand Strategy for America and the World

A review of this volume, covering the foreign policy of the Bush administration, ought to lead us to the conclusion that dramatic and fundamental changes in American foreign policy are necessary. Nothing short of a new American grand strategy must be implemented if for no other reason than "Americans are now disenchanted with Neoconservatism as a foreign-policy doctrine . . . the idea of muscular, unilaterally imposed democratization" that was believed to resonate with American values in a post-9/11 world."[36]

At the center of any new grand strategy there ought to be an attitudinal prism and a series of initiatives that are likely to improve the current situation of American foreign policy by changing it in a fundamental way. A new grand strategy ought to be based on the argument that the Bush presidency left the United States in a substantially weaker position than it has been for a long time; the foreign policy of George W. Bush was "a catastrophic failure" that is "disputed by none today except for a dwindling number of diehards on the neoconservative right."[37] If America is to restore its reputation, prestige, legitimacy, and, most important, its *capacity to lead the world into a better future*, fundamental changes in its foreign policy are essential.

The following grand strategy includes several elements, some procedural in nature but most of them substantive.[38] Those proposed elements address problems on all levels of American foreign policy and deal with both domestic and international dimensions. The grand strategy is formulated as a set of general rules that the United States should explore and possibly implement:

1. Minimize the probability of disastrous self-fulfilling situations by improving the decision-making process. If disastrous situations always follow the wrong definition of the situation, as happened under the Neoconservatives and George W. Bush (chapter 1), how may we avoid them in the future or minimize their probability? A few ideas might be considered, including the following: (a) seek actively *several alternative definitions to any new challenge* (something that was never done openly or quietly by the Bush White House); (b) avoid ideological unity within the decision-making unit, let alone a coercive decision-making process controlled by a single faction within the administration or even a single individual (including the president); (c) think systematically about the long-term consequences of any definition of a new challenge;[39] and (d) avoid overreaction to manageable problems by adopting radical solutions, especially if such solutions involve the use of military force (given that military force tends to produce irreversible results and is generally unpredictable). While those "rules" are general in character, they ought to be applied to any serious challenge to US foreign policy in the future.

   In the case of the Bush administration, foreign policy after 9/11 was framed as a *generalized, timeless "war on terror"*; this image became the one and only acceptable definition of the challenge by the White House, the US bureaucracy, and large segments of the American public. The definition of the situation as "war" required the dispatch of large armies to defeat the "enemy" (in itself ill defined) or anyone presumably associated with the enemy, even if their link to the actual attackers of 9/11 was tenuous and unproven. Alternative definitions of the challenge were not sought or automatically

rejected, ideological unity around the president's definition was strictly en-
forced, and the long-term consequences of the "war" were not assessed.
Thus, 9/11 could have been *alternatively defined as a single attack by a small
terrorist organization* that could be dealt with via law-enforcement and intelligence operations.[40] Under such definition, regimes associated with that organization could have been contained through America's and the West's
superior power, in cooperation with the international community. An operation authorized by the United Nations or even conducted under UN aus-
pices could have been aimed at arresting persons associated with al-Qaeda
and bringing them before an international court.[41] In defining and fighting
the "war on terror" the way it has, the United States lost credibility in the
eyes of the world, found itself in conflict with many of its allies, generated in-
cohesion at home as well as the loss of enormous human and material resources, and probably created more rather than less terrorism. The *lesson for
the future* is that, while we might never be sure that our definition of the situation is correct, we need to minimize the probability of incorrect definitions
by an improved decision-making process.

2. Demilitarize American foreign policy. Rather then viewing the post–Cold
War era as chaotic, dangerous, and threatening (as some Realist observers
have done),[42] or alternatively as opening an opportunity for the extensive
and even unlimited use of American power (as done by the Neoconservatives),[43] the end of the Cold War twenty years ago ought to be looked upon
as a geopolitical blessing, a return from the edge of the nuclear abyss. It
meant that for the first time in over fifty years the United States did not face
a major threat to its security (from Japan, Germany, the USSR, or others).
Such a perspective, much more optimistic than the one provided by the
Neoconservatives, means the possibility of genuine reduction in the level of
militarization of American foreign policy—a reduction in defense appropri-
ations[44] and military presence around the globe,[45] and an increasing reliance
on economic and political instruments in international relations rather than
frequent and extensive deployment of military means. As part of this policy
shift, the United States "must reassure potential allies and foes that it does
not intend to use force to radically change the status quo."[46] It is equally important for the United States to avoid a repetition of a preventive war. Such
a war is "not only a violation of international law but also a repudiation of

America's own traditions."[47] Lind believes that Bush waged "the first—and to date the only—preventive war in American history" and that it was "perfectly consistent with the radical neoconservative variant of US global hegemony strategy."[48]

The recommendation in regard to the use of military force does not amount to the endorsement of a pacifist philosophy, unilateral disarmament, or even reluctance to use military force when needed in well-defined and legitimate situations (such as individual and collective self-defense, UN action to preserve the peace and security of all states, and genocide prevention). Moreover, the American military might continue to be important for certain deterrence purposes. Yet, the United States needs to avoid the feeling of limitless power as well as clinging to the "illusion of control,"[49] the assumption that its military supremacy and new military technologies could solve its foreign policy problems. Neither should it confuse the possession of power (the resources available to it) with influence (the ability of "producing" others). The demilitarization of American foreign policy was not an option during the Bush administration since the United States viewed itself as a hegemonic actor and Neoconservatives, inside and outside the government, assumed that military power should be used extensively.

One of the reasons to avoid the overuse of the military option is that it is an extremely unpredictable instrument; while one might know how war starts, one never knows how it will end. Moreover, "throughout history, states that have pursued aggressive unilateral military policies have paid a heavy price.... Major powers have often balanced against such states."[50] In a general way, it is important for the United States not to overrely on the military, despite the promise of the so-called Revolution in Military Affairs.[51] It is particularly important to note that the Revolution in Military Affairs has limited value in the asymmetric warfare of the contemporary world, where there is a terrorist and insurgent challenge to the United States.

3. Return to the pragmatic, largely nonideological, moderate, and bipartisan Realism that has characterized American foreign policy in the past, and reject the ideological, confrontational policies of the Neoconservatives. While there have been fierce debates on US foreign policy in the post–World War II era (none more so than the debate over the Vietnam War), during most of the past sixty-four years there has been a high degree of agreement over

the main contours of US policy toward the rest of the world—containing the Soviet Union, facilitating free trade, maintaining a large number of international organizations, sustaining strong relationships with countries similar to the United States in terms of their fundamental values (particularly Western European democracies), and using moderation toward countries with which we have fundamental political disagreements (including China and post-Soviet Russia). This consensus was almost completely wrecked by the Neoconservatives and the Bush administration, although bipartisanship based on liberal internationalism declined significantly following the end of the Cold War.

The main issue that ought to be resolved is *the leadership role of the United States* in the post-Bush era. Gone is the Neoconservative dream of establishing an American hegemonic imperium, a situation in which the United States alone decides if and when to use its full military might and do so even in marginal situations. On the other hand, it is hard to conceive of a situation in which the United States would seriously withdraw from its major, leading role in world politics. Such withdrawal is not in America's interest, nor is it in the interest of most other countries and the global society at large. So the main goal of the redrawn, revitalized, and reinvented Washington foreign policy consensus is to *determine the parameters of America's leadership role in the post-Bush world*. Bruce Jentleson creatively identifies three qualities of US leadership for a post-Bush strategy: *mutuality* (not only the United States should benefit from its leadership but also others); *effectiveness* (the level of confidence in "US capacity to help make the world a more secure and just place"); and *vision* (offering an American model that others can believe in).[52]

One particular area around which a new Realist consensus might evolve is in the field of *combating terrorism*. The Neoconservative Bush administration approach of declaring a "war" on terror (despite the fact that terrorism is a tactic, not an actor), using heavily ideological language with historical resonance ("Islamofascism"), focusing on military responses, and announcing regime change as a prime objective ought to be replaced by a more Realistic approach: contain terrorism (as the United States contained the USSR)[53] rather than invade countries; promote fissures between radical Islamic groups and pay close attention to moderate public opinion in Muslim countries; use political and economic tools in the struggle against radicals; emphasize intelligence (especially human intelligence) and law enforcement; and work closely with political elites in targeted countries (such as Afghanistan and Pakistan).

4. Reemphasize the diplomacy of consultation as an alternative to the unilateral use of military force by the United States. The revival of such diplomacy requires a comprehensive historical view. This view rests on the recognition that for most of the post–World War II era the United States found a way of heavily consulting, negotiating, and cooperating with other nations, either within the framework of traditional alliances (such as NATO or ANZUS), close and even special bilateral relations with select countries (UK, Japan, Israel), extensive military and economic aid, action at multilateral international organizations, and so forth. The use of force or threat of force, so enthusiastically recommended by the Neoconservatives, was relatively rare compared with the large numbers of consultative and cooperative initiatives (Vietnam, the Iran 1953 intervention, and a series of interventions in Latin America are among those relatively rare and sometimes regrettable US actions).

The post-Bush era should facilitate the *revitalization of the diplomacy of consultation as the dominant form of American leadership*. Multilateral efforts, alliances, and international institutions are preferable to unilateral military action; they offer the United States both worldwide political legitimacy and significant material resources in cases where action is needed. Such cooperation ought to be institutionalized, but it must "take into account the interests of others in pursuing [American] foreign policy,"[54] not merely the interests of the United States. In the important area of international terrorism, "the United States should try to institutionalize cooperation in the war on terror"[55] and even establish an "anti-terror regime,"[56] shifting its strategy away from "harassing rogue states on the margins of the international system and towards finding a way to lower the domestic costs incurred by leaders of linchpin states when pursuing terrorists."[57]

Another area of cooperation is US activity within the United Nations. Particularly important is the desertion of the campaign against the United Nations carried out by Bush administration officials such as John Bolton and, even more serious, by the occasional US tendency to ignore the will of the international body altogether. While the UN might not always be the appropriate place for carrying out an international action—particularly when a Permanent Member insists on using its veto power in defiance of the international community—whenever it could be used, it should. The UN has the capacity of conferring the ultimate legitimacy on a collective action by the international community. Moreover, the United States itself should avoid ignoring the organization whenever it might be convenient. The new "diplomacy of consultation" ought to be carried out through "overlapping and occasionally competing international institutions that are organized on regional or functional lines."[58] In the context of supporting and further strengthening the UN, it is crucial to avoid efforts designed to weaken it, such as the establishment of a "League of Democracies" or a "Concert of Democracies."[59] Such an organization would be mostly a means to gain legitimacy for Western (probably American) intervention under the cover of democratization while keeping out non-Western nations such as China and Russia. This idea "embodies the same instincts that lie behind the made-to-order multilateralism that the world has grown so tired of under President George W. Bush."[60] "It threatens to circumvent and even undermine real efforts at international cooperation," reflecting a desire "to get around the United Nations."[61]

5. Initiate the era of globalism. The Neoconservative ideological framework offered by the Bush administration was nationalist, patriotic, and exceptionalist, although it made frequent use of high-minded ideals such as the spreading of democracy and freedom. At its core, it was a policy of global hegemony.[62] Adopting that ideology, "the Bush administration had established an in-your-face approach to global diplomacy,"[63] negating international agreements (such as Kyoto, declared "dead on arrival") and international law in general. As such, this administration could never get the support or capture the imagination of the world in developing a new agenda.

A new ideological framework, and possibly even a consensus or near-consensus ought to rest on the assumption that *all or most problems faced by humanity today are by their very nature global*—terrorism and the proliferation of weapons of mass destruction, uneven globalization and differential economic development, health issues and structural poverty, and so forth.

The solution for those problems ought to be found on a global level, internationally and multilaterally, by working toward a worldwide ideological consensus. As part of that consensus, global norms should be codified. In initiating the Global Age, new international institutions capable of dealing with global issues might have to be established and existing international organizations (NATO and the EU, for example) will have to be strengthened, but without accentuating the differences and widening the gaps between nations and groups of nations. The UN Security Council, for example, should be strengthened by adding to its ranks several more permanent members (e.g., Germany, Japan, India, and Brazil) and a few more nonpermanent members (possibly four more).

The "globalism agenda" is, of course, a long-term and complex agenda. It cannot be implemented against the will of the United States and it probably requires the active, enthusiastic leadership of the United States. This agenda must be based on the Realist recognition that today's international institutions simply do not combine effectiveness and legitimacy,[64] but in contrast to the attitude of the Neoconservatives, this recognition should not be used as an instrument to destroy those international institutions but as an invitation for their improvement. In general, multilateral action could be highly effective in some international areas (if not in all). Thus, it could be used for fighting transnational terrorism by "sharing intelligence, cooperating on law enforcement, and freezing terrorists' sources of financial support."[65] Regional organizations, such as the Association of Southeast Asian Nations, the Gulf Cooperation Council, and the African Union, could also be helpful in promoting the global agenda.[66]

6. Refocus American efforts, along with the efforts of others, on solving long-term, severe, "intractable" regional conflicts. First and foremost among these is the Arab-Israeli conflict, but also the conflicts in the former Yugoslavia (especially Kosovo), Sri Lanka, Cyprus, the Sudan (Darfur), and the Caucuses require close and intense international and American attention. Those conflicts should not be left unattended, because they have negative effects both domestically and internationally. Invariably, those conflicts produce resentment, generate violence and reprisals, and waste human lives and economic resources. Issues that are not treated energetically are dangerous in feeding "anarchy."[67] Special attention should be given to so-called

failed states. They should typically be the responsibility of the international community as a whole. As a strategic choice, the United States should work toward the enhancement of self-reliance of various conflictual regions, following the successful European model.

7. Avoid overreaching and overstretching by establishing clearer prioritization of goals and paying more careful attention to the allocation of resources for the achievement of those goals. The graveyard of empires is full of those who overreached beyond their material capacity, including Athens, Britain, the Ottoman Empire, and the Soviet Union.[68] A better sense of the "possible" is required in terms of American foreign and security policy. Neither the United States nor even a coalition of all Western countries has the capability of defeating each and every terrorist group or invading every country in which terrorists might find shelter. What is needed is the development of *a carefully calibrated, calculated, and balanced set of objectives*, a priority list, both in terms of dealing with global terrorism and in terms of the more general goals of American foreign policy. This is a particularly challenging task in the post-Bush era because there is no single, overwhelming, self-evident objective to US foreign policy.[69]

   An example of an issue that apparently has not been given the proper attention by the Bush administration is that of nuclear terrorism. Graham Allison has argued that the next president needs to make this issue an "absolute national priority." More specifically, Allison believes that a president who takes the threat of nuclear terrorism seriously would "assemble the members of the core national security team and work with them to develop a comprehensive strategy, an operational plan, and a specific timetable for achieving measurable objectives."[70] It seems that the investment in Iraq has diverted too many resources from this and other important issues.

8. Deal effectively with the problem of American prominence. The goal of US foreign policy has to be to maintain American leadership, but not imperial hegemony;[71] while the United States is "primus inter pares," in the post-Bush era it will need to regain its image as a "benevolent superpower."[72] American supremacy is inherently problematical since lesser countries tend to coalesce against a dominant power, especially a hegemon. The United States today faces the type of problem Germany had to tackle after 1871 in Europe, a "Bismarckian Dilemma"—how to maintain its leadership role on

the international scene without causing others to coalesce against it. Bismarck adjusted Germany's foreign policy so as to gain the friendship of other great powers in Europe. A variety of strategies that can also be used by the United States has been identified by Josef Joffe. Also, Fukuyama notes that Bismarck was able to "prevent the hostile coalitions that would openly seek to oppose German power."[73] The United Kingdom developed good relationships with the United States and Japan in the early twentieth century, and President Nixon adopted a similar policy with China in the early 1970s, for the same purpose—neutralizing potential rivals and cutting the cost of Great Power competition.

It is clear that the Iraq war was as non-Bismarckian as possible: it managed to unite some of America's ideological opponents (such as China and Russia), some of its traditional friends (including Germany), and practically all others (previously nonaligned nations). Moreover, the Iraq war produced a worldwide, anti-American public opinion. It is in the US interest to avoid such a broad coalition from ever emerging again. Ironically, the American dilemma is "how to maintain prominence despite prominence."

9. Resist the establishment of closed and ideologically based, international coalitions. Ideas such as the establishment of a new "League of Democracies" (raised by Senator John McCain and others) or even the development of a "Western Order"[74] sound like an invitation to divide the world into America's friends versus its enemies, ushering in if not directly provoking a new Cold War, just as an overly aggressive policy on NATO expansion and the development of forward-based missile defense batteries do. Moreover, if the criterion for inclusion in such a new organization is "democracy," it sounds eerily similar to the Neoconservative ideology of democracy expansion. It is one thing to accept the existence of the sixty-year-old NATO as a fixture of the international scene, yet another to initiate new exclusivist "clubs" that could only cause resentment by those left out. Moreover, if there is to be a "Western Order" (and to some extent there already is), it must be liberally open to all, nondiscriminatory, and cooperative in nature.[75]

10. In a world shifting from clear-cut US unipolarity to what might be called "mixed-polar polyarchy," *an American policy of restraint and occasional balancing* is preferred to the policy of primacy and frequent unilateral military action. The United States faces in the post-Bush era a world with no clear

"polarity" and, in fact, mixed-polar polyarchy. In polyarchy there are many actors with diverse relations, interests, and alliances among them.[76] Moreover, the world polarity pattern will continue to be mixed: thus, the United States will continue to be dominant in terms of military power, the economic situation will reflect a multipolar situation (with the US, PRC, and the EU leading the world), and so forth. In such a world, a policy of American "primacy" in any of its variants is unlikely to be successful,[77] while it is likely to be costly (as Iraq has amply demonstrated). On the other hand, a policy of restraint (combined with the diplomacy of consultation and a commitment to a global agenda) is likely to be successful; it is sometimes referred to as "a strategy of offshore balancing," and it is a direct negation of the policy of preventive war.[78] Several factors work in favor of successful restraint, including America's great military and economic power, its ability to project its naval power, the ability to create coalitions with others in order to prevent the emergence of a Eurasian superstate,[79] its considerable soft power, and so forth.

11. Do not avoid moral issues. The Neoconservatives and the Bush administration took the position that the United States could take any unilateral action it deems desirable (as it did in the Iraq invasion). Justification for such unilateral action was frequently given in terms of universal values such as the promotion of freedom and democracy, or in terms of American exceptionalism. In practical terms, the Neoconservatives argued that because no one could stop the United States from acting unilaterally, the Iraq invasion and other such operations could be done "on the cheap" and with insignificant long-term consequences.

    This position has proven to be a shortsighted and self-destructive policy. In issues of war and peace, moral, ethical, and legal issues cannot be avoided or ignored, particularly not in the contemporary world where any and all state actions (especially those taken by the single hyperpower) are exposed to world public opinion. The danger with unilateralist and militarist actions is that they are likely to be costly in terms of international reputation, prestige, and legitimacy. The way to take the moral high ground, if and when a military action is deemed necessary, is to establish genuine, broad-based international coalitions. If wars are to be conducted, and these might not be completely avoidable, most or all elements of the just war tradition, updated to the early twenty-first century, need to be employed. Seyom Brown has argued that in invading Iraq, the United States has carried out a highly controversial preventive war,[80] failing to meet a number of requirements of the just war tradition, including right intention,[81] proper authority,[82] proportionality,[83] last resort,[84] and even probability of success.[85] The majority of sovereign states and public opinions in most countries agreed with this judgment.

One of the most controversial aspects of the Iraq war was the situation created in Iraq as a result of the March 2003 invasion. Although most analysts who looked at the Iraq invasion from a moral perspective analyzed it in terms of the traditional *jus ad bellum* (the right to go to war) or *jus in bello* (the right conduct of war), some thought about it in terms of *jus post bellum*, that is the situation created in Iraq in the aftermath of the war, including the long-term occupation of the country by American forces.[86] Say Williams and Caldwell: "The victor must, in the first place, restore order. Without order, a society can descend into a Hobbesian state of nature in which even the right to life may be impossible to secure."[87] From this perspective, the Iraq war was unjust indeed. It is an important lesson for the future. Above all, it is essential not to ignore the moral dimension.[88]

TOWARD A BETTER FUTURE?

Toward the end of the Bush administration, a new approach to foreign policy had begun to emerge. In fact, the appointment of Condoleezza Rice as secretary of state was the beginning of a shift. It was accompanied by the departure of several Neoconservatives from the Department of State as well as the Department of Defense, the Office of the Vice President, and other key places.

More important, the Bush administration began to adopt significantly more moderate positions on a number of issues, and on several of them it initiated or at least went along with complicated diplomatic, rather than military, efforts. On the issue of nuclear proliferation in North Korea, the administration reengaged in the Six-Party Talks (United States, China, Russia, Japan, South Korea, and North Korea), eventually producing a negotiated deal. While in some ways it was a typical "too little, too late" achievement, where experts thought the United States had missed an opportunity to have this deal in early 2003 before

North Korea went nuclear, it reflected a more moderate, multilateral, and diplomatic attitude, as well as the political defeat of people like Vice President Cheney and John Bolton.

On the issue of Iran, the Bush administration got involved in a multilateral effort along with the UN Security Council, deploying also the E3+3 formula (Britain, France, and Germany, as well as the United States, Russia, and China) in a truly internationalized effort to contain the Iranian regime. While at the time of this writing this effort remains inconclusive, it is generally accepted as a potentially productive initiative.

In terms of the Israeli-Palestinian conflict, the Annapolis meeting, organized by the Bush administration, was followed by intense negotiations between Israel and the Palestinians. In addition to the involvement of those parties, there was an intense involvement of the Middle East quartet (United States, European Union, Russia, United Nations). Also on this issue there was a typical too-little-too-late approach on the part of the Bush administration; it took the administration many years to finally address this important issue in an energetic manner.

On this regional conflict and other conflicts (e.g., Sri Lanka, Darfur, Cyprus, Kosovo), no matter what particular constellation and configuration there might be in regard to a specific dispute, the role of the United States in brokering a deal is *essential* because only it can give specific and substantial *security guarantees* for whatever deal is reached. While the Bush administration lost its capability of being the honest and effective peace broker, often by taking a one-sided (Israel/Palestine), overly militaristic (Iran, North Korea) stance from the start, the next administration must try to recover America's diplomatic role.

The situation in Iraq remains highly volatile. In the summer of 2008, the Bush administration and the Iraqi government announced that they intended to agree on a general "time horizon" for withdrawal of US troops from Iraq. While the words *timetable* and *schedule* were not used in this early announcement, the term *horizon* probably represented a significant shift in the administration's policy. While the final shape of a forthcoming agreement with the Iraqi government is still unknown, we might witness a significant reduction in the size of the American force as well as a change from combat role to training and counterterrorism tasks.[89]

Despite certain improvements in Iraq, both "on the ground" and diplomatically, it had continued to hang over the head of the Bush administration to its very end. It was the "original sin" of the administration, continued to demand countless sacrifices, and, in effect, encapsulated the administration's position on foreign policy. The Iraq invasion and occupation have thrown a long shadow on everything done by the administration. It has put in jeopardy the most important project of the Neoconservatives, the imperial hegemonic project.

Vision

The greatest failure of the Bush administration was its inability to articulate an acceptable vision for the future, either for the United States or for the world at large. Such a vision had to include a set of general objectives and a strategy to achieve those objectives. In general terms such objectives could have included the enhancement of peace and stability in an inherently conflictual and unstable world, increasing the well-being of Americans and others, coordination of international action for dealing with ecological challenges (especially the energy crisis and climate change), and so forth. A convincing program should have included specific means for achieving those objectives.

The irony is that while Bush-41 failed to formulate an overall set of objectives beyond the endorsement of a "New World Order," Bush-43 seemed to be committed to the wrong set of objectives—making the world safe for American hegemony via military means, including regime change in countries perceived as hostile to America. The invasion and subsequent occupation of Iraq were "models," an example to be followed in other places.[90] Interestingly, Bush's strategy to achieve his objectives failed in regard to Afghanistan, Iraq, Iran, North Korea, and other countries to which it was applied.

It thus remains for the next president to put in front of America and the world a new agenda, necessarily global in nature but dealing with the specifics of American foreign policy within the much broader international environment. With so many political, military, economic, and ecological loose ends left untied by the Bush administration, no president in recent memory has ever faced a more daunting agenda than the one called for in the post-Bush era.[91] The ideas raised in this chapter might be useful in formulating such an agenda.

One issue that the next president will have to confront is, *what position in world politics should the United States aspire to?* Given America's truly unique power and influence in global politics, it cannot possibly be, in the foreseeable future, only one of two hundred sovereign units in the world. But then, the possibilities for the *right status* for America are endless. America's unique position in the contemporary world is reflected in notions such as "the sole remaining superpower," the "world policeman," the "Hyperpower,"[92] "the essential (or indispensable) nation,"[93] an "empire," or a "hegemon." Michael Hunt has argued persuasively that the last term is most fitting. Among the ancient Greeks a hegemon was a leader of a federation of states. The hegemon supplies public goods (such as security), and, following Antonio Gramsci, its position is associated also with values and norms of great appeal to others, not only material power.[94] So if a hegemon is more than an empire, the United States since the end of the Cold War has surely been a hegemon.

But one of the most important questions that ought to be asked is the following, essentially normative question: What kind of hegemon (or empire, superpower, or hyperpower) is the United States to be? Is it to be a "benevolent" hegemon or is it to be a unilateralist empire, is it to be a "rogue" superpower or one that benefits the world, as some hegemonic stability theorists believe it should?

The policies adopted by the Bush administration since 2001 have been designed not merely to maintain the American hegemonic position but to enhance it by all means, including coercive ones. For the most part those policies have failed to generate confidence among Americans and non-Americans: they have resulted in the significant loss of life, the enormous waste of economic resources, and the unprecedented decline of legitimacy for the United States. In order to halt the erosion of America's power, aggressive, militaristic, unilateral hegemonism ought to be abandoned as a strategy.

While the United States has not merely a legitimate but necessary role as a leader, possibly even *the* leader, of the democratic world, in today's polyarchic, postpolaric world, hegemony might be a thing of the past. Although America will continue to dominate the world militarily, economically it will be increasingly interdependent, as well as equal, with other states or blocs of states (such as the European Union). This would mean that it would be incumbent on the United States to closely cooperate with other nations, deserting the unilateral modus operandi of the Neocons and the Bush administration.

NOTES

Preface

1. The reference to the Richter scale and to earthquakes here is, of course, merely metaphorical. Earthquakes are often devastating geological events, resulting in terrible human suffering; while historical seismological events might be equally profound in their impact, they have a potential for creating positive developments.

2. Moïsi, "The Land of Hope Again?"

Chapter 1 The Bush Legacy

1. A recent book, Scoblic's *U.S. vs. Them,* furthers the argument that conservatism, rather than Neoconservatism, was responsible for Bush's foreign policy. I strongly disagree with this thesis for reasons fully explained in chapter 3.

2. Zarefsky, "Presidential Rhetoric and the Power of Definition," pp. 607–619. See also Maggio, "The Presidential Rhetoric of Terror," pp. 810–835.

3. For an incisive analysis of those American traditions, see Bacevich, *The Limits of Power.*

4. Merton, *Social Theory and Social Structure,* p. 477. For the application of this idea to Iraq, see Fukuyama, *America at the Crossroads,* p. 181, and chapter 2 of this volume. My own use of the concept is more extensive than Merton's or Fukuyama's.

5. Peleg and Scham, "Israeli Neo-Revisionism and American Neoconservatism," pp. 73–94.

6. On a Manichean perspective, a notion that came from the analysis of religious attitudes, see Culianu, *The Tree of Gnosis.* On this perspective as overwhelmingly relevant for George W. Bush, see Greenwald, *A Tragic Legacy.*

7. On Bush's lack of flexibility, see Draper, *Dead Certain,* as well as many other books and articles.

8. For a similar critical perspective, see Hybel and Kaufman, *The Bush Administrations and Saddam Hussein*. The authors view Bush's decision making as essentially irrational.

9. Daalder and Lindsay, *America Unbound,* p. 2 and p. 189. The authors perceive Bush's foreign policy as revolutionary, although their perception is somewhat narrower than my own. While they emphasize means, I focus on goals. In Bacevich, *The Limits of Power*, the author emphasizes the continuity of US foreign policy under Bush, although he recognizes its radical nature.

10. See, for example, Boyle, "Utopianism and the Bush Foreign Policy," pp. 81–103.

11. Brose, "Twilight of the Idols," pp. 158–159.

12. I share in this regard the assessment of such analysts as Josef Joffe (*Überpower*), Fareed Zakaria (*The Post-American World*), and others.

13. Kupchan and Trubowitz, "Dead Center," pp. 7–44. While liberal internationalism might be understood in a variety of alternative ways, it is the idea of building an international order based on cooperation, free economy, strong international organizations, and limited use of force.

14. On anti-Americanism, see the balanced views of Joffe, *Überpower*.

15. Such an argument is promoted, for example, by accomplished analysts Daalder and Lindsay, *America Unbound,* p. 2.

16. Thus, the Clinton administration was reluctant to intervene in Kosovo. Other interventions, such as the ones in Haiti or even Somalia, were relatively limited.

17. "Statement of Principles," Project for the New American Century, June 3, 1997, www.newamericancentury.org/statementofprinciples.htm.

18. Kagan and Kristol, "Toward a Neo-Reaganite Foreign Policy," pp. 18–32.

19. Krauthammer, "The Unipolar Moment." For a different, more balanced approach, see Zakaria, *The Post-American World*.

20. Such an argument is made, for example, by Dubose and Bernstein in their book, *Vice: Dick Cheney and the Hijacking of the American Presidency*.

21. For emphasis on President Bush's personality, see Greenwald, *A Tragic Legacy*.

22. Fukuyama, *America at the Crossroads,* p. 66.

23. "World Public Says Iraq War Has Increased Global Terrorist Threat," Program on International Policy Attitudes, February 27, 2006, www.worldpublicopinion.org/pipa/articles/home_page/172.php?nid=&id=&pnt=172&lb=hmpg1.

24. "A Year After Iraq War: Mistrust of America in Europe Ever Higher, Muslim Anger Persists," Pew Research Center, March 16, 2004, http://people-press.org/reports/display.php3?ReportID=206.

25. Hoffmann, *Gulliver Unbound,* p. 8.

26. Mearsheimer and Walt, "An Unnecessary War," p. 59.

27. Scowcroft, "Don't Attack Saddam."

28. Buchanan, *Where the Right Went Wrong,* p. 19.

29. The Iraq war, Bush's most important initiative, was more preventive than preemptive, although the president and his advisers presented the war as preemptive. On this issue, see Fukuyama, *America at the Crossroads,* especially pp. 81–88.

30. Chaddock, "A Bush Vision of Pax Americana."

31. Boggs, *Imperial Delusions,* p. 11.

32. Brown, *The Illusion of Control,* p. 8.

33. Daalder and Lindsay, *America Unbound,* p. 199.

34. The impression that the president saw himself as a revolutionary is strengthened in such books as Draper's *Dead Certain: The Presidency of George W. Bush* and McClellan's *What Happened: Inside the Bush White House & What's Wrong with Washington.*

35. Bush's argument in a televised debate with Al Gore reflected that kind of modesty and moderation; his spokespeople (e.g., Condoleezza Rice) expressed similar attitudes.

36. See, for example, Daalder and Lindsay, *America Unbound,* chapters 1–3.

37. Dubose and Bernstein, *Vice: Dick Cheney and the Hijacking of the American Presidency,* p. 177.

38. Ibid, p. 178.

39. Brown, *The Illusion of Control,* especially chapter 3.

40. Peleg, *Democratizing the Hegemonic State.*

41. Brzezinski, *Second Chance.*

42. On the Bismarckian issue, see Joffe, *Überpower.*

43. Allison, *Nuclear Terrorism,* p. 187.

44. For the speech of Prime Minister Tony Blair to the US Congress on July 17, 2003, see *Wall Street Journal,* July 18, 2003.

45. Ibid.

46. Ikenberry, "The Rise of China and the Future of the West," pp. 23–37, especially p. 28.

Chapter 2   The Challenge to America and the World

1. Brown, *The Illusion of Control,* p. 18; Joffe, *Überpower.*

2. Brown, *The Illusion of Control,* p. 2; Zakaria, *Post-American World.*

3. An example of the use of the more nuanced, diplomatic approach was the involvement of Secretary of State Colin Powell in solving the crisis with China following the interception of an American aircraft by the Chinese in 2001.

4. Greenwald, *A Tragic Legacy.* Greenwald is otherwise devastatingly critical of the Bush administration and suggests that the *initial response* of the president and his administration to the events of September 11, 2001, was "a balanced rather than

bloodthirsty approach" (p. 104). He then proceeds to demonstrate that changes in this initial response occurred. This progressively aggressive approach is fully analyzed in chapter 5 of this book.

5. For an effort to present Bush's record as more balanced than it actually was, see Rice, "Rethinking the National Interest," pp. 2–26. Rice, who loyally served Bush as national security adviser when the Iraq debacle was undertaken, argues in the 2008 article for the *peaceful enhancement* of political and economic development of weak and poorly governed states (p. 8), emphasizing "long-term *partnership and mutual responsibility* [emphasis added]" (p. 10). Interestingly, even some renowned Neoconservatives seem to have moved toward a more centrist, Realist position (see, for example, Kagan, *The Return of History and the End of Dreams*).

6. Rice, "Rethinking the National Interest," p. 2.

7. For a critique, see Brzezinski, *Second Chance*, especially chapter 2.

8. See, for example, Mearsheimer, "Why We Will Soon Miss the Cold War," pp. 35–50.

9. See, for example, Kaplan, *Daydream Believers: How a Few Grand Ideas Wrecked American Power*.

10. See, for example, the critique of Carter's national security adviser, in Brzezinski, *Second Chance*.

11. A concept used by pro-American German analyst Josef Joffe.

12. Brzezinski, comparing Bush-41, Clinton, and Bush-43, argues that Bush-43 was clearly the worst among these three post–Cold War presidents. I share his view, although I see Bush-41 and Clinton more positively than Brzezinski.

13. For obvious reasons, journalists (e.g., Maureen Dowd of the *New York Times*) and other observers focused in particular on comparing Bush-41 and Bush-43. This book touches on this issue in chapter 4.

14. Brzezinski, *Second Chance,* p. 82.

15. See, for example, Brown, *The Illusion of Control*, p. 1.

16. See Daalder and Lindsay, *America Unbound,* as well as numerous other sources.

17. See, for example, Ricks, *Fiasco*; see also Gordon and Trainor, *Cobra II*.

18. Thus, the secretary of defense for Clinton between 1997 and 2001, a critical time when the United States carried out the Kosovo operation, was William Cohen, a former Republican senator.

19. Brzezinski, *Second Chance,* p. 192.

20. Ibid., p. 24.

21. Brown, *The Illusion of Control*, p. 3.

22. Ibid., pp. 2–3.

23. Rice, "Rethinking the National Interest," p. 1.

24. Ibid., pp. 1–2.

25. Ibid., p. 5.

26. Ibid.

27. On the emerging balance-of-power system, see Pape, "Soft Balancing Against the United States," especially p. 11.

28. Brown, *The Illusion of Control*, p. 3.

29. Johnson, *The Sorrows of Empire*.

30. See, for example, Mitchell, "NATO Debate: From Big Risk to Sure Thing."

31. See, for example, Johnson, *The Sorrows of Empire*; Baker, "The Year in Ideas"; and Ignatieff, "The American Empire."

32. Ikenberry, "Illusions of Empire."

33. Ray and Kaarbo, *Global Politics*, pp. 185–187.

34. Krauthammer, "The Unipolar Moment," pp. 23–33.

35. Tucker and Hendrickson, "The Sources of US Legitimacy," p. 25.

36. Kaplan, "The Coming Anarchy," p. 24. See also Kaplan, *The Coming Anarchy: Shattering the Dreams of the Post Cold War*.

37. Kaplan, *The Coming Anarchy*, p. xii.

38. Haass, "Defining U.S. Foreign Policy in a Post–Post–Cold War World."

39. Haass, *The Reluctant Sheriff: The United States after the Cold War*.

40. Bovard, *The Bush Betrayal*, p. 11; Agathangelou and Ling, "Power, Borders, Security, Wealth," pp. 517–538; and Crawford, "The Road to Global Empire," pp. 685–702.

41. Most observers saw such a definition as inappropriate if not entirely irrational.

42. The best description of this phenomenon is to be found in Greenwald, *A Tragic Legacy*.

43. Brzezinski, *Second Chance*, p. 141.

44. Daalder and Lindsay, *America Unbound*, p. 116.

45. Dolan and Cohen, "The War About the War," especially p. 47.

46. Ibid., p. 38.

47. Brose, "Twilight of the Idols," p. 158.

48. The evolution of Bush's position was documented in Woodward, *State of Denial*, especially p. 371.

49. Ibid., p. 372.

50. Haass, "Defining U.S. Foreign Policy in a Post–Post–Cold War World."

51. While the vast majority of commentators on the Bush Doctrine have been highly negative, some have been more positive toward it. See, for example, Renshon and Suedfeld, *Understanding the Bush Doctrine*.

52. While some of the principles were openly announced by the president, others could be surmised from his pronouncements and policies.

53. Alexander, "International Relations Theory Meets World Politics: The Neoconservative vs. Realism Debate," in Renshon and Suedfeld, *Understanding the Bush Doctrine*, pp. 39–64, especially p. 39.

54. Jacoby, "What About the Bush Doctrine?"

55. Bacevich, "Rescinding the Bush Doctrine." Preemption reflected US military pre-eminence but, as this volume maintains, ignored other elements of international politics.

56. On preemption and prevention under Bush, see Glad and Dolan, *Striking First,* and Jervis, "Understanding the Bush Doctrine," pp. 365–388. For historical perspective, see Hendrickson, "Preemption, Unilateralism, and Hegemony," pp. 273–287.

57. It is important to note that this goal—spreading democracy—has evolved. While initially linked to the War on Terror, it eventually spread to a war on tyranny all over the world.

58. Brzezinski, *Second Chance,* p. 136.

59. Pape, "Soft Balancing Against the United States," p. 7. Supporters of Bush's unilateralism called it selective multilateralism. See, for example, Renshon and Suedfeld, *Understanding the Bush Doctrine,* p. ix.

60. Peter Suedfeld, Philip E. Tetlock, and Rajiv Jhangiani, "The Psychology of Alliance," in Renshon and Suedfeld, *Understanding the Bush Doctrine,* pp. 105–126.

61. Greenwald, *A Tragic Legacy,* might be the best on this important point.

62. Brady and Peleg, "Carter's Policy on the Supply of Conventional Weapons," pp. 41–68, especially pp. 42–43.

63. Glad, "Black-and-White Thinking," especially p. 33.

64. See, for example, Frum and Perle, *An End to Evil.*

65. Krauthammer, "The Neoconservative Convergence," p. 22.

66. See this argument in Renshon and Suedfeld, *Understanding the Bush Doctrine,* p. ix. Daalder and Lindsay (*America Unbound*) also use this concept in describing such policy makers as Cheney and Rumsfeld. In reality (that is, as policy), the principles leading Neoconservatism and Assertive Nationalism have hardly been distinguishable.

67. Bacevich, "Rescinding the Bush Doctrine." On the other hand, see Kaufman, *In Defense of the Bush Doctrine.*

68. Tucker and Hendrickson, "The Sources of US Legitimacy," p. 24.

69. Fukuyama, *America at the Crossroads,* p. 83.

70. Ibid., p. 84.

71. Stanley A. Renshon, "The Bush Doctrine Considered," in Renshon and Suedfeld, *Understanding the Bush Doctrine,* pp. 1–37. The quote is from p. 20.

72. Patten, "Democracy Doesn't Flow from the Barrel of a Gun."

73. Brady and Peleg, "Carter's Policy on the Supply of Conventional Weapons."

74. Interestingly, this was recognized from the beginning. Even though the Bush administration tried to change the worldwide perception, it was by and large unable to do so.

75. Philip H. Gordon, "The End of the Bush Revolution."

76. Jervis, "Why the Bush Doctrine Cannot Be Sustained," pp. 351–377.

77. See, for example, Guertner, "European Views on Preemption in US National Security Strategy," pp. 31–44.

78. Drumheller and Monaghan, *On the Brink,* p. 56.

79. Pape, "Soft Balancing Against the United States," p. 26.

80. Tucker and Hendrickson, "The Sources of US Legitimacy," p. 24.

81. Woodward, *Plan of Attack,* p. 172.

CHAPTER 3   THE NEOCONSERVATIVE REVOLUTION

1. While the literature on Neoconservatism is vast, among the most impressive efforts to deeply understand this ideology are two volumes by Gary Dorrien, one pre–Bush-43, *The Neoconservative Mind,* and one following the Iraq invasion, *Imperial Designs.* The Neoconservative ideology has been criticized from a conservative perspective by Halper and Clarke in *America Alone* and by many others; even individuals strongly connected to Neoconservatism, such as Francis Fukuyama, have offered sharp criticism of its implementation. Neoconservatism is presented positively and authoritatively by the godfather of the movement, Irving Kristol, in *Neoconservatism: The Autobiography of an Idea* and in "The Neoconservative Persuasion." See also Kagan and Kristol, *Present Dangers.*

2. See Halper and Clarke, *America Alone*; Dorrien, "Consolidating the Empire," pp. 409–428, especially p. 410; and, above all, Kristol, "The Neoconservative Persuasion."

3. In this context, note the title of the most recent book by the leading Neoconservative, Robert Kagan: *The Return of History and the End of Dreams.*

4. Yordan, "America's Quest for Global Hegemony," pp. 125–157.

5. Dorrien, "Consolidating the Empire," p. 414.

6. Such as Albert Wohlstetter, a teacher of such prominent Neoconservatives as Richard Perle and Paul Wolfowitz.

7. Those two contradictory traditions have lived side by side in America since the eighteenth century.

8. Thus, Kagan and Kristol declared triumphantly: "Bush has broken from the mainstream of his party and became a neoconservative in the true meaning of the word" ("An Administration of One").

9. See, for example, Kristol, "The Neoconservative Persuasion."

10. Heilbrunn, *They Knew They Were Right.*

11. Kristol, "The Neoconservative Persuasion"; due to space limitations, I emphasize only some of the ideals mentioned by Kristol, particularly those relevant for the argument promoted in this volume; the focus is on foreign policy.

12. See, for example, Kagan and Kristol, "An Administration of One" and "Toward a Neo-Reaganite Foreign Policy."

13. Fukuyama, *America at the Crossroads,* chapter 1. See also his essay "After Neo-Conservatism."

14. Halper and Clarke, *America Alone*, pp. 11–12.

15. Ibid., p. 26.

16. This analysis is based to some extent on Peleg and Scham, "Israeli Neo-Revisionism and American Neo-Conservatism," pp. 73–94, and on Brady and Peleg, "Carter's Policy on the Supply of Conventional Weapons," pp. 41–68. Yet it is closely applied and further developed by the author for the purpose of highlighting the relevance of Neoconservative ideas for contemporary American foreign policy.

17. Dorrien, *The Neoconservative Mind*, pp. 182–184.

18. See Festinger, Riecken, and Schacter, *When Prophecy Fails*, on the reaction of true believers to a change in the situation.

19. None has been more enthusiastic in regard to such intervention than Kagan and Kristol. See, for example, the introduction to their edited book, *Present Dangers*.

20. Mearsheimer, *The Tragedy of Great Power Politics*.

21. See, for example, Brown, *The Illusion of Control*, chapter 3; Bacevich, *The Limits of Power*, also subscribes to that position.

22. On some of the philosophical ideas of the Neoconservatives, see George, "Leo Strauss, Neoconservatism and US Foreign Policy," pp. 174–202. On the Neocons' tendency toward utopian solutions, see Boyle, "Utopianism and the Bush Foreign Policy," pp. 81–103.

23. Reflected in what became known as the Bush Doctrine.

24. Bacevich, *The Limits of Power*, p. 59.

25. Dunn and Woodard, *The Conservative Tradition in America*; Adam Wolfson, "Conservatives and Neoconservatives," in Stelzer, ed., *The Neocon Reader*, pp. 214–231.

26. See Halper and Clarke, *America Alone*, as well as Buchanan, *Where the Right Went Wrong*.

27. Thus former secretary of state James A. Baker III wrote "The Right Way to Change a Regime."

28. See Tyler, "US Strategy Plan Calls for Insuring No Rivals Develop," p. A14; Daalder and Lindsay, *America Unbound*, p. 41.

29. See Dorrien, *Imperial Designs*, p. 120.

30. Halper and Clarke, *America Alone*, p. 6.

31. See, for example, Boot, *The Savage Wars of Peace*.

32. Halper and Clarke, *America Alone*, pp. 143–144.

33. Kristol and Kagan, "Toward a Neo-Reaganite Foreign Policy," p. 44.

34. Ibid.

35. Kagan, *Of Paradise and Power*, p. 4.

36. Kristol, "The Neoconservative Persuasion," in Stelzer, ed., *The Neocon Reader*, p. 301.

37. On the problematic notion of exceptionalism, see, for example, Lipset, *American Exceptionalism.*

38. Nye, *Soft Power.*

39. Murphy, "The Last Best Hope?" pp. 20–21.

40. On the connection to a previous controversial war, see McCrisken, *American Exceptionalism and the Legacy of Vietnam.*

41. Brady and Peleg, "Carter's Policy on the Supply of Conventional Weapons," documents the use of exceptionalism in promoting Carter's policies on human rights and arms sales.

42. See several biographies of President Woodrow Wilson, such as George and George, *Woodrow Wilson & Colonel House,* and Kupchan and Trubowitz, "Dead Center," on liberal internationalism.

43. Fukuyama, "After Neoconservatism."

44. Ibid.

45. Sanger, "A Speech about Nothing, Something, Everything." Needless to say, Bush's exceptionalist language generated enormous interest beyond America; see, for example, Acharya, " American Exceptionalism," pp. 185–202.

46. See, for example, the introduction to Stelzer, ed., *The Neocon Reader.*

47. Brady and Peleg, "Carter's Policy on the Supply of Conventional Weapons," p. 42.

48. Lipset, *American Exceptionalism.*

49. In trying to "rescue" the Wilsonian connection some analysts have suggested that one can distinguish between "hard Wilsonianism" and "soft Wilsonianism"; this line of argumentation remains unconvincing to this author.

50. Seldin, "Neoconservatives and the American Mainstream."

51. Stuckey and Ritter, "George Bush, Human Rights, and American Democracy," p. 646.

52. Almond, *The American People and Foreign Policy,* p. 50.

53. Sullivan, "The Great Nation of Futurity," pp. 426–430.

54. Dewey, *Liberalism and Social Action,* p. 79.

55. See Turner, *The Frontier in American History.*

56. Potter, *People of Plenty.*

57. Irving Kristol, "The Neoconservative Persuasion," in Stelzer, ed., *The Neocon Reader,* p. 34.

58. Daalder and Lindsay, *America Unbound,* pp. 40–42.

59. Fukuyama, *The End of History and the Last Man.*

60. President Bush's "Mission Accomplished" speech of May 1, 2003, is particularly remembered.

61. Boyle, "Utopianism and the Bush Foreign Policy," pp. 81–103.

62. See in this regard the critique of Neoconservatism by Fukuyama, *America at the Crossroads.*

63. Brzezinski, "America in a Hostile World," p. 81.

64. Hartz, *The Liberal Tradition in America,* p. 58. Hartz's work is a genuine classic on American exceptionalism, but it emphasizes its liberal content.

65. Crabb, *American Foreign Policy in the Nuclear Age,* p. 3.

66. McDougall, *Promised Land, Crusader State.*

67. Mead, *Special Providence.*

68. Kennedy, "What 'W' Owes to 'WW,'" pp. 36–37.

69. Hoffmann, *Primacy or World Order,* p. 216.

70. Ferguson, *Colossus* and "The Unconscious Colossus," pp. 18–33. Other analysts used alternative terminologies to define the status of the United States in the contemporary world (see chapter 6).

71. A speech reported in the *New York Times,* April 13, 2004.

72. Comments made by President Bush at the twentieth anniversary of the National Endowment for Democracy, November 6, 2003, www.whitehouse.gov/news/releases/2003/11/20031106-2.html.

73. On the imperial zest of the Bush administration, see Gurtov, *Superpower on Crusade;* Grondin, "Mistaking Hegemony for Empire"; and Judis, "Imperial Amnesia."

74. Brady and Peleg, "Carter's Policy on the Supply of Conventional Weapons," p. 46.

75. Gregory, "To Do Good in the World: Woodrow Wilson and America's Mission," in Merli and Wilson, eds., *Makers of American Diplomacy,* p. 359; Coles, "Manifest Destiny Adopted for the 1990s," pp. 403–426.

76. Adams, *The Education of Henry Adams: An Autobiography,* p. 33.

77. Rossiter, *The First American Revolution,* p. 65.

78. Ibid., p. 232.

79. Gregory, "To Do Good in the World," p. 366.

80. Crabb, *Policy-Makers and Critics,* p. 34.

81. Brady and Peleg, "Carter's Policy on the Supply of Conventional Weapons," p. 47.

82. Hoffmann, *Gulliver's Troubles or the Setting of American Foreign Policy,* p. 112.

83. See, for example, Kellner, "Preemptive Strikes and the War in Iraq," pp. 417–440.

84. Although Iraq was not the first unilateral operation, it reflected a new level of unilateralism. See Skidmore, "Understanding the Unilateralist Turn in US Foreign Policy," pp. 207–228.

85. Haley, *Strategies of Dominance,* p. 139.

86. Daalder and Lindsay, *America Unbound,* p. 13. See also Monten, "Primacy and Grand Strategic Beliefs in US Unilateralism," pp. 119–138.

87. On John Bolton and the wider implications of his position see Mansell, "John Bolton and US Retreat from International Law," pp. 459–485.

88. Kagan and Kristol, *Present Dangers,* pp. 1–24.

89. Halper and Clarke, *America Alone,* p. 129. Most theorists have not shared the Neocon perspective. See, for example, Brooks and Wohlforth, "International Relations Theory and the Case Against Unilateralism."

90. See Washington, "Once Against Nation-Building, Bush Now Involved."

91. For a useful analysis of different schools of thought in American foreign policy, including the emergent Neoconservative school, see Fukuyama, *America at the Crossroads,* as well as Mead, *Power, Terror, Peace, and War.*

92. George and George, *Woodrow Wilson & Colonel House,* p. 188.

93. Dorrien, "Consolidating the Empire," p. 414.

94. Ibid., p. 418.

95. Nuruzzaman, "Beyond the Realist Theories," pp. 239–253.

CHAPTER 4   THE PERSONALITY OF GEORGE W. BUSH

1. See, for example, Kaplan, *Daydream Believers*; Greenwald, *A Tragic Legacy*; and Weisberg, *The Bush Tragedy,* to mention but some of the most recent books focusing on the personality of the president.

2. Noonan, "To Beat a Man, You Need a Plan."

3. Greenwald, *A Tragic Legacy.*

4. Barber, *Presidential Character.*

5. For "crisis" as a useful analytical concept, see Hermann, "International Crisis as a Situational Variable," pp. 409–421; Hermann, *Crisis in Foreign Policy.* "Crisis" by definition upsets a normal situation and thus enhances the impact of individuals, particularly prominent leaders.

6. See Garfinkle, "Bye Bye Bush," pp. 145–152.

7. Brown, *The Illusion of Control,* chapter 3.

8. Noonan, "To Beat a Man, You Need a Plan."

9. As argued extensively in chapter 3, insofar as George W. Bush is concerned, it seems that he shared individual beliefs and a belief system with what might be called Neoconservatism. At the same time, he was greatly influenced by assertive nationalist "superhawks" such as Dick Cheney and Donald Rumsfeld, and by several evangelicals, such as Michael Gerson.

10. Arnold, "One President, Two Presidencies," makes a distinction between the "conventional presidency" between January 20, 2001, and September 10, 2001, and the "war presidency" after September 11. This distinction is overdrawn. In this chapter, the argument will be made that the pre-9/11 passive aggression of the president and his advisers simply became active aggression after the terrorist attacks.

11. Thus, for example, Bush was ill at ease in front of the camera and hated state dinners, two important parts of his job as president.

12. Abramowitz and Weisman, "Bush Defies Lawmakers to Solve Iraq."

13. Weisberg, *The Bush Tragedy*, covered Bush's family background—probably a key to his personality—in great detail.

14. Kaplan, *Daydream Believers*, p. 114.

15. In fact, *Newsweek* published on December 2001 an article under this title; its author, David A. Kaplan, published it later as a book.

16. Wittkopf, Jones, and Kegley, *American Foreign Policy*, p. 498.

17. Ibid., pp. 500 and 507.

18. Draper, *Dead Certain*, p. 110.

19. Dean, "Predicting Presidential Performance." Dean served as Nixon's legal counsel and thus had a unique perspective on this active-negative president.

20. Carothers, "Promoting Democracy and Fighting Terror," pp. 84–97.

21. Weisberg captured it very well in his book, *The Bush Tragedy*.

22. Daalder and Lindsay, *America Unbound*, p. 19.

23. George W. Bush was extremely conscious of the comparisons between him and his father. Although in public he defended George H. W. Bush, in private he was much more critical. This, for example, was his stance regarding Bush-41's decision not to remove Saddam Hussein from power in 1991 (a position that coincided with that of many in the Neoconservative camp). See, for example, Draper, *Dead Certain*, p. 173.

24. See chapter 5.

25. Brzezinski, *Second Chance*, p. 138.

26. Jervis, "The Remaking of a Unipolar World," pp. 7–19. The quote is on p. 15.

27. Shogan, "Anti-Intellectualism in the Modern Presidency," pp. 295–303.

28. Those issues will be further explored in chapter 5.

29. Daalder and Lindsay, *America Unbound*, p. 20.

30. On a number of occasions Bush assembled his supporters in the White House for what might have looked like "intellectual exchanges." They were not. The assembled were Neocons and others proponents of the president (see note 61).

31. Greenstein, "The Changing Leadership of George W. Bush," pp. 387–396. The quote is on p. 393.

32. See Babington and Milbank, "Bush Advisers Try to Limit Damage." Bush told an interviewer that the United States would do "whatever it takes" to help Taiwan against a Chinese attack, creating the impression that the United States had a new position (which was not the case).

33. Greenstein, "The Changing Leadership of George W. Bush," p. 394.

34. For a systematic comparison between those three presidents, see Brzezinski, *Second Chance*.

35. Draper, *Dead Certain*, p. 157.

36. Brzezinski, *Second Chance*, p. 142.

37. Jervis, "The Remaking of a Unipolar World," p. 15.

38. Kaplan, *Daydream Believers*, p. 118.

39. Ibid., p. 131.

40. Bacevich and Prodromou, "God Is Not Neutral," pp. 43–54. The quote is from p. 43.

41. Ibid., pp. 52–53.

42. Schweder, "George W. Bush and the Missionary Position," pp. 26–36. The quote is from p. 27.

43. Ibid., p. 27.

44. Ibid., p. 35. It is interesting to note that among those supporting the establishment or even expansion of the American empire were several Brits, such as Niall Ferguson and Andrew Roberts.

45. Berggren and Rae, "Jimmy Carter and George W. Bush," pp. 606–632.

46. Stoessinger, *Crusaders and Pragmatists*.

47. For a fuller development of the Neocon ideology, see chapter 3.

48. Jervis, "The Remaking of a Unipolar World," p. 9

49. Conservatives, on the other hand, while often beginning by supporting Bush, ended up highly critical of him. This included commentators such as William F. Buckley and George Will, activists such as Patrick Buchanan and Mickey Edwards, and many others.

50. McClellan, *What Happened*; Paul O'Neill reaffirmed that impression.

51. Lears, "The Arrogance of Power Revisited," pp. 31–46. The quote is from p. 31.

52. Fulbright, *The Arrogance of Power*.

53. Lears, "The Arrogance of Power Revisited."

54. Woodward, *Bush at War*, p. 46.

55. Draper, *Dead Certain*, pp. 132–133.

56. Kaplan, *Daydream Believers*, p. 116.

57. Suskind, "Faith, Certainty and the Presidency of George W. Bush."

58. Brzezinski, *Second Chance*, p. 137.

59. Draper, *Dead Certain*, p. 39.

60. Brzezinski, *Second Chance*, p. 136.

61. Hybel and Kaufman, *The Bush Administrations and Saddam Hussein*, p. 141.

62. Suskind, *The Price of Loyalty*.

63. Ibid.

64. Roberts, *A History of the English-Speaking Peoples Since 1900*.

65. Several accounts of this fascinating meeting were published, including Irwin M. Stelzer, "Reader of the Free World: A Literary Luncheon with the President," and Michael Novak, "Good, Evil, and My Friend Irwin: A Literary Luncheon with President Bush."

66. Chernus, *Monsters to Destroy*.

67. Ibid., p. 79.

68. Maybe the best example is the improvement of crisis management in the JFK White House. See, for example, Janis, *Groupthink.*

69. Thus, Bush's second inauguration address, delivered in January 2005, was an astonishing exercise in daydreaming, totally detached from the reality of world politics. The American crusade for the democratization of the Middle East became a worldwide endeavor even though in reality the United States continued to support a large number of nondemocracies, including Egypt, Jordan, and Saudi Arabia in the Middle East.

70. Suskind, "Faith, Certainty and the Presidency of George W. Bush." See also Suskind, *The Way of the World.*

71. Kaplan, *Daydream Believers,* p. 60.

CHAPTER 5   THE DECISION-MAKING PROCESS

1. Johnson, *Managing the White House.* Johnson's models were applied to foreign and security issues by George in *Presidential Decision-Making in Foreign Policy.*

2. Von Hermann, "Presidential Decision-Making," pp. 13–28.

3. Dobbins, "Who Lost Iraq?" pp. 61–74. The quote is from p. 64.

4. Allison, *Essence of Decision.*

5. Bush himself described his decision-making style as "informed" by instinct, gut reaction, and so forth (see chapter 4).

6. It is still unclear, and maybe will never be entirely clear, the extent to which Bush's decisions were influenced by Dick Cheney. At this stage, it could merely be argued that this influence was substantial.

7. There is an enormous amount of evidence on the link between Cheney and the Neoconservatives, including his chief of staff, Scooter Libby; the evidence linking Bush is much less convincing, although his speeches and policies reflect the impact of Neoconservative thinking.

8. Eisendrath and Goodman, *Bush League Diplomacy.* While the authors emphasize that the policy was "driven by ideology" (p. 174), it was also greatly impacted by the president's personality.

9. On the centrality of definition, see Zarefsky, "Presidential Rhetoric and the Power of Definition," pp. 607–619, and Maggio, "The Presidential Rhetoric of Terror," pp. 810–835.

10. Dobbins, "Who Lost Iraq?" p. 64.

11. Pfiffner, "Did President Bush Mislead the Country in His Arguments for War with Iraq?" pp. 25–46.

12. Ponder, *Good Advice.*

13. Haney, "Foreign Policy Advising," pp. 289–302. The quote is from p. 295.

14. Ibid., p. 298.

15. Pfiffner, "The First MBA President," pp. 6–20.

16. Ibid., p. 7.

17. Ibid., pp. 7–8.

18. See, for example, Suskind, *The Price of Loyalty*.

19. There is still a debate on exactly who authorized the dissolution of the seven-hundred-thousand-strong Iraqi security forces. While the White House argued that it was a decision of Ambassador Paul Bremer, it is impossible to imagine that such an important decision would not have gone through the White House and eventually be made by the president himself. Be that as it may, politically and historically, George W. Bush bears the responsibility.

20. Skowronek, "Leadership by Definition," pp. 817–831, the quote is from p. 817.

21. Ibid., p. 820.

22. See, for example, Hasian Jr., "Dangerous Supplements, Inventive Dissent, and Military Critiques of the Bush Administration's Unitary Executive Theories," pp. 693–716.

23. Yoo, "War and the Constitutional Test," pp. 1–41.

24. Calabresi, "The President, the Supreme Court, and the Founding Fathers," pp. 469–485.

25. Thus, for example, the idea of checks and balances between the decision-making unit (circle 1) and the bureaucracy (circle 2), on the one hand, and the Congress (circle 3), on the other hand, did not work at all; it was the "victim" of national unity in the face of what the administration *defined* effectively as international terrorism.

26. See chapter 2.

27. Thus, several key members of the DMU (including Powell) were simply told that the president had made up his mind about Iraq. Others, including Rumsfeld, were never asked for their recommendations.

28. Although Haass was not closely involved in most decisions.

29. See chapter 3. The emerging Neocons, for example, were strongly opposed to détente between the United States and the USSR, saw the withdrawal from Vietnam as a disaster, and so forth.

30. For such a historical-ideological analysis, see Davis, "Infighting in Washington," pp. 92–122.

31. Ibid., p. 109.

32. While some observers continue to believe that Cheney was opposed to the termination of the war in late February 1991 (e.g., Davis, "Infighting in Washington," p. 110), this was not the case.

33. See Ricks, *Fiasco*, p. 7.

34. Thus, the Neocons achieved control not merely among the "principals" but also among the "deputies."

35. The policy of both the Bush-41 and the Clinton administrations was that of "dual containment"—containing both Iraq and Iran. Between those two, a certain

balance of power existed since the end of their war in 1988, an advantageous situation for the United States, neighboring countries, and the world at large.

36. Ricks, *Fiasco*, p.27.

37. Ibid., p. 30.

38. Isikoff and Corn, *Hubris*, p. 25.

39. Ibid., p. 175.

40. Daalder and Lindsay, *America Unbound*, pp. 57–58.

41. Ibid., p. 59.

42. Other administrations suffered from similar problems, but the consequences have rarely been that dramatic and negative. Thus, for example, during the Carter administration (1977–1981) there were great differences between Secretary of State Cyrus Vance and National Security Adviser Zbigniew Brzezinski.

43. Benjamin and Simon, *The Next Attack*, p. 140. It is important to note, however, that the Neocons were able to appoint John Bolton as a high official in the Department of State, probably against the will of Secretary of State Powell.

44. Ibid., p. 165.

45. Thus, as amazing as it may seem, neither Secretary of State Colin Powell nor Secretary of Defense Donald Rumsfeld were ever asked by Bush whether the invasion of Iraq was advisable. Condoleezza Rice, the national security adviser, was presented with such a question.

46. Thus, for example, a comparison between the decision to invade Iraq—if there ever was such a decision—and the decision to impose a blockade on Cuba in October 1962 reveals enormous differences, the latter being a collective decision.

47. Woodward, *Plan of Attack*, p. 26.

48. Burke, "The Contemporary Presidency," pp. 554–575. The quote is on p. 560.

49. Woodward, *Plan of Attack*, pp. 2–4.

50. Burke, "The Contemporary Presidency," p. 560.

51. Fallows, "Bush's Lost Year," pp. 68–84. The quote is on p. 79.

52. Janis, Groupthink.

53. Benjamin and Simon, *The Next Attack*, p. 172.

54. Hoffmann, *Gulliver Unbound*, p. 11.

55. Isikoff and Corn, *Hubris*, p. 16.

56. Brzezinski, *Second Chance*, p. 141.

57. Buchanan, *Where the Right Went Wrong*, p. 17.

58. Dolan and Cohen, "The War about the War," pp. 30–64. See p. 52 on the debate regarding the number of troops needed for Iraq. See also Fallows, "Blind Into Baghdad," pp. 53–74.

59. Comparing the relationships of Bush and Rumsfeld versus his relationships with Powell is, in this regard, an interesting exercise. The president's relationships with George Tenet are also quite interesting.

60. Pillar, "Intelligence, Policy, and the War in Iraq."

61. Ackerman and Judis, "The Selling of the Iraq War: The First Casualty," and Ackerman and Judis, "The Operator."

62. Woodward, *Plan of Attack*, pp. 269–70.

63. Burke, "The Contemporary Presidency," p. 561.

64. On this particular issue, she was in direct confrontation with the all-powerful Dick Cheney, the leader of the hawks in the Bush administration, and with Neocons such as John Bolton.

65. Thus, for example, US defense expenditures have grown substantially during the Bush administration, by roughly 40 percent in inflation-adjusted terms between 2001 and 2006, according to Roberts, "The War We Deserve," pp. 45–50. The quote is from p. 46.

66. O'Hanlon. "Iraq Without a Plan," pp. 33–45. The quote is from p. 33.

67. Ibid., p. 38.

68. Ibid., p. 36.

69. See, for example, Dubose and Bernstein, *Vice,* p. 178.

70. Benjamin and Simon, *The Next Attack,* p. 171.

71. Daalder and Lindsay, *America Unbound,* p. 59.

72. Isikoff and Corn, *Hubris,* pp. 3–5.

73. Ibid., p. 107.

74. Daalder and Lindsay, *America Unbound,* p. 60.

75. Wilson, *Fair Game.*

76. Eisendrath and Goodman, *Bush League Diplomacy,* p. 177.

77. McClellan, *What Happened.*

78. Dobbins, "Who Lost Iraq?" p. 63.

79. Ibid.

80. Edelman, "Cakewalk in Iran."

81. Thus, for example, Paul Wolfowitz opined that the revenues from Iraqi oil would finance the reconstruction of Iraq.

Chapter 6   Lessons for Future Presidents

1. Yet do not expect President George W. Bush himself to admit to any mistakes; it is not within his personality to do so (see chapter 4)

2. Reflected in her recent article: Rice, "Rethinking the National Interest," pp. 2–26.

3. Although there are exceptions to this claim, including, for example, the works by Dorrien, *The Neoconservative Mind* and *Imperial Designs.*

4. See, for example, Muravchik, "How to Save the Neocons," pp. 64–68.

5. Fukuyama, *America at the Crossroads.*

6. Kagan, *The Return of History and the End of Dreams.*

7. Wattenberg, *Fighting Words.*

8. Thus, Fukuyama studied with some of the movement's founding fathers (e.g., Allan Bloom at the University of Chicago), served as an official in several Republican administrations, and worked closely with some Neoconservative leaders, including Paul Wolfowitz.

9. Fukuyama, "The End of History?"

10. Fukuyama, *The End of History and the Last Man.*

11. Fukuyama's position was, in fact, so unclear that one critic, Anatol Lieven, wrote a review of his book under the title "The Two Fukuyamas."

12. Fukuyama, *America at the Crossroads,* p. 183.

13. Irving Kristol, Norman Podhoretz, and Jeane Kirkpatrick, for example, represented such a position. Podhoretz wrote a full-size book on that theme.

14. Hoffmann, *Gulliver Unbound,* p. 45.

15. Some of this radicalism is rooted in the experiences of some of the founding fathers of Neoconservativism in radical, leftist politics as far back as the 1930s and 1940s.

16. Fukuyama, *America at the Crossroads,* p. 182.

17. While the Weinberger-Powell doctrine emerged at a time of Republican leadership in the White House, it reflected in effect a broad bipartisan consensus. A classic application of the doctrine was the first Gulf War. On the Weinberger-Powell doctrine, see Dolan and Cohen, "The War about the War," p. 39.

18. A right that is explicitly recognized by international law and, more specifically, by the UN Charter (article 51).

19. Halper and Clarke, *America Alone,* p. 6.

20. Haley, *Strategies of Dominance,* p. 176.

21. Hoffmann, *Gulliver Unbound,* pp. 2–3.

22. Demonstrated, for example, in the Camp David Accords of September 1978 and in the Dayton Agreement of November 1995.

23. Fukuyama, *The End of History and the Last Man.*

24. See Boyle, "Utopianism and the Bush Foreign Policy," pp. 81–103.

25. Daalder and Lindsay, *America Unbound,* pp. 46–47.

26. Brzezinski, "America in a Hostile World."

27. These themes are fully developed by Brady and Peleg, "Carter's Policy on the Supply of Conventional Weapons."

28. Isikoff and Corn, *Hubris,* p. 16.

29. Monten, "The Roots of the Bush Doctrine," pp. 112–156. The quote is from p. 143.

30. Tucker and Hendrickson, "The Sources of US Legitimacy."

31. See Brown, *The Illusion of Control,* chapter 3 on polyarchy; Haass, "Regime Change and Its Limits," pp. 66–78.

32. Daalder and Lindsay, *America Unbound,* p. 13.

33. Halper and Clarke, *America Alone,* p. 129.

34. Hoffmann, *Gulliver Unbound,* p. 7.

35. Ibid., pp. 2–3.

36. Drezner, "The Future of US Foreign Policy," pp. 11–35. The quote is from p. 11. See also his "The New New World Order," pp. 34–46.

37. Lind, "Beyond American Hegemony," pp. 9–15. The quote is from p. 9.

38. Due to the dramatic developments over the past few years, many observers have offered ideas under the heading of "grand strategies." See John Lewis Gaddis, "Grand Strategy in the Second Term," pp. 2–15; Mead, "American Grand Strategy in a World at Risk," pp. 589–598; and Posen, "Stability and Change in U.S. Grand Strategy," pp. 561–567.

39. Thus, the Bush administration was warned against the declaration of a "war on terror" as being too ill-defined, unspecific, a war on "tactics," etc., but chose to ignore those warnings. The eminent British military historian Sir Michael Howard argued several weeks after 9/11, when Bush's reaction became clear, that the administration had made a "terrible and irreversible" mistake in calling its antiterrorism campaign "a war." It granted al-Qaeda a status it did not deserve and created overwhelming demand for military action. See Branigan, "Al-Qaida Is Winning War, Allies Warned."

40. For an alternative way of thinking about 9/11, see, for example, Gordon, *Winning the Right War.*

41. Branigan, "Al-Qaida Is Winning War, Allies Warned."

42. Mearsheimer, "Why We Will Soon Miss the Cold War," pp. 35–55.

43. The rise of Neoconservatism as an "applicable ideology" is closely linked to the end of the Cold War.

44. Amounting today to about $700 billion a year, the equivalent of the next largest fifteen to twenty countries in the world.

45. By some estimates, the United States today has about 725 military bases around the world (Johnson, *The Sorrows of Empire*), plus several navies in each of the oceans.

46. Hemmer, "Grand Strategy for the Next Administration," pp. 447–460. The quote is from p. 456. See also Mandelbaum, *The Case for Goliath,* pp. 31–41.

47. Lind, "Beyond American Hegemony," p. 11.

48. Ibid.

49. Brown, *The Illusion of Control.*

50. Pape, "Soft Balancing against the United States," p. 8.

51. Brown, *The Illusion of Control,* chapter 4.

52. Jentleson, "America's Global Role after Bush," pp. 179–200.

53. See, for example, Shapiro, *Containment.*

54. Jentleson, "America's Global Role after Bush," p. 185.

55. Boyle, "The War on Terror in American Grand Strategy," pp. 191–209, especially p. 193.

56. Ibid., pp. 199 and 207.

57. Ibid., p. 200. Pakistan is but the most obvious example of this strategy.

58. Fukuyama, "After Neoconservatism."

59. See Carothers, "A League of Their Own," pp. 44–49.

60. Ibid., p. 46.

61. Ibid., p. 48.

62. Walt, *Taming American Power*, pp. 219–220. Walt contrasts Bush's policy of global hegemony with the policy of selective engagement, which he believes characterized the foreign policy of Bush-41 and Bill Clinton, and the policy of offshore balancing, which he believes has been America's traditional grand strategy.

63. Jentleson, "America's Global Role after Bush," p. 181.

64. Fukuyama, "After Neoconservatism."

65. Kupchan and Trubowitz, "Dead Center," pp. 7–44. The quote is from p. 29.

66. Ibid., p. 42.

67. Kaplan, *The Coming Anarchy*.

68. Kennedy, *The Rise and Fall of the Great Powers*.

69. In fact, one of the major analytical errors on the part of the Bush administration was to make the "war on terror" all-controlling, to the detriment of dealing with other issues such as climate change and other ecological matters.

70. Allison, *Nuclear Terrorism*, p. 205.

71. This issue is dealt with by Brzezinski, *The Choice*.

72. Pape, "Soft Balancing against the United States," pp. 7–45.

73. Fukuyama, *America at the Crossroads*, p. 189.

74. Ikenberry, "The Rise of China and the Future of the West." Ikenberry, however, emphasizes the open nature of the Western-based order, an important consideration.

75. Ibid., p. 30.

76. Brown, *Illusion of Control*, chapter 3.

77. See Posen, "Stability and Change in US Grand Strategy," pp. 561–567. Posen distinguishes between what he calls Clinton's "liberal internationalism" and Bush-43's "national liberalism." For Posen, both strategies are "predisposed to use US power," but disagreements regarding legitimacy, whereby liberal internationalists emphasize more than the national liberals the value of legitimacy. I do not accept Posen's argument that the differences between Clinton's and Bush-43's strategies are relatively small, but his distinction between "primacy" and "restraint" is useful.

78. Boyle, "Utopianism and the Bush Foreign Policy," p. 193.

79. Posen, "Stability and Change in U.S. Grand Strategy," p. 565.

80. Brown, *Illusion of Control*, p. 116; Fukuyama takes a similar position.

81. Ibid., p. 125.

82. Ibid., p. 126.

83. Ibid., p. 129.

84. Ibid., p. 132.

85. Ibid., p. 134.

86. Williams and Caldwell, "Jus Post Bellum: Just War Theory and the Principles of Just Peace," pp. 309–320.

87. Ibid., p. 318.

88. Neuhaus, "Iraq and Moral Judgment," pp. 71–76.

89. See Senator Carl Levin's comments on the new position in McDuffee, "Bush's Time Horizon in Iraq." Levin is the chairman of the Senate Armed Services Committee.

90. In this sense, speeches in which Bush talked about the "Axis of Evil" or democratizing the world (the second inauguration address) are very instructive—they generalize from Iraq to other places.

91. For a reflection of this idea, see the interview of Charlie Rose with Richard Holbrook on National Public Radio (August 2008) as well as Holbrook's article in the September–October 2008 issue of *Foreign Affairs* ("The Next President: Mastering a Daunting Agenda").

92. Or the *hyperpuissance,* as France's foreign minister, Hubert Védrine, called it.

93. A concept used by US Secretary of State Madeleine Albright.

94. Hunt, *The American Ascendancy.*

REFERENCES

Abramowitz, Michael, and Jonathan Weisman. "Bush Defies Lawmakers to Solve
  Iraq." *Washington Post*, January 27, 2007.

Acharya, Sukanta. "American Exceptionalism." *International Studies* 43, no. 2 (January
  1, 2006): pp. 185–202.

Ackerman, Spenser, and John B. Judis. "The Operator." *New Republic* (September 22,
  2003): pp. 18–22.

_____. "The Selling of the Iraq War: The First Casualty." *New Republic* (June 30,
  2003): pp. 14–23.

Adams, Henry. *The Education of Henry Adams: An Autobiography*. Cambridge, MA:
  Riverside Press, 1918.

Agathangelou, Anna M., and L. H. M. Ling. "Power, Borders, Security, Wealth:
  Lessons of Violence and Desire from September 11." *International Studies Quarterly*
  48, no. 3 (September 2004): pp. 517–538.

Albright, Madeleine. "Good Versus Evil Isn't a Strategy." *Los Angeles Times*, March 24,
  2006.

Alexander, Gerard. "International Relations Theory Meets World Politics: The
  Neoconservative vs. Realism Debate." In *Understanding the Bush Doctrine:
  Psychology and Strategy in an Age of Terrorism*, edited by Stanley Allen Renshon and
  Peter Suedfeld, pp. 39–64. New York: Routledge, 2007.

Allison, Graham T. *Essence of Decision: Explaining the Cuban Missile Crisis*. Boston:
  Little, Brown, 1971.

_____. *Nuclear Terrorism: The Ultimate Preventable Catastrophe*. New York: Times
  Books/Henry Holt, 2004.

Almond, Gabriel A. *The American People and Foreign Policy*. New York: Frederick A.
  Praeger Publishers, 1950.

Arnold, Peri E. "One President, Two Presidencies: Bush in Peace and War." In *High
  Risk and Big Ambition: The Presidency of George W. Bush*, edited by Steven E. Schier,
  pp. 145–166. Pittsburgh, PA: University of Pittsburgh Press, 2004.

Babbin, Jed. "Prisoners of Evil." *National Review*, March 23, 2003. National Review
  Online, www.nationalreview.com/babbin/babbin032303.asp.

Babington, Charles, and Dana Milbank. "Bush Advisers Try to Limit Damage: No
  Change in Policy toward Taiwan." *Washington Post*, April 27, 2007.

Bacevich, Andrew J. *The Limits of Power: The End of American Exceptionalism*. New York: Metropolitan Books, Henry Holt and Company, 2008.

————. "Rescinding the Bush Doctrine." *Boston Globe*, March 1, 2007.

Bacevich, Andrew, and Elizabeth Prodromou. "God Is Not Neutral: Religion and US Foreign Policy After 9/11." *Orbis* 43, no. 1 (Winter 2004): pp. 43–54.

Baker, James A., III. "The Right Way to Change a Regime." *New York Times*, August 25, 2002.

Baker, Kevin. "The Year in Ideas: A to Z; American Imperialism, Embraced." *New York Times*, December 9, 2001.

Barber, James David. *The Presidential Character: Predicting Performance in the White House*. Englewood Cliffs, NJ: Prentice Hall International, 1992.

Bar On, Bat-Ami. "Terrorism, Evil, and Everyday Depravity." *Hypatia* 18, no. 1 (Winter 2003): pp. 157–163.

Baum, Matthew A. "How Public Opinion Constrains the Use of Force: The Case of Operation Restore Hope." *Presidential Studies Quarterly* 34, no. 2 (June 2004): pp. 187–226.

Beeson, Mark, and Richard Higgott. "Hegemony, Institutionalism in US Foreign Policy." *Third World Quarterly* 26, no. 7 (October 2005): pp. 1173–1188.

Benjamin, Daniel, and Steven Simon. *The Next Attack: The Failure of the War on Terror and a Strategy for Getting It Right*. New York: Henry Holt, 2006.

Berenskoetter, Felix Sebastian. "Mapping the Mind Gap: A Comparison of US and European Security Strategies." *Security Dialogue* 36, no. 1 (2005): pp. 71–92.

Berggren, D. Jason, and Nicole C. Rae. "Jimmy Carter and George W. Bush: Faith, Foreign Policy, and an Evangelical Presidential Style." *Presidential Studies Quarterly* 36, no. 4 (December 2006): pp. 606–632.

Boggs, Carl. *Imperial Delusions: American Militarism and Endless War*. Lanham, MD: Rowman & Littlefield, 2005.

Boot, Max. *The Savage Wars of Peace: Small Wars and the Rise of American Power*. New York: Basic Books, 2002.

Bostdorff, Denise M. "George W. Bush's Post–September 11 Rhetoric of Covenant Renewal: Upholding the Faith of the Greatest Generation." *Quarterly Journal of Speech* 89, no. 4 (November 2003): pp. 293–319.

Bovard, James. *The Bush Betrayal*. New York: Palgrave Macmillan, 2004.

Boyle, Michael. "Utopianism and the Bush Foreign Policy." *Cambridge Review of International Affairs* 17, no. 1 (2004): pp. 81–103.

Brady, Linda P., and Ilan Peleg. "Carter's Policy on the Supply of Conventional Weapons: Cultural Origins and Diplomatic Consequences." *Crossroads* 15 (Winter 1980): pp. 41–68.

Branigan, Tania. "Al-Qaida Is Winning War, Allies Warned." *Guardian*, October 31, 2001.

Brodkin, Joel. "Herman Wouk: The First Neoconservative." *New Politics* 10, no. 3 (Summer 2005): pp. 110–117.

Brooks, Stephen G., and William C. Wohlforth. "International Relations Theory and the Case against Unilateralism." *Perspectives on Politics* 3, no. 3 (September 2005).

Brose, Christian. "Twilight of the Idols." *National Interest* 72 (Summer 2003): pp. 157–163.

Brown, Seyom. *The Illusion of Control: Force and Foreign Policy in the 21st Century.* Washington, DC: Brookings Institution Press, 2003.

Brzezinski, Zbigniew. "America in a Hostile World." *Foreign Policy*, no. 23 (Summer 1976): pp. 61–96.

_____. *The Choice: Global Domination or Global Leadership.* New York: Basic Books, 2005.

_____. *Second Chance: Three Presidents and the Crisis of American Superpower.* New York: Basic Books, 2007.

Buchanan, Patrick J. *Where the Right Went Wrong: How Neoconservatives Subverted the Reagan Revolution and Hijacked the Bush Presidency.* New York: St. Martin's Griffin, 2005.

Burke, John P. "The Contemporary Presidency: Condoleezza Rice as NSC Advisor: A Case Study of the Honest Broker Role." *Presidential Studies Quarterly* 35, no. 3 (2005): pp. 554–575.

_____. "The Neutral/Honest Broker Role in Foreign-Policy Decision Making: A Reassessment." *Presidential Studies Quarterly* 35, no. 2 (2005): pp. 229–258.

Bush, George W. *George W. Bush on God and Country: The President Speaks Out about Faith, Principle, and Patriotism.* Fairfax, VA: Allegiance, 2004.

Calabresi, Steven G. "The President, the Supreme Court, and the Founding Fathers: A Reply to Professor Ackerman." *University of Chicago Law Review* 73 (2005): pp. 469–485.

Cameron, Fraser. *US Foreign Policy After the Cold War: Global Hegemon or Reluctant Sheriff?* London and New York: Routledge, 2005.

Cantori, Louis J., and Augustus Richard Norton. "Evaluating the Bush Menu for Change in the Middle East." *Middle East Policy* 12, no. 1 (Spring 2005): pp. 97–122.

Carothers, Thomas. "The Backlash Against Democracy Promotion." *Foreign Affairs* 85, no. 2 (March–April 2006): pp. 55–68.

_____. "A League of Their Own." *Foreign Policy* 167 (July–August 2008): pp. 44–49.

_____. "Promoting Democracy and Fighting Terror." *Foreign Affairs* 82, no. 1 (January–February 2003): pp. 84–97.

Carter, Ashton B. "America's New Strategic Partner?" *Foreign Affairs* 85, no. 4 (July–August 2006): pp. 33–44.

Chaddock, Gail Russell. "A Bush Vision of Pax Americana." *Christian Science Monitor*, September 23, 2002.

Chernus, Ira. *Monsters to Destroy: The Neoconservative War on Terror and Sin.* Boulder,
    CO: Paradigm Publishers, 2006.

Clinton, Hillary Rodham. "Security and Opportunity for the Twenty-first Century."
    Foreign Affairs 86, no. 6 (November–December 2007): pp. 2–19.

Coe, Kevin. "No Shades of Gray: The Binary Discourse of George W. Bush and an
    Echoing Press." *Journal of Communication* 54, no. 2 (June 2004): pp. 234–252.

Cohen, David. "From the Fabulous Baker Boys to the Master of Disaster." *Presidential
    Studies Quarterly* 32, no. 3 (September 2002): pp. 463–483.

Coles, Roberta L. "Manifest Destiny Adapted for the 1990s." *Sociology of Religion* 63,
    no. 4 (Winter 2002): pp. 403–426.

_____. "War and the Contest over National Identity." *Sociological Review* 50, no. 4
    (November 2002): pp. 586–609.

Cook, Steven A. "The Right Way to Promote Arab Reform." *Foreign Affairs* 84, no. 2
    (March–April 2005): pp. 91–102.

Crabb, Cecil V., Jr. *American Foreign Policy in the Nuclear Age*, 3rd ed. New York:
    Harper & Row, 1972.

_____. *Policy-Makers and Critics: Conflicting Theories of American Foreign Policy.*
    New York: Praeger Publishers, 1976.

Crawford, Neta C. "Just War Theory and the US Counterterror War." *Perspectives on
    Politics* 1, no. 1 (March 2003): pp. 5–25.

_____. "The Road to Global Empire: The Logic of US Foreign Policy after 9/11."
    Orbis 48, no. 4 (Fall 2004): pp. 685–702.

Culianu, Ioan. *The Tree of Gnosis: Gnostic Mythology from Early Christianity to Modern
    Nihilism.* San Francisco: HarperCollins, 1992.

Daalder, Ivo H., and James M. Lindsay. *America Unbound: The Bush Revolution in
    Foreign Policy.* Washington, DC: Brookings Institution Press, 2003.

_____. "Does the Bush Foreign Policy Revolution Have a Future? In Search of
    Monsters." *The World Today* 60, no. 1 (January 2004): pp. 7–9.

Davis, John. "Infighting in Washington: The Impact of Bureaucratic Politics on US Iraq
    Policy." In *Presidential Policies and the Road to the Second Iraq War: From Forty-One
    to Forty-Three,* edited by John Davis, pp. 92–122. Aldershot, UK: Ashgate, 2006.

_____, ed. *Presidential Policies and the Road to the Second Iraq War: From Forty-One
    to Forty-Three.* Aldershot, UK: Ashgate, 2006.

Dean, John W. "Predicting Presidential Performance: Is George W. Bush an Active-
    Negative President Like Nixon, LBJ, Hoover and Wilson?" FindLaw.com, May 22,
    2004.

"Defending and Advancing Freedom: A Symposium." (Discussion) *Commentary* 120,
    no. 4 (November 2005): p. 21. (Composed of contributions from various authors.)

Desch, Michael C. "Bush and the Generals." *Foreign Affairs* 86, no. 3 (May–June 2007):
    pp. 97–108.

Dewey, John. *Liberalism and Social Action.* New York: Capricorn Books, 1963.

Dietrich, John W., ed. *The George W. Bush Foreign Policy Reader: Presidential Speeches and Commentary.* Armonk, NY: M. E. Sharpe, 2005.

Dobbins, James. "America's Role in Nation-Building: From Germany to Iraq." *Survival* 45, no. 4 (2003): pp. 87–109.

————. "Who Lost Iraq?" *Foreign Affairs* 86, no. 5 (September–October 2007): pp. 61–74.

Dockrill, Saki Ruth. "Dealing with Fear: Implementing the Bush Doctrine of Preemptive Attack." *Politics & Policy* 34, no. 2 (June 2006): pp. 344–373.

Dodge, Toby. *Inventing Iraq: The Failure of Nation-Building and a History Denied.* New York: Columbia University Press, 2005.

Dolan, Chris J., and David B. Cohen. "The War about the War: Iraq and the Politics of National Security Advising in the G. W. Bush Administration First Term." *Politics & Policy* 34, no. 1 (March 2006): pp. 30–64.

Dorrien, Gary J. "Consolidating the Empire." *Political Theology* 6, no. 4 (October 2005): pp. 409–428.

————. *Imperial Designs: Neoconservatism and the New Pax Americana.* New York: Routledge, 2004.

————. *The Neoconservative Mind: Politics, Culture, and the War of Ideology.* Philadelphia: Temple University Press, 1993.

Dosal, Paul. "The Latinamericanization of American Foreign Policy." *Journal of Developing Societies* 21, nos. 3–4 (2005): pp. 253–269.

Draper, Robert. *Dead Certain: The Presidency of George W. Bush.* New York: Free Press, 2007.

Drew, Julie. "Identity Crisis: Gender, Public Discourse, and 9/11." *Women & Language* 27, no. 2 (2004): pp. 71–77.

Drezner, Daniel W. "The Future of US Foreign Policy." *Internationale Politik und Gesellschaft* 15 (January 2008): pp. 11–35.

————. "The New New World Order." *Foreign Affairs* 86, no. 2 (March–April 2007): pp. 34–46.

Drumheller, Tyler, and Elaine Monaghan. *On the Brink: An Insider's Account of How the White House Compromised American Intelligence.* New York: Carroll & Graf, 2006.

Dubose, Lou, and Jake Bernstein. *Vice: Dick Cheney and the Hijacking of the American Presidency.* New York: Random House, 2006.

Dunn, Charles W., and J. David Woodard. *The Conservative Tradition in America.* Lanham, MD: Rowman & Littlefield, 1996.

Durham, Martin. "The Republic in Danger: Neoconservatism, the American Right and the Politics of Empire." *Political Quarterly* 77, no. 1 (2006): pp. 43–52.

Edelman, Ken. "Cakewalk in Iran." *Washington Post,* February 13, 2002.

————. "Cakewalk Revisited." *Washington Post,* April 10, 2004.

Edwards, John. "Reengaging with the World." *Foreign Affairs* 86, no. 5 (September–October 2007): pp. 19–36.

Eisendrath, Craig R., and Melvin A. Goodman. *Bush League Diplomacy: How the Neoconservatives Are Putting the World at Risk.* Amherst, NY: Prometheus Books, 2004.

Fallows, James. "Blind into Baghdad." *Atlantic Monthly* 293, no. 1 (January–February 2004): pp. 52–74.

————. "Bush's Lost Year." *Atlantic Monthly* 294, no. 3 (October 2004): pp. 68–84.

Ferguson, Niall. *Colossus: The Price of America's Empire.* New York: Penguin Press, 2005.

————. "The Unconscious Colossus." *Daedalus* 134, no. 2 (Spring 2005): pp. 18–34.

Festinger, Leon. *When Prophecy Fails: A Social and Psychological Study of a Modern Group That Predicted the Destruction of the World.* New York: Harper & Row, 1964.

Frank, Justin. *Bush on the Couch: Inside the Mind of the President.* New York: HarperCollins, 2004.

Frum, David, and Richard Perle. *An End to Evil: How to Win the War on Terror.* New York: Random House, 2003.

Fukuyama, Francis. "After NeoConservatism." *New York Times Magazine*, February 19, 2006, pp. 62–71.

————. *America at the Crossroads: Democracy, Power, and the Neoconservative Legacy.* New Haven, CT: Yale University Press, 2006.

————. "The End of History?" *National Interest* 16 (Summer 1989): pp. 3–18.

————. *The End of History and the Last Man.* New York: Avon Press, 1993.

Fulbright, William. *The Arrogance of Power.* New York: Random House, 1966.

Fullilove, Michael. "All the President's Men." *Foreign Affairs* 84, no. 2 (March–April 2005): pp. 13–18.

Gaddis, John Lewis. "Grand Strategy in the Second Term." *Foreign Affairs* 84, no. 1 (January–February 2005): pp. 2–15.

————. *Surprise, Security, and the American Experience.* Cambridge, MA: Harvard University Press, 2004.

Garfinkle, Adam. "Bye Bye Bush: What History Will Make of 43." *Foreign Affairs* 87, no. 2 (March–April 2008): pp. 145–52.

Gause, F. Gregory, III. "Can Democracy Stop Terrorism?" *Foreign Affairs* 84, no. 5 (September–October 2005): pp. 62–76.

George, Alexander L. *Presidential Decision-Making in Foreign Policy: The Effective Use of Information and Advice.* Boulder, CO: Westview Press, 1980.

George, Alexander L., and Juliette L. George. *Woodrow Wilson and Colonel House: A Personality Study.* Mineola, NY: Dover, 1964.

George, Jim. "Leo Strauss, Neoconservatism and US Foreign Policy: Esoteric Nihilism and the Bush Doctrine." *International Politics* 42, no. 2 (2005): pp. 174–202.

Giuliani, Rudolph W. "Toward a Realistic Peace." *Foreign Affairs* 86, no. 5 (September–October 2007): pp. 2–18.

Glad, Betty. "Black-and-White Thinking: Ronald Reagan's Approach to Foreign Policy." *Political Psychology* 4 (Spring 1983): pp. 33–76.

Glad, Betty, and Chris J. Dolan, eds. *Striking First: The Preventive Doctrine and the Reshaping of US Foreign Policy.* New York: Palgrave Macmillan, 2004.

Gordon, Michael R., and Bernard E. Trainor. *Cobra II: The Inside Story of the Invasion and Occupation of Iraq.* New York: Pantheon Books, 2006.

Gordon, Philip H. "Can the War on Terror Be Won?" *Foreign Affairs* 86, no. 6 (November–December 2007): pp. 53–66.

_____. "The End of the Bush Revolution." *Foreign Affairs* 85, no. 4 (July–August 2006): pp. 75–86.

_____. *Winning the Right War: The Path to Security for America and the World.* New York: Times Books, 2007.

Gray, Christine. "The Bush Doctrine Revisited: The 2006 National Security Strategy of the USA." *Chinese Journal of International Law* 5, no. 3 (2006): pp. 555–578.

Greenstein, Fred. "The Changing Leadership of George W. Bush: A Pre- and Post-9/11 Comparison." *Presidential Studies Quarterly* 32, no. 2 (June 2002): pp. 387–396.

Greenwald, Glenn. *A Tragic Legacy: How a Good vs. Evil Mentality Destroyed the Bush Presidency.* New York: Three Rivers Press, 2007.

Grondin, David. "Mistaking Hegemony for Empire: Neoconservatives, the Bush Doctrine, and the Democratic Empire." *International Journal* 61, no. 1 (Winter 2005): pp. 227–241.

Guertner, Gary L. "European Views of Preemption in US National Security Strategy." *Parameters* 37, no. 2 (Summer 2007): pp. 31–44.

Gurtov, Mel. *Superpower on Crusade: The Bush Doctrine in US Foreign Policy.* Boulder, CO: Lynne Rienner, 2006.

Haass, Richard N. "Defining US Foreign Policy in a Post–Post–Cold War World." U.S. Department of State, April 22, 2002, www.state.gov/s/p/rem/9632.htm.

_____. "Regime Change and Its Limits." *Foreign Affairs* 84, no. 4 (July–August 2005): pp. 66–78.

_____. *The Reluctant Sheriff: The United States After the Cold War.* New York: Council on Foreign Relations, 1997.

Haley, P. Edward. *Strategies of Dominance: The Misdirection of US Foreign Policy.* Baltimore, MD: Woodrow Wilson Center Press/Johns Hopkins University Press, 2006.

Halper, Stefan A., and Jonathan Clarke. *America Alone: The Neo-Conservatives and the Global Order.* Cambridge, UK: Cambridge University Press, 2004.

Haney, Patrick. "Foreign-Policy Advising: Models and Mysteries from the Bush Administration." *Presidential Studies Quarterly* 35, no. 2 (June 2005): pp. 289–302.

Hartz, Louis. *The Liberal Tradition in America.* New York: Harcourt, Brace, and World, 1955.

Hasian, Marouf, Jr. "Dangerous Supplements, Inventive Dissent, and Military Critiques of the Bush Administration's Unitary Executive Theories." *Presidential Studies Quarterly* 37, no. 4 (December 2007): pp. 693–716.

Heilbrunn, Jacob. *They Knew They Were Right: The Rise of the Neocons.* New York: Doubleday, 2008.

Hendrickson, David C. "Preemption, Unilateralism, and Hegemony: The American Tradition?" *Orbis* 50, no. 2 (Spring 2006): pp. 273–287.

Herman, Arthur. "How to Win in Iraq—and How to Lose." *Commentary* 123, no. 4 (2007): pp. 23–29.

Hermann, Charles F. *Crisis in Foreign Policy: A Situation Analysis.* Indianapolis: Bobbs Merrill, 1969.

_____. "International Crisis as a Situational Variable." In *International Politics and Foreign Policy*, rev. ed., edited by James N. Rosenau. New York: Free Press, 1969.

Hoffman, Stanley. *Gulliver's Troubles, or the Setting of American Foreign Policy.* New York: McGraw-Hill, 1968.

_____. *Gulliver Unbound: The Imperial Temptation and the War in Iraq.* Lanham, MD: Rowman & Littlefield, 2004.

_____. *Primacy or World Order: American Foreign Policy since the Cold War.* New York: McGraw-Hill, 1978.

Holmes, Kim. "Ensuring a Legacy." *National Interest* 87 (January–February 2007): pp. 21–27.

Huliaris, Asteris. "Evangelists, Oil Companies, and Terrorists: The Bush Administration's Policy Towards Sudan." *Orbis* 50, no. 4 (Fall 2006): pp. 709–724.

Hunt, Michael H. *The American Ascendancy: How the United States Gained and Wielded Global Dominance.* Chapel Hill: University of North Carolina Press, 2007.

Hybel, Alex Roberto, and Justin Matthew Kaufman. *The Bush Administrations and Saddam Hussein: Deciding on Conflict.* New York: Palgrave Macmillan, 2006.

Ignatieff, Michael. "The American Empire: The Burden." *New York Times Magazine*, January 5, 2003.

Ikenberry, G. John. "The End of the Neo-Conservative Moment." *Survival* 46, no. 1 (2004): pp. 7–22.

_____. "Illusions of Empire: Defining the New American Order." *Foreign Affairs* 83, no. 2 (March–April 2004): pp. 144–154.

_____. "The Rise of China and the Future of the West: Can the Liberal System Survive?" *Foreign Affairs* 87, no. 1 (January–February 2008): pp. 23–37.

Isikoff, Michael, and David Corn. *Hubris: The Inside Story of Spin, Scandal and the Selling of the Iraq War.* New York: Random House, 2006.

Jacoby, Jeff. "What About the Bush Doctrine?" *Boston Globe*, May 28, 2008.

Janis, Irving L. *Groupthink: Psychological Studies of Policy Decisions and Fiascoes.* Boston: Houghton Mifflin, 1982.

Jentleson, Bruce W. "America's Global Role after Bush." *Survival* 49, no. 3 (Autumn 2007): pp. 179–200.

Jervis, Robert. *American Foreign Policy in a New Era.* London and New York: Routledge, 2005.

_____. "The Remaking of a Unipolar World." *Washington Quarterly* 29, no. 3 (2006–2007): pp. 7–19.

_____. "Understanding the Bush Doctrine." *Political Science Quarterly* 118, no. 3 (Fall 2003): pp. 365–388.

_____. "Why the Bush Doctrine Cannot Be Sustained." *Political Science Quarterly* 120, no. 3 (Fall 2005): pp. 351–377.

Joffe, Josef. *Überpower: The Imperial Temptation of America.* New York: W. W. Norton, 2006.

Johnson, Chalmers A. *The Sorrows of Empire: Militarism, Secrecy, and the End of the Republic.* New York: Metropolitan Books, 2004.

Johnson, Richard T. *Managing the White House.* New York: Harper & Row, 1974.

Judis, John B. "Imperial Amnesia." *Foreign Policy* 143 (July–August 2004): pp. 50–59.

Kagan, Frederick W. "The U.S. Military's Manpower Crisis." *Foreign Affairs* 85, no. 4 (July–August 2006): pp. 97–110.

Kagan, Robert. *Of Paradise and Power: America & Europe in the New World Order.* New York: Knopf, 2003.

_____. *The Return of History and the End of Dreams.* New York: Knopf, 2008.

Kagan, Robert, and William Kristol. "An Administration of One." *Weekly Standard,* December 1, 2003, pp. 7–8.

_____. *Present Dangers: Crisis and Opportunity in American Foreign and Defense Policy.* San Francisco: Encounter Books, 2000.

_____. "Toward a Neo-Reaganite Foreign Policy." *Foreign Affairs* 75, no. 4 (July–August 1996): pp. 18–32.

Kaplan, Fred M. *Daydream Believers: How a Few Grand Ideas Wrecked American Power.* Hoboken, NJ: John Wiley & Sons, 2008.

Kaplan, Lawrence. "Bush's Split Personality." *New Republic,* July 7, 2003.

Kaplan, Lawrence F., and William Kristol. *The War Over Iraq: Saddam's Tyranny and America's Mission.* San Francisco: Encounter Books, 2003.

Kaplan, Robert D. "The Coming Anarchy: How Scarcity, Crime, Overpopulation, Tribalism, and Disease Are Rapidly Destroying the Social Fabric of Our Planet." *Atlantic Monthly,* February 1994.

_____. *The Coming Anarchy: Shattering the Dreams of the Post Cold War.* New York: Random House, 2000.

Kaufman, Robert G. *In Defense of the Bush Doctrine*. Lexington: University Press of Kentucky, 2007.

Keller, William W., and Gordon R. Mitchell, eds. *Hitting First: Preventative Force in US Security Strategy*. Pittsburgh, PA: University of Pittsburgh Press, 2006.

Kellner, Douglas. "Bushspeak and the Politics of Lying: Presidential Rhetoric in the 'War on Terror' (George Bush)." *Presidential Studies Quarterly* 37, no. 4 (December 2007): pp. 622–645.

_____. "Preemptive Strikes and the War on Iraq: A Critique of Bush Administration Unilateralism and Militarism." *New Political Science* 26, no. 3 (September 2004): pp. 417–440.

Kengor, Paul. *God and George W. Bush: A Spiritual Life*. New York: HarperCollins, 2004.

Kennedy, David M. "What 'W' Owes to 'WW': President Bush May Not Even Know It, but He Can Trace His View of the World to Woodrow Wilson, Who Defined Diplomatic Destiny for America That We Can't Escape." *Atlantic Monthly* 295, no. 2 (March 2005): pp. 36–37.

Kennedy, Paul M. *The Rise and Fall of the Great Powers: Economic Change and Military Conflict from 1500 to 2000*. New York: Random House, 1987.

Krahmann, Elke. "American Hegemony or Global Governance?" *International Studies Review* 7, no. 4 (2005): pp. 531–545.

Kramer, Ronald, R. Michalowski, and D. Rothe. "The Supreme International Crime: How the US War in Iraq Threatens the Rule of Law." *Social Justice* 32, no. 2 (Summer 2005): pp. 52–81.

Krauthammer, Charles. "The Neoconservative Convergence." *Commentary* 120, no. 1 (July–August 2005): pp. 21–26.

_____. "The Unipolar Moment." *Foreign Affairs* 70, no. 1 (1990): pp. 23–33.

Kristol, Irving. *Neoconservatism: The Autobiography of an Idea*. New York: Free Press, 1995.

_____. "The Neoconservative Persuasion." *Weekly Standard* 8, no. 47 (August 23, 2003): pp. 23–25.

_____. "Toward A Neo-Reaganite Foreign Policy." *Foreign Affairs* 75, no. 4 (July 1996): pp. 18–32.

Kumar, Martha Joynt, and Terry Sullivan, eds. *The White House World: Transitions, Organizations, and Office Operations*. College Station: Texas A&M University Press, 2003.

Kupchan, Charles, and Peter Trubowitz. "Dead Center: The Demise of Liberal Internationalism in the United States." *International Security* 32, no. 2 (Fall 2007): pp. 7–44.

Kurth, James. "Ignoring History: US Democratization in the Muslim World." *Orbis* 49, no. 2 (2005): pp. 305–322.

Lampe, John R. "The Lessons of Bosnia and Kosovo for Iraq." *Current History* 671 (March 2004): pp. 113–118.

Laver, Harry S. "Preemption and the Evolution of America's Strategic Defense." *Parameters* 35, no. 2 (2005): pp. 107–120.

Lears, Jackson. "The Arrogance of Power Revisited." *Raritan: A Quarterly Review* 26, no. 1 (Summer 2006): pp. 31–46.

Lennon, Alexander T. J., and Camille Eiss, eds. *Reshaping Rogue States: Preemption, Regime Change, and US Policy Toward Iran, Iraq, and North Korea*. Cambridge, MA: MIT Press, 2004.

Levi, Michael. "Stopping Nuclear Terrorism: The Dangerous Allure of a Perfect Defense." *Foreign Affairs* 87, no. 1 (January–February 2008): pp. 131–140.

Lieven, Anatol. "The Two Fukuyamas." *National Interest* 84 (July 2006): pp. 123–130.

Lind, Michael. "Beyond American Hegemony." *National Interest* 89 (May–June 2007): pp. 9–15.

Lipset, Seymour Martin. *American Exceptionalism: A Double Edged Sword*. New York: W. W. Norton, 1996.

Lowry, Richard. "Reaganism v. Neo-Reaganism." *National Interest* 79 (Spring 2005): pp. 35–41.

MacDonald, Scott. "Hitler's Shadow: Historical Analogies and the Iraqi Invasion of Kuwait." *Diplomacy & Statecraft* 13, no. 4 (2002): pp. 29–59.

Maddox, Graham. "The 'Crusade' Against Evil: Bush's Fundamentalism." *Australian Journal of Politics and History* 49, no. 3 (September 2003): pp. 398–411.

Maggio, J. "The Presidential Rhetoric of Terror: The Re(Creation) of Reality Immediately after 9/11." *Politics & Policy* 35, no. 4 (December 2007): pp. 810–835.

Mann, Bonnie. "How America Justifies Its War: A Modern/Postmodern Aesthetics of Masculinity and Sovereignty." *Hypatia* 16, no. 4 (2003): pp. 147–163.

Mann, James. *Rise of the Vulcans: The History of Bush's War Cabinet*. New York: Viking Press, 2004.

Mann, Michael. *Incoherent Empire*. London and New York: Verso, 2005.

Mansell, Wade. "John Bolton and the US' Retreat from International Law." *Social & Legal Studies* 14, no. 4 (December 2005): pp. 459–485.

Mansfield, Stephen. *The Faith of George W. Bush*. New York: Tarcher, 2003.

Marty, Martin E. "The Sin of Pride." *Newsweek,* March 10, 2003.

Mazarr, Michael J. "George W. Bush, Idealist." *International Affairs* 79, no. 3 (May 2002): pp. 503–522.

———. "The Long Road to Pyongyang." *Foreign Affairs* 86, no. 5 (September–October 2007): pp. 75–94.

McCain, John. "An Enduring Peace Built on Freedom." *Foreign Affairs* 86, no. 6 (November–December 2007): pp. 19–34.

McClellan, Scott. *What Happened: Inside the Bush White House and Washington's Culture of Deception*. New York: PublicAffairs, 2008.

McCrisken, Trevor B. *American Exceptionalism & the Legacy of Vietnam*. New York: Palgrave MacMillan, 2003.

McDougall, Walter A. *Promised Land, Crusader State: The American Encounter with the World Since 1776*. Boston: Houghton Mifflin, 1997.

McDuffee, Allen. "Bush's Time Horizon in Iraq." *The Nation*, August 5, 2008.

McLaren, Peter, and Gregory Martin. "The Legend of the Bush Gang: Imperialism, War and Propaganda." *Cultural Studies* 4, no. 3 (2004): pp. 281–303.

Mead, Walter Russell. "American Grand Strategy in a World at Risk." *Orbis* 49, no. 4 (Fall 2005): pp. 589–598.

————. *Power, Terror, Peace, and War: America's Grand Strategy in a World at Risk*. New York: Knopf, 2004.

————. *Special Providence: American Foreign Policy and How It Changed the World*. New York: Knopf, 2001.

Mearsheimer, John J. *The Tragedy of Great Power Politics*. New York: W. W. Norton, 2001.

————. "Why We Will Soon Miss the Cold War." *Atlantic Magazine* 266, no. 2 (August 1990): pp. 35–50.

Mearsheimer, John J., and Stephen Walt. "An Unnecessary War." *Foreign Policy* 134 (2003): pp. 50–59.

Merli, Frank J., and Theodore A. Wilson, eds. *Makers of American Diplomacy*. New York: Charles Scribner's Sons, 1974.

Merton, Robert K. *Social Theory and Social Structure*. New York: Free Press, 1968.

Mitchell, Alison. "NATO Debate: From Big Risk to Sure Thing." *New York Times*, March 20, 1998.

Moens, Alexander. *The Foreign Policy of George W. Bush: Values, Strategy & Loyalty*. Aldershot, UK: Ashgate, 2005.

Moïsi, Dominique. "The Land of Hope Again? An Old Dream for a New America." *Foreign Affairs*, 85, no. 5 (September–October 2008): pp. 140–146.

Monten, Jonathan. "Primacy and Grand Strategic Beliefs in US Unilateralism." *Global Governance* 13, no. 1 (January–March 2007): pp. 119–138.

————. "The Roots of the Bush Doctrine: Power, Nationalism, and Democracy Promotion in US Strategy." *International Security* 29, no. 4 (Spring 2005): pp. 112–156.

Mueller, John. "The Iraq Syndrome." *Foreign Affairs* 84, no. 6 (November–December 2005): pp. 44–54.

Muravchik, Joshua. "How to Wreck NATO." *Commentary* 107, no. 4 (April 1999): pp. 29–33.

_____. "Operation Comeback: How to Save the Neocons." *Foreign Policy* 157 (November–December 2006): pp. 18–20.

_____. "The UN on the Loose." *Commentary* 114, no. 1 (July–August 2002): pp. 29–32.

_____. "What Use Is the UN? Fifty Years on, the World Organization Has Proved Militarily, Diplomatically, and Morally Bankrupt." *Commentary* 101, no. 4 (April 1996): pp. 51–62.

Murphy, Bruce F. "The Last Best Hope? The Perils of American Exceptionalism." *Commonweal* 17 (2004): pp. 20–21.

Neuhaus, Richard. "Iraq & Moral Judgment." *First Things: A Monthly Journal of Religion and Public Life* 156 (October 2005): pp. 71–76.

Noon, David Hoogland. "Operation Enduring Analogy: World War II, the War on Terror, and the Uses of Historical Memory." *Rhetoric & Public Affairs* 7, no. 3 (Fall 2004): pp. 339–364.

Noonan, Peggy. "To Beat a Man, You Need a Plan." *Wall Street Journal*, September 15, 2006.

Norris, Andrew. "'Us' and 'Them.'" *Metaphilosophy* 35, no. 3 (2004): pp. 249–272.

Novak, Michael. "Good, Evil, and My Friend Irwin: A Literary Luncheon with President Bush." *Weekly Standard*, March 14, 2007, www.weeklystandard.com/Content/Public/Articles/000/000/013/408pahsi.asp.

Nuruzzaman, Muhammad. "Beyond the Realist Theories." *International Studies Perspectives* 7, no. 3 (2006): pp. 239–253.

Nye, Joseph S., Jr. "The Decline of America's Soft Power." *Foreign Affairs* 83, no. 3 (May–June 2004): pp. 16–20.

_____. *Soft Power: The Means to Success in World Politics*. New York: PublicAffairs, 2004.

_____. "Transformational Leadership and U.S. Grand Strategy." *Foreign Affairs* 85, no. 4 (July–August 2006): pp. 139–149.

Offner, Arnold A. "Rogue President, Rogue Nation: Bush and U.S. National Security." *Diplomatic History* 29, no. 3 (June 2005): pp. 433–435.

O'Hanlon, Michael E. "Iraq Without a Plan." *Policy Review* 128 (December 2004–January 2005): pp. 33–45.

Ornstein, Norman J., and Thomas E. Mann. "When Congress Checks Out." *Foreign Affairs* 85, no. 6 (November–December 2006): pp. 67–82.

Panofsky, Wolfgang K. H. "Nuclear Insecurity." *Foreign Affairs* 86, no. 5 (September–October 2007): pp. 109–118.

Pape, Robert A. "Soft Balancing Against the United States." *International Security* 30, no. 1 (Summer 2005): pp. 7–45.

Patten, Chris. "Democracy Doesn't Flow from the Barrel of a Gun." *Foreign Policy* 138 (September–October 2003): pp. 40–45.

Peleg, Ilan. *Democratizing the Hegemonic State: Political Transformation in the Age of Identity*. Cambridge, UK: Cambridge University Press, 2007.

Peleg, Ilan, and Paul Scham. "Israeli Neo-Revisionism and American Neoconservatism: The Unexplored Parallels." *Middle East Journal* 61, no. 1 (Winter 2007): pp. 73–94.

Perkovich, George. "Giving Justice Its Due." *Foreign Affairs* 84, no. 4 (July–August 2005): pp. 79–93.

Pfiffner, James P. "Did President Bush Mislead the Country in His Arguments for War with Iraq?" *Presidential Studies Quarterly* 34, no. 1 (March 2004): pp. 25–46.

_____. "The First MBA President: George W. Bush as a Public Administrator." *Public Administration Review* 67, no. 1 (January–February 2007): pp. 6–20.

Podhoretz, Norman. "Is the Bush Doctrine Dead?" *Commentary* 122, no. 2 (September 2006): p. 17–31.

Pillar, Paul R. "Intelligence, Policy and the War in Iraq." *Foreign Affairs* 85 (March–April 2006): pp. 15–28.

Ponder, Daniel E. *Good Advice: Information and Policy Making in the White House*. College Station: Texas A&M Press, 2000.

Porch, Douglas. "Occupational Hazards: Myths of 1945 & US Iraq Policy." *National Interest* 72 (Summer 2003): pp. 35–47.

Posen, Barry R. "Stability and Change in US Grand Strategy." *Orbis* 51, no. 4 (Fall 2007): pp. 561–567.

Potter, David M. *People of Plenty*. Chicago: University of Chicago Press, 1954.

Prendergast, John, and Colin Thomas-Jensen. "Blowing the Horn." *Foreign Affairs* 86, no. 2 (March–April 2007): pp. 59–74.

Quinn, Adam. "The Great Illusion: Chimeras of Isolationism and Realism in Post-Iraq US Foreign Policy." *Politics & Policy* 35, no. 3 (2007): pp. 522–547.

Ray, James, and Juliet Kaarbo. *Global Politics*, 9th ed. Boston: Houghton Mifflin, 2007.

Renshon, Stanley Allen, and Peter Suedfeld. *Understanding the Bush Doctrine: Psychology and Strategy in an Age of Terrorism*. New York: Routledge, 2007.

Rhodes, Edward. "The Imperial Logic of Bush's Liberal Agenda." *Survival* 45, no. 1 (March 2003): pp. 131–154.

Ribuffo, Leo P. "George W. Bush and the Latest Evangelical Menace." *Dissent* 53, no. 4 (Fall 2006): pp. 42–49.

Rice, Condoleezza. "Promoting the National Interest." *Foreign Affairs* 79, no. 1 (January–February 2000): pp. 45–62.

_____. "Rethinking the National Interest: American Realism for a New World." *Foreign Affairs* 87, no. 4 (July–August 2008): pp. 2–26.

Ricks, Thomas E. *Fiasco: The American Military Adventure in Iraq*. New York: Penguin, 2006.

Roberts, Alasdair. "The War We Deserve." *Foreign Policy* 163 (November–December 2007): pp. 44–50.

Roberts, Andrew. *A History of the English-Speaking Peoples Since 1900.* New York: HarperCollins, 2007.

Ross, Dennis. "Remember Statecraft? What Diplomacy Can Do, and Why We Need It More Than Ever." *American Scholar* 76, no. 3 (Summer 2007): pp. 47–60.

Ross, Gregory. "To Do Good in the World: Woodrow Wilson and America's Mission." In *Makers of American Diplomacy*, edited by Frank J. Merli and Theodore A. Wilson, pp. 259–283. New York: Charles Scribner's Sons, 1974.

Rossiter, Clinton. *The First American Revolution.* New York: Harcourt, Brace, and World, 1956.

Rubin, Barnett R. "Saving Afghanistan." *Foreign Affairs* 86, no. 1 (January–February 2007): pp. 57–78.

Sanger, David. "A Speech About Nothing, Something, Everything." *New York Times*, January 23, 2005.

Schier, Steven E., ed. *High Risk & Big Ambition: The Presidency of George W. Bush.* Pittsburgh, PA: University of Pittsburgh Press, 2004.

Schmidt, John R. "Can Outsiders Bring Democracy to Post-Conflict States?" *Orbis* 52, no. 1 (Winter 2008): pp. 107–122.

Schuman, Howard, and Amy Corning. "Comparing Iraq to Vietnam." *Public Opinion Quarterly* 70, no. 1 (Spring 2006): pp. 78–87.

Schweder, Richard A. "George W. Bush and the Missionary Position." *Daedalus* 133, no. 3 (Summer 2004): pp. 26–36.

Scoblic, J. Peter. *U.S. vs. Them: How a Half Century of Conservatism Has Undermined America's Security.* New York: Viking Books, 2008.

Scowcroft, Brent. "Don't Attack Saddam." *Wall Street Journal*, August 15, 2002, p. 22.

Seldin, Zachary. "Neoconservatives and the American Mainstream." *Policy Review Online* 124 (April–May 2004): pp. 29–39.

Shapiro, Ian. *Containment: Rebuilding a Strategy Against Global Terror.* Princeton, NJ: Princeton University Press, 2007.

Sharpe, Kenneth. "Realpolitik or Imperial Hubris: The Latin American Drug War and U.S. Foreign Policy in Iraq." *Orbis* 50, no. 3 (Summer 2006): pp. 481–499.

Shatz, Adam. "Lessons from Algiers." *The Nation* 277, no. 11 (October 2003): p. 8.

Shogan, Colleen J. "Anti-Intellectualism in the Modern Presidency: A Republican Populism." *Perspectives on Politics* 5, no. 2 (June 2007): pp. 295–303.

Skidmore, David. "Understanding the Unilateralist Turn in US Foreign Policy." *Foreign Policy Analysis* 1, no. 2 (2005): pp. 207–228.

Skowronek, Stephen. "Leadership by Definition: First Term Reflections on George W. Bush's Political Stance." *Perspectives on Politics* 3, no. 4 (2005): pp. 817–831.

Smidt, Corwin E. "Religion and American Attitudes toward Islam and an Invasion of Iraq." *Sociology of Religion* 66, no. 3 (Fall 2005): pp. 243–262.

Spence, Keith. "World Risk Society and the War Against Terror." *Political Studies* 53, no. 2 (June 2005): pp. 284–302.

Spielvogel, Christin. "You Know Where I Stand." *Rhetoric & Public Affairs* 8, no. 4 (2005): pp. 549–570.

Spiro, Peter J. "The New Sovereigntists—American Exceptionalism and Its False Prophets." *Foreign Affairs* 79, no. 6 (November–December 2000): pp. 9–15.

Steinberg, James. "The Bush Foreign Policy Revolution." *New Perspectives Quarterly* 20, no. 3 (Summer 2003): pp. 5–14.

Stelzer, Irwin M. "Reader of the Free World: A Literary Luncheon with the President." *Weekly Standard* 12 (Issue 25), March 12, 2007.

_____, ed. *The Neocon Reader*. New York: Grove Press, 2004.

Stoessinger, John G. *Crusaders and Pragmatists: Movers of Modern American Foreign Policy*. New York: W. W. Norton, 1979.

Stuckey, Mary E., and Joshua R. Ritter. "George Bush, Human Rights, and American Democracy." *Presidential Studies Quarterly* 37, no. 4 (December 2007): pp. 646–667.

Sullivan, John L. "The Great Nation of Futurity." *United States Democratic Review* 6, no. 23 (1839): pp. 426–430.

Suskind, Ron. "Faith, Certainty and the Presidency of George W. Bush." *New York Times Magazine*, October 17, 2004.

_____. *The One Percent Doctrine: Deep Inside America's Pursuit of Its Enemies Since 9/11*. New York: Simon & Schuster, 2006.

_____. *The Price of Loyalty: George W. Bush, the White House, and the Education of Paul O'Neill*. New York: Simon & Schuster, 2004.

_____. *The Way of the World: A Story of Truth and Hope in an Age of Extremism*. New York: HarperCollins, 2008.

Tracy, James. "Bearing Witness to the Unspeakable." *Journal of American Culture* 28 (November 2005): pp. 85–99.

Tucker, Robert, and David Hendrickson. "The Sources of US Legitimacy." *Foreign Affairs* 83, no. 6 (November–December 2004): pp. 18–32.

Turner, Frederick Jackson. *The Frontier in American History*. New York: Henry Holt, 1920.

Tyler, Patrick E. "US Strategy Plan Calls for Insuring No Rivals Develop." *New York Times*, March 8, 1992, p. A14.

Von Hermann, Denise. "Presidential Decision-Making: Three Models and the Road to War in Iraq." In *Presidential Policies and the Road to the Second Iraq War: From Forty-One to Forty-Three*, edited by John Davis. Aldershot, UK: Ashgate, 2006.

Wallace, Iain. "Territory, Typology and the Christian Scriptures." *Geopolitics* 11, no. 2 (2006): pp. 209–230.

Walt, Stephen. *Taming American Power: The Global Response to US Primacy.* New York: W. W. Norton, 2005.

Washington, Wayne. "Once Against Nation-Building, Bush Now Involved." *Boston Globe,* March 2, 2004.

Wattenberg, Ben. *Fighting Words: A Tale of How Liberals Created Neo-Conservatism.* New York: St. Martin's Press, 2008.

Weisberg, Jacob. *The Bush Tragedy.* New York: Random House, 2008.

Williams, Michael. "What Is the National Interest?" *European Journal of International Relations* 11, no. 3 (2005): pp. 307–337.

Williams, Robert E., Jr., and Dan Caldwell. "Jus Post Bellum: Just War Theory and the Principles of Just Peace." *International Studies Perspectives* 7, no. 4 (2006): pp. 309–320.

Wilson, Valerie Plame. *Fair Game: My Life as a Spy, My Betrayal by the White House.* London: Simon & Schuster, 2007.

Wittkopf, Eugene R., Christopher M. Jones, and Charles W. Kegley. *American Foreign Policy: Pattern and Process,* 7th ed. Belmont, CA: Thomson/Wadsworth, 2008.

Wolfson, Adam. "Conservatives and Neoconservatives." In *The Neocon Reader,* edited by Irwin M. Stelzer, pp. 213–231. New York: Grove, 2004.

Woodward, Bob. *Bush at War.* New York: Simon & Schuster, 2002.

———. *Plan of Attack.* New York: Simon & Schuster, 2004.

———. *State of Denial.* New York: Simon & Schuster, 2006.

———. *The War Within: A Secret White House History, 2006–2008.* New York: Simon & Schuster, 2008.

Yankelovich, Daniel. "The Tipping Points." *Foreign Affairs* 85, no. 3 (May–June 2006): pp. 115–125.

Yoo, John C. "War and the Constitutional Test." *University of Chicago Law Review* 69 (2005): pp. 1–41.

Yordan, Carlos. "America's Quest for Global Hegemony." *Theoria* 110 (August 2006): pp. 125–160.

Yoshihara, Toshi, and James R. Holmes. "China's Energy-Driven 'Soft Power.'" *Orbis* 52, no. 1 (Winter 2008): pp. 123–137.

Zakaria, Fareed. *The Post-American World.* New York: W. W. Norton, 2008.

Zarefsky, David. "Presidential Rhetoric and the Power of Definition." *Presidential Studies Quarterly* 34, no. 3 (2004): pp. 607–619.

Zoysa, Richard de. "America's Foreign Policy: Manifest Destiny or Great Satan?" *Comparative Politics* 11, nos. 2–3 (2005): pp. 133–156.

INDEX